To Paul — tha
the blessing
and your friendship

Graham

I thought that my voyage had come to its end at the last limit of my power – that the path before me was closed, that provisions were exhausted and the time come to take shelter in silent obscurity.
But I found that thy will knows no end in me, and when old words die out on the tongue, new melodies break forth from my heart; and where old tracks are lost, new country is revealed with its wonders.

Gitanjali
Rabindranath Tagore

On the Road
with Heitor

Journeys of Hope, Healing and Peace

Graham J Macey

Mazo Publishers

On the Road with Heitor

ISBN: 978-1-946124-59-3

Contact The Author
Email: graham@nomadshuffle.co.uk
Website: www.grahamjmacey.com

Mazo Publishers

Email: mazopublishers@gmail.com
Website: www.mazopublishers.com

Cover Design by D'art Design of Cranleigh

To Julie

Thank you
for your never failing
encouragement and love.

To my daughters Hannah and Laura,
to my brothers Duncan and Stuart,
to my family and friends,
and to all those who believed in me…

… long before I learnt
to believe in myself.

Contents

Part Three
Through The Storm ~ 137

Part Four
The Other Side Of Midnight ~ 206

Part Five
Into the Light ~ 257

Coda
Of Angels Singing ~ 299

Preface

This book is a book of journeys, each one of them rooted in darkness and despair, but each one leading, in the end, to healing, reconciliation and peace.

It is set in a small suburban Surrey bungalow where, in 2012, I came to be the full-time carer for my 89 year old mother, and the joint custodian of our deeply troubled relationship.

This book began, not as a book, but as nothing more than a clumsy attempt to make sense of it all. Slowly, as the words followed their own wilful yet fractured path, it became clear that the pain of the present was inextricably entwined with the pain of the past and it was here, and only here, that the seeds of healing were to be found and nurtured.

This book is not the product of a garlanded 'writer' employing all of their skills and talents to bring the past, the present and the future to life. It is the desperate attempt to release and to mirror on the page all the sorrows and confusions of a tortured mind – not to invite the reader to wallow with me there, but in the firm hope and faith that we may come to walk together into the light of healing and love. For I see no point in asking for the reader's time and patience, if it is not for the purpose of leaving them with a little more hope than that with which they started.

I offer the portrait of a life of relentless failure and shame, a life, at times, brought as low as it is possible to fall, a life crushed by the weight of things buried and unresolved – all the corrosive inheritance of so many previous generations – a life of broken dreams to be sure – but a life, nevertheless, of ultimate acceptance, fulfilment and peace.

And yet, as I write these words, it is clear to me now, that the focus of this book is not myself at all, but my mother – and more than that – it is the enduring and the flowering of her love.

I have come to understand that everything my mother has ever done has been an expression of her passion and her love and her gratitude and her childlike humility before the Gift of

Life – before the wonder of simply being alive.....

..... but sadly, and tragically, because of her broken-ness and the ever vigilant and violent patterns of self-defence that she was forced to assume, that same love was forever trapped in a web of relentless contortion and turmoil – even to the point of becoming actively and helplessly destructive.....

..... and how does this story of my mother's broken love resonate now with our own lives – with the lives of those around us – with all the frustrated aspirations for 'good' of the world in which we live.

In the last few years of her life, my mother rose above all that had blighted her love, as she learned to embrace that part of her which experience had convinced her to believe was never hers to embrace.

My mother learned to exercise the power of choice – slowly and falteringly and most probably without clear conscious decision – but steadfastly and resolutely nevertheless.

My mother 'chose' to let go to broken patterns of behaviour – to resentment and self-pity, to habit and to fear, and to all that would stand between a mother and her sons.

As a ninety year old woman, my mother discovered the power of her will to lead her step by step, from the darkness of her childhood into the light and the peace and the simple liberation and joy of her passing.

And so it was – and continues to be – that my mother's love was able to inspire me with the hope and the courage I so desperately needed to complete the journey of my own healing.

A love redeemed, restored and radiant..... free at last to nurture and to cherish – to teach and to protect – to guide and to set free.....

..... a Mother's Love indeed.

Eastbury Manor
28th September 2019

Introduction

Come – sit with me awhile – let us succour each stolen breath – let us pause before the incontinent splendour – the aching profundity of winter's veiled address.....

..... we will talk of warmer days – of paths familiar and roads as yet undiscovered – of wild flowers reaching out to lithesome hearted travellers – of shy maidens in piecemeal undress, radiant in tongues of careless desire – still shining in the stars, of a hundred youthful summers.....

..... we will wink at hedgerows and glimpse the dawn through archways of filigreed constraint – we will wander unscathed through parks of quiet attendance – while insects shimmer in patterned sunlit crevices – and roses compete for any other names.....

..... come sit with me – as the children dance homeward and distant carriages define our lost horizons – we will drink deep the scent of magnificent uncertainties – and we too will dance, on carpets buoyant with trumpeted abandon..... wrapped in the languid armour of posterity – we will posture our wisdom with care.....

..... make haste my friend – flowers are fading in tenement conceits – the adventure is afoot..... resonant with motifs of resplendent heartaches – we will kneel before the passing of silent moons.....

..... come – we will write together..... as constancy stammers through the vacant particles of my breath..... we will write together – and you will save me from words and intent.....

..... I am but a fellow fugitive from the tyrannies of pretension and the fetters of expectation – these pages – nought but a lifeline – cast out in the hope of finding your hand.....

..... my friend – through the song in your heart – and the lingering touch of your patience – save me I pray – from words and intent.

Buckfast Abbey
November 2013

*Let's just drive
while the sat nav
sorts its life out*

My daughter Hannah

Part One

From The Darkness

1

From Dreams To Reality… And Back Again

You can never impart a truth
until it has become alive within yourself

anon

The mist in the half-light is trembling – before the covered murmur of the big straight six – dignified and poised in its venerable restraint – the lightest touch of my foot – the only request that it seeks, to calmly address the affairs of the day – with authority and grace – my trusted old companion – hand in hand through the dust of our winter years – down these vacant tracks of my restless surrender – this ragged journey back to the dawn of my days…..

….. the poppy fields are shimmering – to the soft dance of a solitary summer breeze – I stop to embrace this wide Tuscan landscape – the red of each flower – echoing with the red of my chariot – metallic particles sparkling in the untouched glory of the early morning sunlight…..

….. I wrap my arms around the beauty – as I too am wrapped in its warm caress….. all is still – all is waiting – expectant – full of shapeless promise….. I stand as a conductor before the song of ages – I raise my arms to its orchestrated rapture – I hold my breath and wait…..

….. far out across the swollen hills – a slow murmured cry – rising from deep within the jilted heart of the God's lovelorn creation….. the gentle cry becomes a troubled groan – rhythmical – cyclical – rising and falling – in crescendoed insistence….. the sky darkens as I cling to the coat tails of its fading light….. but they slip between my fingers – and I am torn away – to the beat of the march that comes trampling through my senses…..

….. to remain here – just to remain here – by all that is born of mercy and grace – please God – just to remain here – for a little while longer…..

..... mis-shaped complexities crash the wasted horizon – I pause before the timeless collision – my lover is waiting – in fields of anxious surrender – unknowing and unknown – my hand forever naked – fingertips in conscious abandon – tracing and exploring – tapestries of wonderment – all laid at my door..... the vortex approaches – all is lifted – all is beyond – in a moment – an eternal moment – all is lifted and all is passing..... into this moment we fall – through folds of breathless collusion – the last act of stoic aspiration – to straighten and defy – in statued liberty – the eagled stance – the whispered hallelujah..... touchstones for a wanton imagination.....

..... he is now fully awake – eyes wide open and fixed on the shadowed lines of the painting before his bed – the sounds from the room next door can be ignored no longer – they fill the house – rhythmical – cyclical – in crescendoed insistence..... and yet – and yet – he doesn't move – he doesn't feel.....

..... he reaches out to the proud sensuality of the flamenco dancer – washed in shades of blue as she rises from the canvas – the canvas whose threads can no longer contain her – he touches her arm in vain appeal – to be lifted up into her dance – to slide without trace into her beauty and her passion.....

..... but his breath is getting heavy now – the waters are closing above his head – dark and bitter – still he cannot move – the dancer has flown and he is left alone with the empty frame – lines and hues devoid of life – she has escaped – in the nick of time.....

..... every breath now is a weight lifted from the darkness of a long forgotten tomb – a tomb wherein lie the bones of a broken child – he struggles beneath the chains that are coiling above his chest – he is sweating – in shards of anger and merciless guilt..... and yet – in the same moment – he hears but cannot hear the cries through the wall – he feels but cannot feel – if he goes now – then he will have to go the next night and every night that follows – as to an irksome child – he cannot give in – he cannot allow the compassion to rise up..... he has trained himself well – for the longest of times.....

..... he does not feel – and yet – his soul writhes twisted and contorted within the straight-jacket calm of his aching flesh..... will he go or will he stay – it makes no difference – not to him – not to her..... he turns into the pillows and closes his eyes as he closes his heart..... the seeker of distant landscapes returns to his sleep..... the crying fades – the house is still – haunted but still – haunted but still..... haunted..... but still.

2

Heitor Villa-Lobos

Heitor Villa-Lobos (March 5, 1887-November 17, 1959) was a Brazilian composer, described as "the single most significant creative figure in 20th-century Brazilian art music". Villa-Lobos has become the best-known and most significant Latin American composer to date. He wrote numerous orchestral, chamber, instrumental and vocal works. His music was influenced by both Brazilian folk music and by stylistic elements from the European classical tradition, as exemplified by his Bachianas Brasileiras.

Heitor Villa-Lobos was born in Rio de Janeiro. His father, Raul, was a civil servant, an educated man of Spanish extraction, a librarian, an amateur astronomer and musician.

Around 1905 Villa-Lobos started explorations of Brazil's "dark interior", absorbing the native Brazilian musical culture. Serious doubt has been cast on some of Villa-Lobos's tales of the decade or so he spent on these expeditions, and about his capture and near escape from cannibals, with some believing them to be fabrications or wildly embellished romanticism.

After this period, he gave up any idea of conventional training and instead absorbed the musical influences of Brazil's indigenous cultures, themselves based on Portuguese and African, as well as American Indian elements. His earliest compositions were the result of improvisations on the guitar from this period. Villa-Lobos played with many local Brazilian street-music bands; he was also influenced by the cinema and Ernesto Nazareth's improvised tangos and polkas. For a time Villa-Lobos became a cellist in a Rio opera company and his early compositions include attempts at Grand Opera.

Villa-Lobos underwent very little formal training. After a few abortive harmony lessons, he learnt music by illicit observation from the top of the stairs of the regular musical evenings at his house arranged by his father. He learned to play the cello, the guitar and the clarinet. When his father died suddenly in 1899 he earned a living for his family by playing in cinema and theatre orchestras in Rio.

In 1912, Villa-Lobos married the pianist Lucília Guimarães, ended his travels, and began his career as a serious musician. His music began to be published in 1913.

In June 1959, Villa-Lobos alienated many of his fellow musicians by expressing disillusionment, saying in an interview that Brazil was "dominated by mediocrity".

In November he died in Rio; his state funeral was the final major civic event in that city before the capital transferred to Brasília. He is buried in the Cemitério São João Batista in Rio de Janeiro.

When touring Europe with his music he said, "I don't use folklore, I am the folklore" and "I have not come to learn, I have come to show what I have made up to now."

Wikipedia

It is said that Heitor Villa-Lobos disliked being referred to as 'the Brazilian composer Villa-Lobos' – he would say that no-one speaks of the Austrian composer Mozart or of the German composer Beethoven..... it is also said that, during his one and only encounter with Hollywood – having completed his score to the film Green Mansions – a fellow composer asked why he was leaving – Villa-Lobos replied that the score was finished – they could now fit the film around his music.....

..... I know nothing of the veracity of these stories – and nothing of the character they portray..... I know only the wild generous spirit that for forty years has walked patiently beside me – tending to my broken hands and my broken heart..... he alone in this world of men has kept safe the memory of my wholeness – never condemning – never intimidating – never judging – never mocking ..... but always accepting – always encouraging – always nurturing – the silenced song within my heart – the stammering dance of my fingers..... when doctors and healers – wise men and counsellors – wives and accusers – when all had fallen away – the Brazilian composer Villa-Lobos never faltered.....

3

The Story Begins

The musk is in the deer, but it seeks it not within itself;
it wanders in quest of grass

Kabir

I arrived on April the First 2012 – a suitable portent for what lay ahead, or at least, for the first few years of my confinement. During the days that would follow, I would often try and remember just how and when the decision was made – leaving my work, my friends, my life in Devon – to care for my ageing mother, back beneath the gull free skies of the Surrey hills.

I cannot recall any attempts at deliberation, there had been no weighing up of pros and cons, no talking things through..... there were precipitating circumstances for sure, my mother's hip operation and her aversion to being cared for by strangers, my stepfather's long planned escape to be with his family in

Somerset, my brother's health being brought dangerously low by the stress of it all….. but a decision, a conscious exercising of 'choice' – definitely not.

It just sort of happened, but then, does anything 'just sort of happen'. I have come to understand that decisions are always made, choices always exercised – but maybe not in the ways and at the times we think.

When that moment comes for a decision to be made, have not the foundations already been laid, the freedom to choose already been used and exhausted….. the stage already set.

We think we are guiding our actions, our responses – that we are masters of our destinies, but in truth, the seeds were sown long before….. the cards that now lay before us have already been stacked – we have become bystanders before the inevitable outpouring of everything that we have persistently chosen to hold in our hearts – for good or for bad.

….. we choose to entertain and indulge our anger and our impatience, then we ask 'how could it happen that we were so reckless as to run a red light'….. we choose to open our hearts to lusts and fantasies, to selfish desires, then we ask 'how could it be that we have come to betray the one that we love'….. and is this not how heroes are born….. not in a moment of wild self-sacrifice but in all the countless moments when the needs of others have been put before their own, when compassion and love and 'right' have been chosen over apathy and self-concern.

Nothing comes from nothing….. and so it was that I found myself amidst the Range Rovers and the Food Banks of Cranleigh….. deep within, beyond acknowledgment or acceptance, I had yearned to be the man who would take care of another in their vulnerability and their need – I was far from being that man, and could see no way of becoming like him – but when the moment came, the decision was already cast – I had no idea how it could possibly work out – but in faith, and much trepidation, I took the first step.

4

Simple Pleasures

Give me a Jeep. It's not perfect, but neither are we or we'd be able to afford Maserati Quattroportes. The Jeep is straight, square, forthright. It reminds us of something that makes us feel good. And, if being reminded of WWII makes us feel good compared with what other cars remind us of, those are some damn creepy cars. At least the Jeep looks like a motor vehicle, not a netsuke* or a plush toy or what the computer-styling software did when the cat went to sleep on the keyboard..... Okay, we're a little crazy to have a Jeep for a daily driver. But if we go off our meds, we might wind up in a Prius.

P J O'Roarke

Not from hallowed halls did you come - not from any lofty heights from which perfectly manicured architects look down with careless disdain - their hearts and their passions long since sucked away down the bottomless abyss of computer interfaces..... no - you were born in bars - traced on beer mats and cigarette packets while your creators laughed and spoke of adventures and wild sunlit trails..... you were born, not of committees or contrived intent, but of generous passions and midnight banter - you spare me the burdens of pride and envy - you are without pretence, humble of heart and I cherish the sharing of our simple pleasures.

* A *netsuke* (pronounced "nets-keh") is a small sculptural object which has gradually developed in Japan over a period of more than three hundred years.

5

'School' – Day One

Nothing outside can ever help you or reveal anything until it finds its answer within.

anon

The boy is 4 years old – it is his first day at Park Nursery School – it is full of strangeness and mystery..... he is sitting in the front room of a large old house surrounded by vast impenetrable Rhododendron bushes – mysteries within mysteries..... the teacher is sitting at a table in the middle of the room while six or so children are arranged around her in an innocent and compliant semi-circle..... so far so good.....

..... it is the end of a lesson in Arithmetic – they have been given crisp new exercise books with pages all divided into small squares into which the numbers can, and must, be squeezed in order to create lots of neat little parallel rows.....

..... he likes the squares and he likes the sums and he especially likes his name on the cover....... soon it is time to hand in their 'work' – one by one – all around the semi-circle – the children slide their books across the table to the waiting arms of the teacher.... it is his first day – he watches carefully and he follows the example of his classmates – he is happy to feel part of the group – to have got through the lesson so triumphantly – soon he would be going home – his first day safely ticked off on the register..... he slides his book across the table to the teacher – a lamb to the slaughter..... she stands up in a sudden violent explosion and shouts at him – just him – he is alone – set apart – confused and shaking – and he doesn't understand why.....

..... many years will pass before he comes to understand the meaning of the word 'disrespectful' – the word so abruptly scorched into his memory.....

….. he doesn't know then that this scene will become the first of many such horrors to fall upon him, throughout the endless incomprehension of 'School' and beyond – and he will never understand why – and he will never notice or mourn as the noble quest for knowledge will, for him, become slowly trampled before a single, solitary yearning….. to become silently and irretrievably invisible.

I am aching and wondering in divine proportion – as the nights come and go – prescient with the knowledge of sorrow's passing…..

….. later….. much later….. in the beguiling moments of certainty….. when all is quiet and dangerous – I make my escape – my midnight flight – far from this cackling brood – this lawless crowd – flaked with its petulant liturgies – its tarnished boughs and rusted blades – sated yet forever hungry – rushing like madness to disrobe at last – from the final ragged vestments of conscience and regard…..

Ah….. the folly of discarding so proudly – for as the perfect breath of dawn trembles the darkness – the incumbent collaborator returns – tainted and tired – falling once more from side-shows of numbed regret….. a stranger here – a stranger amongst strangers – eyes forever fixed on incandescent horizons – feet forever poised on margins of clay…..

6

There Must Be Something More

... there is a crack in everything
– it's where the light gets in

Leonard Cohen

Meditations

I am reaching out – beyond these walls of time and space – these winds that would tear the flesh from my bones – these orphaned hours that would surely destroy me.....

I am reaching out through the words – to the fragrant promises that shimmer and beckon beneath this hallowed paucity of anthems and creeds.....

I am reaching out for the beauty within the beauty – the laughter within the laughter – for the tears within the tears.....

..... reaching through the mist to that which seems remote and obscure – yet always familiar – closer than my own breath.....

..... watching as it rises, without reproach, through the debris of my humbled submission – all gentleness and light – like a flower in the desert..... like a whisper on the storm.....

I am reaching out to touch the song....... the song within the song ..... it is here – now – behind this veil that shivers like gossamer on a warm night breeze....... it is the herald for all who would hear ..... that there is a *truth* in all things..... its light shining through the cracks..... shining to guide us home.....

..... but wherein lies this *truth* – on what golden dawn does she rest her head..... I would lay beside her there – and make my home, where the tyrannies of intellect can never assail or deceive.....

I am reaching out – across the chasm of my own heart – to that place of artless wonder – where the world outside becomes silent and still and all my words begin to shine.....

….. for the child whose blood still wanders through my veins – whose heartbeat echoes in my wearied chest….. the child whose trust is forever perfect…..

….. where is he now – the child you formed with tenderness and grace – where is your child….. I can still hear him calling from far across the years – calling from behind this broken mask….. the faithful keeper of my ageless self…..

….. we are not set apart by time's clawing fingers – he is not torn away through the whirlpools of space – our fingertips still touch and the strands of our breath remain forever entwined…..

….. our eyes are searching the same horizons – our steps meandering through the same cloistered halls….. we have wandered between cradle and Lyre – close yet unknowing – through these years of exile and aimless sorrow…..

….. the charge that he placed in the womb of my soul has kept me alive and ever restless – he set a candle to the spark – and before his simple faith I could almost believe – that I am not just the measure of these timorous reflections – the tortured palpitations of this broken heart…..

….. I am reaching out…..

….. or maybe….. maybe I am falling – into that holy distance where lovers kiss and the Garden rests for evermore in unsullied contentment…..

….. where all is drawn together – where all is reconciled – where all is *one*….. will you catch me there – am I falling into your arms….. or am I just falling….. into the empty void of my own wishful imaginings…..

I wait for the fear – but the fear does not come – I wait for the doubts – but they remain silent – I wait for the mocking finger – but it lies unmoving before me….. my heart is still – washed in the beauty and the unfathomable nearness of the moment…..

There is an ocean beneath this ocean – where forgiveness and trust are met together – where rainbows touch and heroes weep and honey eyed children dance on rhythms of light…..

..... there is a laughter between the tides..... no ear could ever steal - no lips ever betray - its wonder or its delight.....

..... I will let the stirring of summer's reveries take me in its arms - I will run through its valleys and chase the silent echo of eternity - there between its wistful glades.....

..... I will rest in the hollows where continents drift - and kneel beside streams where the leaves of healing grow..... with my heart overflowing - and the song of ages forever on my tongue - I will return to that timeless hearth that was never lost or forgotten.....

..... and as the sun falls upon the passing day - the fading light casts one last spell - and one by one - as shadows turn to blue...... once again..... once again..... love comes through.....

All that I was - all the days of my youth and beyond.....

... denying the undeniable...

... resisting the irresistible...

... holding my hand out against the tides...

... my life tossed and broken on the rocks of selfish abandon...

... I can run no more...

... my blindness is now spent - my foolishness exposed - my solitary shelter all washed away...

... and here in the silence - at last - I wait...

... in fragile expectation...

... between these hours - these precious hours - that frame the sacred gate...

... waiting - always waiting...

... for your hand to lead me through...

He speaks - 'I will no longer seek to explore the mystery - but rather - I will wait for its timely embrace... I will no longer aspire to be a seeker after truth - but rather - I will rest here - and wait for its consuming breath'.

7

The Past Reveals The Present

Non, je ne suis jamais seul
avec ma solitude

Georges Moustaki

He stands before the front door of a pleasantly non-descript 1970's bungalow..... he is reaching out.....

.... but as the key touches the lock – he hesitates – like an animal before the scent of a hunter – he can feel it – like electricity through the glass..... on the other side of the door – all is not well.....

..... somewhere within the darkened rooms she is brooding – spoiling for a fight..... he hesitates – he is remembering – he stands un-moving – cold and haunted.....

The boy is seven years old – it is Saturday morning – and as with the dawn of every weekend he awakens to the sound of his mother's screams.....

His father has become a master of passive weekday diplomacy..... he returns late from work – eats – then falls asleep on the sofa..... there is no space left for confrontation – within his heavy childlike slumbers he is inviolate – beyond reproach or resentment..... but the violence will bide its time – the madness will have its way.....

..... even his father has no answer, no defence, no strategy for the atrocity of Saturday mornings..... the boy hears the screaming even before he is fully awake..... a week – or maybe a lifetime of repressed anger and frustration – coursing through the house without restraint or opposition .....

..... a father and his sons – clinging by their fingernails to the flotsam of normality – storm-tossed on waves of hysteria – helpless before the ensuing onslaught.....

..... and so it starts – the weekend narrative.....

"Why are you cleaning the car when there are shelves to be put up?"

"Why are you putting up shelves when the lawn needs mowing?"

"Why are you mowing the lawn when the car needs cleaning?"

And then with terrifying inevitability the madness turns towards the boy and his brother – childhood offers no immunity to the violence….. it is not safe to be caught sitting or reading or – sin of sins – dreaming ….. nothing is safe….. there is nothing now but screaming…..

"Why are you sitting down when I have so much to do?"

"Why are you so lazy?"

"When I was a child we had nothing – we had no toys or books but I was happy to help my mother – we weren't allowed to sit around doing nothing"

"How dare you read when there is so much to be done – must I do everything myself?"

"You are a wicked, selfish, ungrateful child – get up and do the hoovering"

"When I was a child we had nothing – when I was a child – when I was a child….."

everything is wrong….. everything is always wrong…..

The boy learns the blessed sanctuary of the garage roof – the furthest of the old tumble-down buildings at the end of the garden – here he will lie – out of sight from the house – the screaming now, just a muffled cry…..

….. here is safety – peace – quietness….. apart from the thumping of his heart – the weight upon his chest through which he strains to lift each measured breath – the betrayal of his father and brother as he condemns them to face the madness alone – the horror of his eventual return….. but even these pernicious intruders to his tranquillity will slowly surrender to the warm embrace of this beloved haven – this 'time out of time out of time'…..

The risky business of dreaming

..... he stares up into the vast umbrella of the old oak tree – he longs to climb up into its gently waving branches – to be held there forever in its strength and its timeless dignity..... never to come down.....

..... and so it goes..... the tree in its seductive majesty – the screaming and the madness below – the boy on the roof between heaven and hell..... just a normal Saturday morning.....

He stands before the door – his senses finely tuned and quivering – he knows he must open the door and enter – he is no longer a child – there is nowhere to hide – he has chosen to be here – to care for her – somehow – somehow – to persevere and stay.....

He steels his heart and he steels his patience – he opens the door and enters in.....

She is now 89 years old – the violence has been tempered by the constraints of old age..... but not a lot.....

8

Three Childhood Dreams – 1

Our poisoned inheritance – our chalice of guilt..... sins of the fathers – shame of the sons – the pen forever cherishing the testament of tears..... all our fine misgivings – all our noble cheers – all our savage delights – collide now in dormitories of silent defeats – sanctified somehow through the disdain of their fallen vanity.....

..... flags are weeping half-masted over cuckolded empires – the creatures have all left for the lights of distant towers – children wait in forgotten cradles – before the ticking of the penitentiary clock – we scrape the barrel for the edge of reason – all is still – all is waiting – I pass the time..... to you.....

1

The boy is holding a single grain of sand in the outstretched palm of his left hand..... at the same moment – the grain of sand is the size of a large planet – it weighs down upon his chest – it pins him to the ground – crushing the life from his body.....

Once again..... at the very same moment – he is perched on the top of a narrow pole – he is looking down in terror at the earth – a small round circle far below..... the pole beneath him disappears into the clouds – it sways from side to side – he stands alone in the cold dark emptiness of space – clinging to his tiny purchase – knowing nothing but the fear of falling.

9

I Fall In Love

Heaven's not a place – no, 'tis a dance
where love perpetual, rhythmical, musical maketh advance
loved one to lover

Evelyn Vanderbilt

January 1975

She is standing in the kitchen doorway of a dishevelled old farmhouse – her gaze is distant and unbroken – and in the midst of the clamour that surrounds her – she stands apart – untouched and unseeing – robed in the yearning for the sacred worlds within her heart – worlds that he may only come to glimpse – in the veiled depths of her dark brown eyes.....

..... she is a child – beautiful – graceful – and infinitely gentle..... she is without pretension or guile..... and although he cannot feel it then – she has reached out and touched his heart – she has made it her own – she has placed a seed there which, in time, will grow to consume him.....

..... but before that time..... there will be years of abeyance and simple closeness – there will be nights that arch out across the hours – touching the dawn without effort or design – full of words and song – of cigarettes and coffee – of lingering glances and the meeting of fingertips.....

..... there will be meadows and streams and banks of wild flowers..... there will be sleeping on sofas beside fine old Red Setters – with casual manners and Spanish names..... there will be trespassers on fields ripe and golden – with angry farmers and timid retreats..... there will be highways taught with the voice of her calling and partings and distances and letters and longing.....

..... slowly and tenderly – she will come to walk beside him –

and though he will never find that place of enchantment within her eyes – in fleeting moments – to the song of children's laughter – he will be lifted into the radiance of her beauty and her love…..

….. for a little while – he will hold her close – and she like a stolen jewel – clenched in the palm of a blind man's hand…..

….. for just a little while – he will abide beneath the touch of her smile….. but for the longest of days – and through the darkest of nights – as time looks on without pity or grace….. he will kneel to mourn her passing…..

… meanwhile…

… on the other side of the house…

… another dance is stirring…

Five Preludes

Crashing into his world – without any semblance of decorum or reserve – comes a spirit of impatience and captivating charm – of wild extravagance and heart-rending tenderness…..

….. without hesitation – his shallow pretensions are exposed one by one – the anaemic rhythms and the tepid refrains of a spoilt young white boy's conceit….. it is too late to run for cover – music that is warm and generous and recklessly unguarded – is arrowed at his heart with merciless precision….. even if he wanted….. he is helpless to turn from the voice that is calling…..

"Come now – why do you tarry? – I come to you freely – to offer up melodies sweet and sublime….. melodies that you may learn to caress – just as you would trace with a lingering kiss – the perfect miracle of a woman's thigh….."

"….. listen to me now….. do not fear – for just when the sweetness holds in her sights – chances for vanity and proud self-assurance – we will cast off her finery – and in a careless moment we will escape her stifling restraints…..

"….. we will run in search of alleyways and bars – of full-hearted companions and maidenly charms….. we will drink together – and dance on tables – and as we watch the dawn through lines of wasted content….. we will offer a hymn to the mystery – while we cast our empty glasses into the smouldering ashes of yesterday's already forgotten certainties….."

"I will not abandon you or ask what you cannot give – I am faithful….. if a little capricious….. we will walk through the years – and we will fall together – ever deeper into the heart of all things….."

….. and so they collide….. the most unlikely of confidants….. the most improbable of friends…..

….. HVL has arrived…..

….. and though it will take a lifetime for the dance to breakthrough his sullen flesh….. the invitation has been made – and will not be withdrawn.

10

The Daily Routine

You who would search for love –
let love be your carriage.

The days are falling, slowly and alarmingly, into a restless, yet amicable, blur – with the daily round of shopping, sleeping and old TV crime repeats helping my brain to find a, not unwelcome affinity with my regular morning bowl of porridge.

I have just returned from my early morning swim, my antidote to the relentless encroachments of age. My mother is on the phone to her friend Hazel. I have already grown wary of returning to find that she has been calling her friends – it's often a sign that she's sulking at my absence and ringing round to find a likely victim – I mean, candidate – to take her out for tea.

This time, however, the call seems relatively goodhearted. They are going through a checklist of bodily functions, to compare what is or isn't working, what has been taken away, replaced, or just simply misappropriated, and what general maladies have befallen them since the last roll-call.

It sounds suspiciously like a competition, with the prize going to the one who's lost the most bits – the most easily quantifiable measure of discomfort and pain.

High on the list are, predictably – memory, teeth, hearing, bowel movements and eyesight, but included amongst these are some unexpected maladies – or at least, unexpected enough to keep me listening – such as, a seemingly endless and colourful raft of medication side effects, inner ear infections and wild hallucinations.

(I make a mental note to avoid old age, if at all possible).

Hazel is 98 and has just bought a new, and very ornate, baby grand piano, concurrent with her plans to be playing well in to her next century. She still plays the odd (I choose the word 'odd' with care) gig, and takes a keen interest in the Brooklands Race Track Society.

We have found that we all have an interest in the Napier Railton land speed car which is based at Brooklands. Hazel, because her husband Nick once worked on it, me because I had my photograph taken whilst sitting in the car with my father and brother at the age of nine, and my mother, because she gave birth to a boy who had his photo taken sitting in a Napier Railton.

We have all agreed that we must go and see it again sometime.

This is turning out to be an exciting morning, it is nearly lunch-time and I still haven't felt the need to feign weariness (after swimming) in order to gain concerned permission to withdraw to my room for a few precious moments of solitude and peace.

Oh, the holy and exalted estates of sickness and fatigue – childhood retreats without the need for garage roofs – trump cards to the relentless and ubiquitous insanity that surrounded us – blessed oil on the troubled waters of the terrifying volatility of everyday family life.

I'll take it

It was simple – like magic – to be instantly transported to a place of normality and order, where all my words were suddenly laden with purpose and dignity and the symptoms of my afflictions shone proudly like badges of honour.

In this childhood paradise, I could say things like…..

"I'm not hungry"

….. or make spectacularly selfish demands like…..

"Can I have the window open?"

….. amazingly, miraculously , these words would not be met by screaming or castigation or lectures on starving children in Africa – no – there would be replies like…..

"Of course"

"Oh dear"

"I'll do it right now"

or – bliss upon bliss…..

"You poor thing"

….. and still, to this day, the magic weaves its spell…..

"I'm sorry, I'm not feeling too good"
"Oh dear, you must go and lie down"
"I'm feeling a bit tired"
"I'll try not to disturb you"
"I'm feeling a bit achy" – (a real winner)
"Shall I bring you a cup of tea – maybe you'd like a biscuit with it"

I am suddenly free, lying in saintly repose, in an oasis of perfect calm and serenity..... however, there is, and was, a catch.....

This powerful wizardry must be used sparingly and only in times of great need – lest the treachery be discovered – lest the deceit be unmasked.....

..... and as the days fulfil their aimless rambling – life bestows upon us its welcome punctuations – like footholds in the snow – like paper trails through the forest.....

..... meal times and weather reports, market days and post, rubbish collections and doctor's appointments – we move from one to the other, with care and respect..... lest we fall through the gaps and are lost forever to this world.

Today is a good day, but it is not wise, nay reckless, to let down one's guard.

The darkness is ever watching – ever waiting.

The quiet times are the most dangerous of times, but it will take me a few years yet to fully learn this lesson – to live as if there is a demented creature imprisoned in the attic and to tip toe around the house accordingly, ever mindful and fearful of waking her.

I am living as a leaf blown by the storm.

Today, the leaves are sitting in neat little piles at the end of the garden..... but who knows what tomorrow may bring.

11

Café Daydreams

Love perceives
as never a man sees

anon

The easy virtues of dawn are slipping through my fingers as I search the narrow skyline for guidance and light – the domes and spires so easily mapped from the hills above, now lie hidden and obscured behind these ancient canyons of glass and stone.....

..... the warm wistful breezes of autumn have moved on – the wind is now a harsh and brittle thing – it moves like a hunter – stalking these empty streets for unwary souls to mock and to scatter.....

..... the early morning sun – delicate and ravishing – seems unwilling to share any warmth from within her slow sleepy awakening..... her flaxen hair – lying cold and unmoving across the pillows of my simple contentment.....

..... here and there, small intrepid groups of tourists are sheltering – and while their eyes may question the wisdom of their seasonal choices – the words remain un-spoken before the stoic resolve of each day's planned explorations..... paintings and statues – books and manuscripts – cafés and restaurants..... they huddle over charts that flap and flutter in the wind – like the wings of captive birds – like the coats of shuffling day-dreamers – all plaintively searching for liberty and release.....

..... I turn my collar to the retreating dawn and let the low winter sunlight blur my vision – like an old 50's cinematic filter falling golden across my sleep filled eyes.....

Sounds of the waking day echo tentatively behind closed shop doors and shutters – but for now – I am un-hindered – to shuffle and to day-dream – alone with the romance, that are the streets and the alleyways and the avenues of Florence.

But as I walk – I am quietly mindful that I am not alone…..

….. somewhere – high above – amongst the hilltops that look down as from the rim of a smouldering volcano….. somewhere behind the rising mist – there is a long white villa – a place of enchantment and simple childhood dreams…..

Here my love would play and sing – chasing down corridors with her sister and her friends – in search of mysteries and untold adventures – running along verandas resonant with the sounds of children's unfettered laughter….. here my love would play and sing….. here my love – would play and sing…..

….. a long white villa on a foreign hillside….. just an image on a small faded photograph – faded and forgotten….. yet forever imprinted on the tissues of my mind…..

….. I imagine her walking here as I am walking now – her hand in the hand of her father – loving and proud – with his elegant charm and his suave sensibilities – the father who was always leaving – leaving to follow his own adventures…..

….. until the day that he left and did not return – taking her laughter with him – to keep him warm on this, his final adventure…..

Did they walk here together – along paths strewn with the hopes and dreams of distant ancestors – to the song of their far off cadences – sweet and beguiling – ever calling to lead them home…..

….. if I listen hard enough – maybe I will hear her footsteps still….. and if I linger long enough – maybe I will see her passing by…..

….. for caught amongst these tangled streets – there is a child forever searching – for the hand of her beloved papa – for the laughter that he never did return….. she runs from door to bolted door – her thick dark hair veiling her troubled face…..

The day has passed – I am climbing once again to the perfect vistas of the Piazza Michelangelo – as the evening sun collides upon the shrouded hills….. I find the steps where my daughter and I sipped from bottles of thin Italian birra – I trace the paths where we threaded our way through the shining crowds of sunset voyeurs – to the songs of the street musicians – beneath the heady aromas of a warm summer's night..... here we searched the horizon for an image – an image from an old faded photograph – and here we gave silent thanks to the memory and the beauty of her song.....

I lift my eyes to the coffee that has grown cold before me..... I lift my step to re-join the passing parade..... and as the ghosts of my present rise to welcome me back – I am thinking still of a little girl – her dark eyes wet and sorrowed – forever wandering through deserted avenues – pausing before each hollowed doorway – alone and fragile – armoured only with a single refrain – the last clinging memory from the fluency of her carefree childhood tongue.....

'*Domani, vuoi venire a grocare con me?*'

..... I would hold her now – and lay my solace soft upon her heart – her head upon my shoulder – my hand upon her hand – and in the meeting of our eyes – we would know each other there..... far beyond the reason of a lost and broken generation – far beyond the reach of cold and bitter words.....

My love – my beloved..... I would hold you now.....

where everything and everything
has fallen by the way
and only love...
and only love
remains.

12

I Seek The Safety Within

I watch from afar – between the calloused reaches of your weary indifference – beneath the thriving contempt of so many fallen dreams.....

..... from behind closed repentant gestures I watch – as the river beckons and moves on – bloated with its unrepentant lusts.....

..... sunshine on bleached flagstone..... angels and rust.....

..... what must I do..... to be loved by you

The boy is five years old – he has been waiting in the car now for over two hours – whilst inside Spinney Hill Post Office his mother is talking – and talking..... and talking.....

..... every day – or so it seems – on the homeward journey from nursery school – the ordeal is repeated – and although he doesn't know it then – it will become the pattern – the grotesque and inviolable pattern for endless years to come.....

..... he is screaming inside – the boredom is excruciating – unbearable – there is nothing to read – nothing to listen to – there are no distractions to ease the pain..... he has no alternative now – save to sit and watch the ghastly ritual – through the small square window panes of bulls eyed glass.....

The back seat of the old Morris has become his prison cell ..... he is forgotten – beneath the senseless noise spewing from her mouth..... he knows that it will continue unabated until closing time – and if not for closing time – then for how long would he wait ?

..... he shudders violently at the thought.....

But this is a day like none before it – this is the moment when all will change – his patience has finally come to its end….. he opens the door and steps on to the pavement – he waits for the screaming and the wrath to fall – but she doesn't notice his wilfulness – she is oblivious to everything but the need for 'chatter'….. for this, he is now strangely grateful…..

….. he is suddenly free – he is five years old – and he is walking alone for the first time – along pavements and alleyways – past hedgerows and fences – across roads and ditches….. he walks the half mile to his home – full of fear for the fury that he will have unleashed – yet triumphant and confident – in the sure knowledge that his courageous escape will have 'brought her to her senses' – and will have finally broken the bonds of his torment…..

But nothing has changed – nothing will ever change….. the next day and forever he will wait….. in silent screaming he will watch and wait….. while his mother talks – and talks….. and talks…..

Although he doesn't realise it then – the world outside has begun to slowly slip away – the world in which he is helpless – dumb – degraded….. without planning or comprehension he is learning to escape to the warmth and the safety within himself – to that place of reason and self-determination – where, in an instant, everything seems suddenly possible…..

Many years later – the child will re-emerge – but until then there is a world that is calling – and, for now, he has no strength nor will to resist.

13

My Father

God is love
and he that dwelleth in love
dwelleth in God – and God in him

1 John 4:16

It stands in the driveway like a proud old guard dog – poised and ready – although, like an old guard dog – it has probably long forgotten what it's supposed to be poised and ready for.

It is a 1999 Jeep Cherokee 4 litre Orvis – the last of a series of XJ's that stretch back over a period of 18 years to 1984 – it is the final fling of a dying breed.

Although its classic lines still hold their own amid the complex computer generated curves of contemporary fashion – beneath its Chilli Pepper Red panels – it has more in keeping with the plucky little green workhorses of WW2 than it does with the homogeneous marvels of technology that currently fill our roads and by-ways.

Sometimes it taunts me with work that I have yet to finish, but mostly, it speaks of sweepings hills, of passing villages, of rivers and valleys and tree lined avenues reaching out to distant horizons – its very presence assuring me that one day I will be free.

It does not subscribe to this age of conformity and dispensability – it was designed to allow for repair and long service – and whatever words I may use to describe it – bland and boring would not be amongst them.

There is a saying that has served me well, and saved me from many a disaster…..

When you're workin on a Yank – if it don't come apart easy – then you ain't doin it right!

Above all, its 'old' technology allows me to fulfil the long dormant need within me – to experience once more the simple and immediate pleasures and rewards of 'working with my hands'.....

..... the ritual preparation of tools and parts – of spaces and clothing..... and the arching of the mental picture, like musical phrase marks over all the notes and rhythms of the day's endeavours – holding it all together into a single coherent whole.

Each time I open a bonnet, or pick up a spanner, I feel my father beside me – with his words of advice and his endless exhortations for 'perfection'.

After all these years, I think I understand him now – how he saw only the beauty in 'making' and how he was unwilling and unable to reduce it to the crass everyday requirements of jobs and money.

Maybe he had more in common with the world of the artist than he did with the world of engineering. For him, the design and sculpture of cutters and components held their own fascinations and fulfilments – pure and undefiled by the impenetrable contortions of 'business'.

My father's needs in life were few and modest.....

..... to stand and work at his favourite lathe – to play with his St. Bernard – for his children to remain forever children – to live at peace as far away from bills and bank statements and 'paperwork' as possible – and to receive in return, just a little of the honesty, trust, humility and kindness that he himself gave out so freely.

He was a man who sought only to love and be loved and to be accepted for who he was – which, of course, led naturally to his affection for animals and his deep rooted affinity with all things cuddly and soft.

He had no thoughts for wealth or possessions – although he would have dearly loved to have been reunited with his Bugatti P35 – stolen from his garage in the first few months of the war – and to drive it just once at the Prescott hill climb.

He had no defence against the sharks that never ceased to

circle and prey upon his naïve childlike trust and gullibility.

Through the times of hopelessness and hardship that they inflicted, ironically, it was my mother's grit and courage and the energy of her now aptly focused anger that pulled us through.

It was her that held us together and spared her children the truth and the fear of each imminent abyss, and it was her that rallied all the forces at her command, so that each and every time, we were able to start again.

My father loved my mother from the start, and in his way, I believe that he understood her broken-ness and accepted and cherished her just as she was.

As I stare out at the driveway, I can picture him at the wheel of my ruby red chariot – pushing himself back into the driver's seat – straining hinges and brackets to the limit of their strength and integrity….. and maybe beyond.

I can see him listening and nodding approval at the velvet tones of the in-line 6 and the near seamless changing of the auto-box – and I can see myself sitting beside him as he slows once again to check the faithfulness of the steering geometry.

This was his favourite – he would choose a suitably straight piece of road and then he would take his hands off the steering wheel. If we did not career into the nearest ditch but continued in a straight line, then he would nod and smile – and I knew that, in that perfect moment, everything in my father's world was just fine.

Until the day of his death, my father never learnt to become hard or cynical – 'smart' or wise….. he never once stooped to understand the world that surrounded him…..

….. in all things – he remained as he had always been – so that – surely….. when, on the 8th of January 1980, his tender heart finally succumbed…..

….. it was not us – but God himself – who reached down to inscribe upon his simple headstone…..

Here Lies A Gentle Man

14

Ottershaw Infant School 1957-1959

See John in the boat.
John is in the big boat.
let me come, John.

Come in, Janet.
Come in and play.
Let us play in the big boat.

Janet and John – Book 1

My transition from nursery to infant school proved to be abrupt and confusing and was not made any easier by my curt introduction to the true, and hitherto hidden, purposes of the classroom ruler.

It soon became apparent, that the presence of all the little lines and numbers, so fastidiously engraved along its length, was, in fact, a ruse to entice small unsuspecting children into a false and misplaced sense of security.

Its actual role in their education was to induce fear and obedience through the inflicting of pain and lingering red marks to their naked flesh.

This twelve inch piece of malevolence showed its true colours on my very first day when – as I waited with the other children at the large green door that lead to the school entrance hall – my innocent musings were suddenly cut short by the sound of whistling air and a sharp burning pain to my leg, all of which were instantly followed by the severe and violent admonishments of a stooping red-faced teacher to 'get in line'.

As far as I was concerned, things had gone quite well up to this point – being dropped off without too much drama or chatter – finding some equally anxious chums to run about with – and then, without any problems whatsoever, being able to determine exactly when and where to join the queue for morning assembly and the start of lessons.

So far in my life, I had experienced very little in the way of physical assaults. My mother preferred the emotional kind and my father, when at home, preferred sleeping.

Here I was having not inconsiderable pain inflicted on me by a total stranger. It all seemed very odd and unpleasant, and whilst I was willing to try and put it all behind me, it soon became clear, for all of us, that this was not an isolated nor random act of sudden irritation.

The ruler, it seemed, was the teachers' flexible friend and was equally at home causing misery to the hands and fingers as it was to the buttocks and legs.

The upturned palm was always a popular choice – usually as a punishment for talking when we shouldn't, or at least, when the teacher deemed that we shouldn't – two very different things.

To stand in front of the class with an outstretched hand seemed to me, even at the time, to be a bizarre act of collusion and assent with the whole unsavoury process – a sort of S and M for beginners – I guess.

Surely, the only sane and rational response would be to hide ones hands firmly and resolutely behind ones back.

Anyway, this inauspicious start to 'proper schooling' actually proved to be, thankfully, unrepresentative of the fairly pleasant course of the next two years.

Altogether, I have just four surviving memories from my time at Ottershaw Infant School.

My second recollection is of the two 'what we did on our holidays' projects, one a painting and the other, an essay. The picture that I painted turned out to be well received and was entered into an inter-school competition sponsored by a company that supplied painting materials. My representation of a fictional fairground won a prize which, not surprisingly, turned out to be a box of watercolour paints.

However, these encouragements to my fledgling creative

impulses proved to be premature and unwise as, for my essay, I chose to throw all constraints of reality out the window and write about my visit to the factory where they made Avro Lancaster bombers.

Not long afterwards I discovered the folly of inexperienced poetic licence, in that the Lancaster had ceased production soon after the Second World War and the last one had been made over 10 years before my unfortunate composition.

I felt that this was a cruel trick on the part of the armaments industry, but nevertheless, I have been waiting for the repercussions of this blatant deceit ever since.

Thirdly, there is the 'Traumatic Starter Motor Incident'.

Our big black Morris had now been replaced by a long sleek Studebaker Champion Saloon, also in black, but adorned with a copious array of shiny chrome plating, which, although discreet by American tastes, still lifted the car into the world of the exotic.

My mother, who was, and continues to be, a beautiful woman, complimented the Studebaker like an archetypal 'American Dream' billboard – something that she was probably far too innocent to be aware of.

The US auto industry was always pushing the boundaries of design and innovation, but before the advent of computer chips, sophisticated systems that we now take for granted, such as climate control and memory seats etc. were only made possible by labyrinthine complexities of rods and levers, of vacuum pipes and motors, of wires and cables and huge amounts of positive thinking.

Often these innovations were impressive and admirable in theory, but in practice, proved to be over optimistic in terms of the limits of the contemporary technology – the accelerator pedal of the Studebaker Champion being an excellent example.

To ask this heroic little pedal to control the engine speed was just fine and, after all, the prime purpose of its existence – to ask it to operate the accelerator jets and the gearbox 'kickdown' was also in keeping with its job description, although when that gearbox turned out to be a manual one, things were beginning

An American billboard'

to get a little risky.

However, the people at Studebaker obviously thought that it would be a real wheeze if the accelerator pedal could be enticed to control the starter motor as well – somewhere amongst the tangle of levers and bushes something inevitably had to give….. and so it proved on this fateful summer's day in 1958.

My mother had parked the car directly opposite the school gates and, as I made the short eager journey to the car, I had no idea of just how quickly feelings of pride and good cheer could turn to disbelief and horror.

All was fine right up to the moment that my mother pressed the accelerator pedal to start the engine. Instead of engaging with the flywheel, the starter motor began to emit an alarmingly loud screeching noise, and to make things worse, we were soon faced with the mortifying truth that there was no way of switching it off or shutting it up.

Almost immediately, we were surrounded by a large group of parents and teachers and, of course, children, all showing signs of concern but actually doing little to hide their cruel appreciation of the ironic comedy of our predicament.

The noise of the runaway starter motor was to continue unabated for what seemed like hours until the battery finally gave up – but even then, the motor didn't stop immediately – it milked every second of its new found celebrity status as it wound down ever so slowly, like a small apathetic air-raid siren after the planes had passed.

By this time, most of the onlookers had drifted away, but not until their smiles and the hysteria of my mother – as she ran round the car in helpless panic – had pushed me to the only course of action left open to me..... to pray to a loving and merciful God to let me die right there and then.

It was in this way that I was introduced to the 'dark' side of cars, and it was probably no coincidence at all, that shortly afterwards, I started walking to school – but I was soon to discover that even this was not without peril.

My final memory of infant education is the way that I was introduced, without any warning whatsoever, to the tragic dichotomy of bullying.

... and therefore, never send to know for whom the bells tolls...

All through the 1950's, an epidemic of Polio ran freely through the towns and villages and cities of England, and although my brother and I escaped the ravages of this insidious disease, the boy who lived across the road did not.

He was a few years older than I was, and bore the evidence of his suffering in the wearing of a single clumsy and noisy leg brace, and strangely, as I think about him now, I feel ashamed at no longer being able to remember his name or his face.

My parents, my father's mother, my brother and I, all lived in a big old red brick house surrounded by gardens that backed on to fields and woodlands and were always on the verge of returning to their wild and natural existence.

The gardens at the front were bordered by tall hedges and trees and two large white wooden gates that had to be opened and closed each time we drove in or out (the fact that my parents could regularly park a car in the middle of a main road while they did this, surely offers a significant and nostalgic clue as to the scale of the traffic that we experienced in those days).

Across the road from our home ran a long line of 'council houses' and although there was no railroad between us, I see clearly now, how we all lived on two very different 'sides of the tracks'.

What nobody from those houses could have realised then, was that our privileged but tenuous way of life was only made possible through the callous self-concern and the relentless emotional blackmail of my father's parents – but that is another story.

For now it is enough to know, that through the years ahead I was to become slowly but surely aware of the resentment that lingered just across the street.

This resentment first impacted my life when on a perfect spring morning, the boy with the leg brace jumped out in front of me as I was walking alone to school.

He had concealed himself behind a gap in a hedge and now stood there before me, blocking my path with eyes of thinly concealed hatred and contempt.

Pre-disposed as I was to day-dreaming, this confrontation was akin to the sudden and violent awakening of a sleep-walker, which made the encounter all the more shocking and disarming.

Strangely, very little was said – his objective it seemed, was simply to keep me standing there for as long as possible and to hold me in a state of terror and submission until he got bored with it all and allowed me to pass.

And so it was, that all through my final summer term at infant school, my solitary journeys to and from school were filled with the fear and the horror of these encounters.

I told no-one, and sought no support or explanation – my feelings were only concerned with my abiding sense of shame and disgrace.

As it all comes back to me now, I realise that there are questions that I have never asked, questions that might now allow some light to enter in upon the darkness and confusion of those troubled days.

How was it that he was free to stalk me in such a way – did he not go to school – did his parents not worry about his absence and his vulnerability..... what did he do on the days that I went by car – how long did he wait..... what sort of pain did he put himself through in order to reach the place of my tormenting.....

Most of all I wonder what kept me standing there when I could have so easily run, or even walked away..... what power did he have over me..... and why did I submit so easily to his will.

Was it the power of his own sense of injustice and the need for redress..... did I feel guilty and compelled to somehow make amends for my own lack of disability.

Although the tenor of our meetings was undoubtedly aggressive – was he, in fact, just reaching out for friendship.

For the seven year old boy from the better side of the tracks there were no such questions or considerations, just the over-riding sense of relief when, at the ending of the summer term, he was able to move up to the primary school and be free at last from the hold of his accuser.

As for me – I feel the heart of an old man growing heavy for the child who, deep down, probably just wanted someone, anyone, to give him an answer to his question..... the question that he was to no doubt carry with him for the rest of his life.....

Why me God..... why me ?

15

Three Childhood Dreams – 2

Like falling stars from the universe we are hurled
down through the long loneliness of the world
until we behold
the pain becomes the pearl

Emmylou Harris

2

He is running from the house and from the faceless terror that is chasing him…..

….. he is running through the front garden to the four huddled fir trees that offer him his first hope of shelter from the cold dark shadow that follows…..

….. before him now there is a rusted wrought iron gate that opens to the road and to his chance of escape…..

….. he struggles to fight the stupor that is now flooding through his body….. his breath crashing upon his chest as waves upon the jagged rocks of his fear…..

….. there are three roads that stretch out in front of him – three roads – three choices – each with its own curving and its own promise of safety and freedom…..

….. to the left – the road rises upon a small hill – as it passes the summit there is a ditch and a thick dark forest beyond…..

….. ahead of him – the road is lined with houses – until it reaches a sharp right hand corner – and then disappears from sight…..

….. to his right – the road leads to a gentle curve upon which there is a narrow track leading to open fields and hedgerows…..

….. he knows that he must reach the bend in one of these without being seen – so that his unknown pursuer will not know which path he has chosen…..

….. every night it is the same – the same frantic flight – the same three choices – the same desperate search for sanctuary…..

….. on this night, he chooses the hill to the left….. he reaches the ditch and lies there waiting – quiet and still – cold – in silence trembling…..

… on fields of dew torn chaos…

… the children are marching – while soldiers sleep…

… somewhere on a twisted hill…

… a boy remains quiet and undiscovered…

… this time

Memo

… and what sort of people are we

that we would

send out our little ones

to stand and defend

the front line

alone

against

the falling darkness

16

A Night In Rio de Janeiro

Choro is the true incarnation of Brazilian soul.
> Heitor Villa Lobos

*Choro is classical music played with bare feet
and callus on the hands.*
> Aquiles Rique Reis

Suite Populaire Bresilienne

1

Mazurka-choro*

Beneath the falling dusk – lovers are shuffling – sanguine and sentient and blissfully content within their slow meandering processions.....

Now and then, they pause and turn to each other – with easy laughter and teasing kisses.....

..... the streets are gently stirring.....

There is a soft sultry song in the air – from down through the years it comes to us now – intimate and sensuous..... we follow its siren call as it moves to invite us in.....

..... to love's bitter sweet dance we come.....

Tonight we would all be lovers

..... this is its promise..... that somewhere among these *ruelas*

---

* Choro, popularly called chorinho ("little cry" or "little lament"), is an instrumental Brazilian popular music genre which originated in 19th century Rio de Janeiro.

Despite its name, the music often has a fast and happy rhythm. It is characterized by virtuosity, improvisation and subtle modulations, and is full of syncopation and counterpoint. Choro is considered the first characteristically Brazilian genre of urban popular music. The serenaders who play Choros are known as Chorões. (Wikipedia) *e avenidas* – love is waiting….. that somewhere here – there are arms waiting to enfold us – lips waiting to kiss our eyes…..

….. and when the dawn comes – it will find us bound and bewitched – in threads of glorious consent – loved one to lover…..

….. this is its promise – and who are we to question or to doubt…..

The narrow street opens into a lively square – punctuated with tables and chairs – with coloured canopies and the smell of fresh coffee…..

….. a small band of musicians call to us with their dancing smiles and with the seductive swaying of their bodies…..

….. their song is noble and proud…..

….. we feel the blood begin to stir in our sleepy veins…..

….. but still – we pass amicably by…..

….. for now we are content with the *canto* of the streets and the soft echo of our own footsteps…..

Somewhere high above the rooftops – a melody is floating – sinuous and sweet – we pause just in time to catch its falling supplications…..

It is the whisper of all who have passed this way before…..

….. in their endless searching for love and light – they speak of joys and heartaches – of laughter and tears – of holding close and letting go – of tender endearments and bitter dissensions….. of bright hellos and dark farewells…..

We are caught for a moment within their ghostly refrain…..

….. but the night is young – all is possible – and for now – we would hear nothing of sadness or foreboding…..

2

Schottisch-choro

She fills the night with her dance…..

She runs as if searching – sometimes hesitant and cautious – sometimes eager – without care or restraint….. searching for distances that she alone can see…..

She is a ballet dancer – a ballerina – delicious and irresistible

- playful and profound - distant yet mercilessly intimate.....

She runs towards the wings - sometimes quickening - sometimes slowing - her feet stuttering to a halt - her arms raised behind her as if to pull her back from the edge.....

She plays with the beat of the music - like a kitten with a ball of wool..... her arms now swaying like reeds and rushes to the eddies of unseen currents and tides.....

In the entrancing lightness of her step - gravity has no part - nor wanting - nor entreating - nor sexual allure.....

She rises above them all - above and beyond..... in another time..... in another place.....

..... and we who came freely - are now held here in her spell.....

..... we who sit and watch - with our hands before us and our hearts safe within..... we are undone - and in our undoing - we are more..... so much more than we were - each moment before.

3

Valsa-choro

We have left the music and the chatter to linger here beside the quiet water - we gaze out into the darkness - lights flickering like candles all across the black broken mirror of the bay.

From somewhere in the distance we hear the solitary calling of a church bell - measured and sorrowful - and for a moment, we are not really sure whether it is real or whether it exists only inside our minds.

From the streets behind us - we can hear laughter and the clinking of glasses - calling us back..... but for now we are contented to be alone - we have stepped off the carousel for a moment - to wait and to ponder.

There is a beauty and a sadness here - it comes to remind us that within the euphoria of love there exists always the fear and the certainty of loss - tears are always waiting - it seems - to baptise our finer feelings.

We are lifted into the glory within the hallowed reaches of a deeper melancholy.

The echo that we heard high above the dusk filled streets – has now returned to disquiet us once again.

But there is no teasing this time – no frivolity – the sensuous mazurka is now a serious and sombre waltz – gone are the playful syncopations – with all their promises of romance and erotic delight.

This is another kind of dance – a dance for lovers – yes – but this dance would lead us to a garden and a hill and to a lonely wooden cross.....

..... for high above – with arms outstretched – ever waiting and ever watching – Love looks down – and weeps.....

4

Gavota-choro

We have fallen back into the now crowded streets – we are running – just for the joy of it – we have no plans – no destinations – we run – we sing – we are drunk on the wine of love.....

..... but wine would ever have its way.....

..... our running becomes heavy and stumbling – we stop – breathless but elated – we look around for a place to rest.....

5

Chorinho

We descend into a midnight bar – the lights are dim and the air is filled with a thick blue haze of cigarette smoke – we have stumbled into a scene from Les Miserables it seems – young men raising their glasses to the glories of future victories – hopes and dreams aroused and exalted through injustice, alcohol and the unassailable optimism of late night camaraderie.

They sing of freedom and equality – arm in arm – they would man the barricades still – as young men have always done and always will.

But in the midst of their bustling anthems – a single melody rises above – plaintive and achingly beautiful – for a moment all is still – mesmerized – enchanted.

A lone voice sings of a freedom that will never be found in the taking of walls and barricades but only in the giving of mercy and love – it sings of an equality that will never be revealed in any victory but only in the willing surrender of a humble and forgiving heart.

We know that we have been touched by truth – but laughter and good cheer are not so easily confounded.

The melody is drowned by wild-eyed speeches and the breaking of glasses – once again – arm in arm the young men join together to dance – kicking and stamping they circle around us.....

..... *while the young women look on in reserved admiration – in bemused but enthralled fascination.....*

The single graceful melody returns once more – for one last encore.

The revellers climb slowly and triumphantly into the street – we follow and watch as their singing and their laughter fade into the night.....

The dawn is stirring.....

We are suddenly alone – without words or intention.....

..... and so.....

we stand at last...

in the simple unspoken humour of being together...

without reason or understanding...

just to shine upon each other...

here in the half-light...

... the whole of existence...

... defined in a smile.

17

Three Childhood Dreams – 3

I am hanging in the balance
of a perfect finished plan
like every sparrow falling,
like every grain of sand.

Bob Dylan

3

He is standing at the edge of a large open field.....
He stands beneath a clear blue sky – the air warm and sweet with the scent of the long green grass.....

All is washed in the golden light of late autumn sunshine.....

All is quiet and strangely still.....

For beneath the silence, the scene is charged with an all pervading presence – that would reach out now to draw him in.....

..... a presence quite unlike the dark malevolent form of his nightmare pursuer – this is loving and good – and with every part of his being he yearns to follow its calling.....

He walks slowly to the centre of the field – his fingers stroking the tips of the grass as he goes.....

He reaches his chosen spot and kneels to lie down – curling foetus like – while the meadows wash over him and hold him in their tender benediction.....

He feels himself pressed into the soft compliant earth and in an instant he is consumed by a warm light flooding through his body.....

There is nothing now but the overwhelming desire to let go – and as he does so – he feels himself to be at one with all things.....

A lifetime later – he will find himself walking by just such a field – beneath just such a sky.....

..... feeling foolish and self-conscious – he will walk to the centre of the field and curl like a child.....

..... and in that moment – as the chains of this world slip away.....

..... the man will become the child once more – and the child will become the man.....

..... the promise of a distant dream – now the guiding light for all that he would seek to be.

18

First Attempts At Driving Backwards

Motion is tranquillity

Stirling Moss

The boy is two years old and he is about to have his first, and completely unexpected, experience of driving a real-life motor car.....

He is perched on the driver's seat of a big old black Morris 25.....

..... constrained by his tender years – he is just able to reach up and touch the steering wheel – and although he has yet to discover the starter button – he is happy to content himself with imitating the sound of a running engine.....

'*brrmm brrmm – brrmm brrmm*'

His mother leans to take his photograph through the open driver's door..... (the photograph that would later become the much vaunted 'mug-shot' of a budding young law-breaker)

Isn't he sweet?

Places to be, people to see

….. a few moments later – he is not so sweet…..

….. a few moments later – he has managed to release the handbrake and the car is now beginning to slip calmly, but purposefully, backwards down the driveway…..

As it gathers pace – it threads itself effortlessly through the two large white gates that access the main road beyond…..

….. the very same large white gates which – for reasons that would later be the topic of loud, prolonged and heavily accusatory 'discussions' – have been left neglectfully and 'unforgivably' open…..

The outing is dramatic but short-lived – the car and its reckless young driver soon come to rest in the middle of Murray Road…..

Slowly but inexorably – the consequences of this arrant wilfulness leach through the quiet surrey morning like a spreading stain…..

The world outside of the car becomes permeated with a

growing cacophony of car horns, intemperate recriminations and an atmosphere of general panic and confusion.....

..... but within the car – hidden safely below the window line – in perfect peace and seclusion – a happy little boy continues with his cheerful chanting.....

'brrmm brrmm – brrmm brrmm'

... but all too soon...

... all too soon...

... his innocent reveries would be cut short by one of life's harsher and more brutal lessons...

... after the fun...

... the fall-out.

19

Surrey In The 1950's

"... and who is my neighbour"

Luke 10:29

For the inhabitants of a small Surrey village – the 1950's were a time of simplicity and order – of stability and easy going security..... life was predictable and self-contained – comfortable and contented.....

Aspirations, as far as they existed, were insular and unwittingly modest..... within the borders of the village – at least in the world outside of our front doors and garden gates – all was exactly as it should be.....

..... 'Tranquilité' indeed.....

..... or so it seemed to little boys – desperately searching for reason and repose amongst the thorns and briers of their wild and tortuous confusions.....

A tacit consent allowed the Church and God (in that order) to preside quietly over our lives – and although religious matters were never discussed in polite company – spirituality was ever humming quietly away in the hinterlands of our collective consciousness.....

Life had boundaries and reassuring parameters..... shops were open from 9am to 5pm every day except Sunday – each day they would shut for a 'Lunch hour' and on Wednesdays they would remain shut for 'Early closing'.....

These opening hours were not mere guidelines – they defined the margins of our lives like benevolently towering stone columns – keeping us from harm – from ourselves – allowing us to enjoy a world, beyond their time-honoured demarcations, that remained quietly and stoically 'shopping free'.

At Christmas shops would close for up to a week – which seemed to suggest conspiratorial undertones to any child who had been given a Christmas present requiring a battery or batteries in order to infuse it with life.....

How interminable the days following Christmas seemed for such a child – watching and waiting as a long coveted toy lay motionless and silently useless before them – patiently waiting until the one and only shop that sold batteries finally opened its doors – thus allowing this bleak and desultory period of battery abstinence to come to an end.....

Shops were small, friendly and dependable..... they seemed happily at ease with the titles above their doors – grocery shops sold groceries – vegetable shops sold vegetables – bakers shops sold bread and cakes – chemist shops sold whatever it was that chemist shops sold and, most importantly, toy shops sold toys.....

Groceries, meat, fish and newspapers could be delivered – if required – by boys on strange looking bicycles with large baskets and tiny front wheels..... each shop was a proud domain unto itself – no one seemed concerned or inclined to duplicate or to step on another's toes.....

Strange as it may seem to us now – garages catered solely for the essential needs of cars, motorbikes, vans and lorries..... the sale of petrol and oil was nearly always accompanied by an amenable cave-like workshop and, in the case of our own Trident Garage – a small but shiny car sales showroom.....

Forecourts were staffed by friendly attendants (made all the more friendly, no doubt, by the practice of tipping) who filled petrol tanks from pumps that stood over us like grandfather clocks – with large dials and ponderously revolving hands..... if asked, he (it was always a he) would check the oil and clean the windscreen before disappearing into his 'office' for change.....

At no point in the proceedings were customers required to wait patiently in line at the petrol pumps whilst the owners of the cars before them – with effortless and carefree indifference to their fellow man – became blithely and irretrievably lost in the slow and discerning acquisition of the week's family shopping.....

Even the weather acceded to the simple and reliable scheme of things – at least as remembered through the eyes of a child.....

Summers were long and hot with the sun forever shining through clear blue skies..... (except, of course, for holidays by the sea – which were equally reliably cold and wet.....)

At the end of each stifling day – once out of sight of the school gates – caps were stuffed defiantly into blazer pockets – and blazers were thrown jauntily and provocatively over arms and shoulders.....

..... essential to this wickedness was the necessity to identify and research likely routes home that would be free from the passing surveillance of teachers and staff – not to mention parents.....

Fields and forests and hedgerows teemed with bugs and bees and endless varieties of butterflies – 'Nature Studies', however, always seemed to be demanding that their elusive beauty be committed to paper – with descriptions and borders and marking by teachers in bright red ink – thus stealing away the simple pleasures of merely being witness to their easy and glorious existence.....

Likewise – our eager abandonment to the ever-present explosion of colours and aromas and general good cheer was always tempered by the need for vigilance towards the constant lurking menace of wasps and, more especially, maybugs – with their menacing drone and their total disrespect for the time limiting implications of their name.....

Autumn coincided with returning – not only to school – but to a new and scary form-room..... and for this reason its colours and hues were always appreciated with some reserve.....

Consolations came with the advent of the conker season and being able to kick our way home from school through growing piles of golden leaves.....

But, in truth, on every child's mind – and heightened by the ever deepening chill in the evening air – was the slow and thrilling build up to Firework night – the surreal gateway through which we all entered in to the dark cold mysterious world of winter.....

..... the lurid yellow smogs that brought our lives to sudden and welcome halts – cobwebs laced with frost and the rush to make the first footprints in the perfect morning snowfall – gloves and scarves and woollen hats – and waking to ice on the inside of our bedroom windows upon which we would bravely scratch our names..... snowballs and sledges forever unfinished – and more kicking homeward – but through thick grey slush this time.....

All would pass imperceptibly from view – as if on one single day the awakenings of spring had filled both the landscapes of our village and the landscapes of our hearts with a sudden single brush stroke of colour and birdsong.....

Easter would mark the moment when coats and jumpers were packed away – never to be seen again until October – as children returned to the summer term – they did so in shirts and blazers – in summer dresses and sandaled feet – walking as only children can – in the quiet knowing of their shared rebirth with all living things.......

And so..... in the village of Ottershaw.....

..... all was as it should be.....

As well as the dozen or so shops – the village had a single telephone box – which was situated across the road from Hunts the Coal Merchants and as far as possible, it seemed, from the village centre..... what it lacked in numbers, it easily made up for by its commanding presence – standing like a miniature cathedral – with its domed roof – its small square glass window panes and its name in large plastic panels that lit up at night like beacons in a storm.....

The 'telephone box', as it was known, became the regular host of those young boys easily given to curiosity and feelings of awe and wonder..... they came singularly, or in pairs – not to make telephone calls – but to stand reverently before the altar of its regal red magnificence.....

Behind its heavy sprung door there hung a shiny black box with large chrome A and B buttons and slots for the receiving and the giving of coins – on the wall above there were lists of mysterious and vaguely conspiratorial sounding numbers and codes – and of course, on the counter top – there was the telephone handset itself – resting authoritatively in its cradle and with its sliding tray beneath – whose true purpose has, to this day, remained persistently and artfully hidden.....

Everything about the telephone box suggested mystery and subterfuge – which led a child's imagination easily and inevitably to the certain conclusion that telephone calls were just a front for a far deeper, and possibly darker, reason for its existence.....

..... a suspicion that was to become fully vindicated by the BBC on the 23rd November 1963.......

Many years later – teenagers would gleefully share the secret of how to take advantage of this distinguished member of the community – calls could be made for free by tapping the receiver in a certain and practised manner – but I was never really happy with this deceit – not through any innate sense of honesty – but because I felt like I was stealing from an old and trusting friend – and anyway – I always managed to get the wrong number…..

At home – there was an equally large shiny black apparatus that stood majestic and aloof on its own 'Telephone Table'…..

Children, with any sense of self preservation, instinctively understood that telephone calls were the sole domain of adults – and an obvious and constant cause of their frustration and irritation….. these same adults were often to be found slamming down the receiver whilst angrily complaining of busy numbers or the blatant selfishness of the other 'Party Line' members….. the whole situation sounded awful and best avoided for as long as possible…..

Telephones came with numbers that were three digits long….. ours was 'Ottershaw 401' – and it was the source of great satisfaction and pride – as well as identity – at a time when all reinforcements to one's identity were greedily and gratefully received…..

To be sure….. the 1950's were a time of simplicity and order – of stability and easy going security…..

….. for some…..

For as with any successful 'club' – are not the needs and the well-being of the eligible addressed and catered for at the expense of those deemed ineligible….. can a club truly exist without maintaining the notion of the 'outsider'…..

In truth – is there not an equation that we would all rather not consider – let alone accept…..

….. that someone – somewhere – no matter how distant and hidden their plight – will always be paying the price for another's privilege – and that long before thoughtless complacency descends to conscious exploitation – are they betrayed…..

In the 'new beginnings' of post war Britain – it must have seemed reasonable and plausible that one hard fought-for victory over injustice and inhumanity would naturally lead to a consensus and a fervour for further such victories…..

In the fertile soil of these hopes and visions were nourished the tender shoots of fairness and equity – of inclusivity and justice….. and as they gave flower – the noble aspirations of Equality and Political Correctness – of Religious Tolerance and Human Rights emerged…..

How far we have come since then….. how far we have fallen….. and yet – the power and the 'veto' of their long lost worthiness remains…..

For in the hunger and thirst for 'right' – once again – once again – forgiveness and mercy lay trampled and contemptuously discarded….. as if they may be summoned back when they are needed – at some other more convenient time and place…..

And so we all now bear witness to the timeless futility of attempting to carve our humanity with tools that have been purged of the tiresome virtues of compassion and love…..

We stand helpless and watch – as the victim becomes the aggressor once more – and the aggressor becomes the victim….. as the sickening circle remains forever unbroken…..

….. as the tender green shoots become warped and contorted by the cankers of bitterness and vengeance….. in the place of graceful flowers – a poison ivy has taken root – strangling and suffocating – blind and senseless in its craving for revenge and satisfaction – forcing us all to stagger and fall beneath its uncompromising assertions of moral superiority and its frantic need for control…..

….. but what do I know…..

….. what can a man with two healthy children and a roof above his head really know about pain and suffering – and what can a white middle class kid really understand about injustice and intolerance…..

Whatever affinities I may have with the 'outsider' – tenuous though they may be – were born over a half century ago in a large red brick house – in a small Surrey village – in a time of 'simplicity and order'…..

….. just a small defenceless outpost of a society in which the Truth of the ages still resonated – however faintly – in the hearts of the many….. a society carelessly and unknowingly watching

– as the last dying breaths of its spiritual memory fade into the night.....

In vain it whispers of a love for our neighbour – a love for our world – a love for ourselves – that can never come through the oppressive constraints of the laws of Man – no matter how profuse – no matter how enticing they may be.....

..... it cannot be contrived – it cannot be imposed – it cannot be manipulated – and it cannot be feigned.....

..... the tragic impotence at the very heart of the socialist dream.....

..... that in supplanting Love with Reason.....

..... it is Reason itself – that withers and dies.

... I think that we can't go around measuring our goodness by what we don't do, by what we deny ourselves, what we resist, and who we exclude.

I think we've got to measure goodness by what we embrace, what we create... and who we include.

Father Père Henri

Memo

If we do not seek

to protect

our

humanity

then what

do we really think

we have left

that is worth

our protection

Part Two

The Die Is Cast

20

Home Sweet Home

Mid pleasures and palaces though we may roam
Be it ever so humble, there's no place like home
A charm from the skies seems to hallow us there
Which seek thro' the world, is ne'er met elsewhere
Home! Home!
Sweet, sweet home!
There's no place like home
There's no place like home!

John Howard Payne

A year before my birth – my father and my mother and my father's parents – all moved into a large red brick house called West Dene.

Unfortunately for my father and mother – it was not the happy event that it might have appeared to anyone happening to be passing that way.....

..... for it was not so much a move – but more a final phase – in the relentless scheming and manipulation that would keep my parents trapped and compliant for the next 18 years.

For my mother – the years of her late teens and early twenties had brought with them a brief but precious taste of freedom and adventure.....

As if tripping through a magic wardrobe – she had fallen into a world of laughter and dancing – of innocent reverie and shy romance – of enticing dreams and easy friendships..... of open hearted suitors and all the sparkling ephemera of 'young love'.

Faces – young – radiant and shining.....

I have lived always as a witness to their star-crossed fortunes – as they reach out across the years – on the wings of small black

A brief taste of freedom

and white photographs – forever whispering of what might have been.

My father met my mother in 1945 whilst picking up drawings from Vickers Armstrong where she worked as a short-hand typist and later, as private secretary to Major Atkinson, their Chief Test Pilot.

It is a sad likelihood that the kindness, encouragement and respect that she received from this man was her first, and possibly only, glimpse of what a fatherly love might look like.

The name that he called her – 'the child' – was either a gentle and affectionate endearment – or a perceptive insight into the fragile secrets of her innermost soul….. or, most probably, both.

My father's only real crime – in the sordid unravelling of events that followed – was simply to fall in love….. it was his parents, and other family conspirators, who 'decided' upon my mother and then proceeded to employ every dark device they could evoke (as was their nature) to lure and capture her.

It was them that followed her in order to discover the wanton 'conspiracy' of her violin lessons – and it was them that contrived – through accusations of unfaithfulness and betrayal – to have them stopped.

My mother 'liked' my father – she was drawn to his gentleness and his simple modesty….. but she was not in love….. maybe this would come later….. but within the crucible of the moment – it was deemed to have no relevance or importance by the powers that now guided her life.

All through the days of late '45 – while a nation celebrated – and its people gave themselves to strange forgotten feelings of optimism and hope…..

….. all through these days of light – a web of darkness was falling upon my mother from which she would never again be free.

And so it was – that on the 4th September 1948 my father and mother were duly married…..

….. and that – at the age of 25 years – my mother – like a child to the gallows – came to exchange one malevolent incarceration – for another.

However….. she was soon to discover that, as far as her marriage was concerned, the scheming had barely begun…..

My grandfather – who owned a large building company in Hersham (though considerably depleted from the depression of the 1920's) allowed my father to use a workshop at the end of his garden to run a small engineering business.

The plan was simple yet fiendishly effective….. my father was warned that – if he decided to leave home with his new bride – then he would be taking his machinery with him.

At the time – buying or even renting another workshop was out of the question for my father – for implicit in the threat, was that there would be no forthcoming financial support from his parents to help him on his way.

From this moment on – my grandfather set about consolidating his hold on my father by building a large new factory in Oyster Lane, Byfleet – by sad chance or by malicious design – directly opposite the Vickers Armstrong site where my parents first met and where my mother was no longer allowed to work.

My grandfather had obviously considered it expedient and concordant with his plans, to move from the building trade to engineering – for by the time the building was finished and occupied, he had come to establish a regime of complete control and regulation over every aspect of my father's life – both at work and at home.

Moving to West Dene was his answer to my mother's continuing pleas for 'a place of their own'….. thus – not the happy event that it might have appeared to anyone happening to be passing that way.

My grandfather celebrated his triumph by attempting to 'force himself' on my mother soon after they all moved in.

My father, who had come home early from work, and to his eternal credit, struck my grandfather in the face – knocking him to the ground.....

..... but his glorious moment of assertion was short-lived and no doubt paid for many times over during the months to come – for, by the very next day, all was back to 'normal' and this atrocious betrayal was never spoken of again.

Many years later, though, it did come to light, through my father, that my grandfather had tried the very same thing with all three of my father's previous girlfriends – all of whom had made hasty retreats, and were never seen again.

It is surely a fair conclusion that my grandfather, having learnt from his mistakes, waited this time, until my mother was securely married, before attempting to lay his sly depravity upon her naïve and unsuspecting heart.

Such was the happy family into whose bosom I was received in the last days of February 1952.

The only memory that I have of my grandfather – is of him lying on his side – beneath the frantic attentions of my parents, my grandmother and our local doctor – on what was soon to become his deathbed.*

I had erringly strayed into his bedroom – at the age of 4 years old – whilst trying to find my parents – and although I was very quickly and firmly 'encouraged' to leave – the memory and, in particular the smell, of his dying – has remained with me – even to the day.

The stories of my grandfather – as passed on by my mother – unquestionably paint a sordid and woeful picture..... but it is a

---

* Following his death – my grandfather's beloved black Spaniel Toby, retreated to the end of the garden, lay down outside his master's workshop, and remained there pining – refusing to eat, drink or be moved – until his own death three days later.

picture – certainly not redeemed – but possibly enlightened – by the many images of my grandfather and myself that lay hidden within the dust of our many family photo albums.

Beaming from the pages there – is the face of a short stocky man – with a large smile and an even larger moustache – playing with his small shiny faced grandson – in the thick crumpled clothes of an unapologetic working man – the pride and the joy of grandfather hood oozing from every pore.....

In the midst of a garden – wild and unpretentious – they share the secrets of a laughter that only they can hear – as the old man pushes the little boy in his very own small grey-painted wheelbarrow..... just one of the exquisite wooden toys that lay scattered across the grass – all patiently and lovingly crafted by my grandfather – in the mysterious depths of his workshop.

As these small faded photographs lay plaintively before me – they seem to be asking the question..... are we not each and every one of us – a conundrum – vile and glorious – precious and tainted....

Who is there that would tell my grandfather's story – who will speak for him and for all of those that have gone before..... who will speak – and who will listen.....

..... from all the moments of his life – I am obliged to choose the darkest – for it is not the best, but the worst in him – that lives here among us – within these broken hours that I now share alone with my mother .....

As I stand here – torn between the pillars and posts of forgiveness and scorn – I am wondering..... from all the moments of my life – for which will I be remembered.....

..... from all the moments of *our* lives – for which will we be judged.....

..... and if it is only for the iniquity of our darkest hours – then who would not now bow their heads in shame at the thought of it.....

Our garden – despite my mother's occasional concerted

efforts – never seemed to rise above the wild and unpretentious stage of horticultural development.

My father's reluctant but dutiful contribution to the world outside of his workshop – was to mow the lawns and, from time to time, to plant things…..

However – my father didn't really get the whole idea of 'scattering the good seed on the land'….. whereas, for most people, the process of planting will usually involve things like flowers and shrubs – or even vegetables and herbs….. my father's attempts at planting involved cast off motor cars and various, redundant garden machinery…..

The earliest victims of this strange obsession – were a breathtakingly beautiful pre-war Lago Talbot – and a large – but not so breathtakingly beautiful – garden rotavator…..

The French built Lago Talbot – whose name still falls like honey from the tongue – was 'planted' many years before it was able to register upon a small child's perception – by which time it was well on its way to returning to the dust from whence it came…..

But even in these final stages of decay – it retained an elegance and a dignity that caused anyone walking by – to instinctively lower their voices in awe and respect…..

This was not the case with the garden rotavator….. this bestial and terrifying machine was, without doubt, the product of a deeply disturbed mind – for it was not so much a machine – but more an experiment in mechanical vivisection…..

On to the front half of a tractor – had been grafted a pair of simple lawn mower handles – beneath which were suspended a set of extremely lethal looking rotary blades…..

With only two wheels – the hapless operator was left to support the back half (trying not to step on the whirling blades) while the snarling beast at the front dragged him helplessly around the garden 'rotavating' everything in its path…..

After nearly killing my grandfather by pinning him to a tree – the monster was left to rot where it stood….. of all the sorry vehicles that my father dreamed of resurrecting – I have no doubts that the garden rotavator was definitely not included .....

Through the years of my early childhood – various additions were made to this surreal garden exhibition..... the trusted old Morris inevitably took its place – closely followed by a special aluminium bodied MG – a large four wheeled concrete mixer – an MG WA – an MG VA – and too many engines and gearboxes to list.....

By the late fifties – my father had reluctantly succumbed to the notion that cars could actually be sold..... although two weeks after selling our Studebaker Champion to a 'friend' – it was ignominiously driven into a ditch and written off.....

..... so maybe my father's first inclinations were right after all.....

Much later – we came to understand that, in my father's mind, all these rotting corpses were never actually destined for such a fate – no matter how they appeared – they were all, in fact, in a state of transition and the subjects of bold and elaborate plans for modification and improvement and the redeeming to a life of mechanical glory.....

However – the meeting place between dreams and reality – was never really a strong point for my father..... and so – they rotted.....

There is a postscript to this episode that is worth relating before moving on.....

The special aluminium bodied MG – known as the GMG – was bought for a specific reason – to develop and test a front suspension system that my father had designed and machined meticulously out of solid pieces of alloy.

He had managed to find financial backing and enthusiastic support for the project from a friend who was both a film director and an amateur racing driver.

All looked promising until the film director crashed and killed himself whilst flying his own light aircraft – leaving the project, inevitably, to flounder and to die.

The story goes that – within a short space of time – the very same design had been developed and tested by someone else and was soon included as standard equipment on every modern day racing car.

For my father – the success that so cruelly eluded him – must have taunted him daily – in the dismantled remains of the GMG and the exquisitely crafted components that were condemned to remain forevermore on the bottom shelf of his workbench.

As a postscript to this postscript – I find that I am unable to silence the voice of my father's mother-in-law in my ear – the indisputable queen of negativity – when she surely proclaimed:

"a very good thing too..... he would only have made lots of money – bought a fast car – and killed himself..... a very good thing indeed".

In keeping with the way that life can often resemble a revolving door..... in September 1955 – a year before the death of my grandfather – my 'middle' brother was born.

After a few years of basic training – he proved to be a useful addition to the family line-up (assuming that the rest of us could be described as 'useful additions') in that, he enabled me to explore all sorts of boyish activities hitherto denied to an only child.

For two young boys – the garden surrounding West Dene – was not so much an area of lawns and trees and flowerbeds and bushes..... but rather – a series of disconnected portals – mystical doorways through which they could pass to worlds beyond.

The portal of choice – was always the magnificent Cherry tree that stood across the lawn from the side of the house..... it had grown in a thoughtful manner – anticipating the needs of intrepid young explorers – to be able to climb, branch by branch, to the very top.

In the spring – its falling blossom garnished the garden like a flurry of soft pink snowfall – and in the summer – it graced our dining room table with bowls of luscious fruit..... it was indeed a prince amongst trees – benevolently watching over us – through all the days and seasons of our formative years.

There was the narrow gravel track that led from the infamous

Work work work

white gates to the garages at the end of the garden – bordered by Apple trees and exotic Japanese Maples – it would become a thinly disguised race-track for budding young rally drivers – curiously trusted with putting the cars away in the garages at night.

There was the tumble-down old Summer House that no one ever sat in – and the Pampas Grass that soaked up cricket balls like a hungry and vengeful sponge.....

.....and then there were the garages themselves – like Aladdin's Caves – bursting with endless assortments of carburettors and steering wheels and huge chrome-plated headlamps that were often inclined to launch themselves from the shelves above onto the heads of unsuspecting 'intruders'.....

..... there was the honeysuckle arch and the well and the mint lined crazy-paving path.....

..... as it all comes flooding over me – I feel both comforted and disturbed in the remembering of it all.....

..... for – although the times spent in the garden – were surely the lightest and happiest of times..... as much as I want to – I cannot say the same – about our lives within the red brick walls of West Dene.

On roadside misdemeanours
the children swop form

while far across the golden distance
gently wanders a dusty caravan...

... as we gaze in studied distrust
from the borders of our contentment

the song of a passing wayfarer
echoes listlessly
beneath vaulted expectations

while ever marked in the cross-hairs
of our brazen defeats

gently wanders the dusty caravan

Once let out into the garden..... (In the appropriate clothing – in the appropriate good health – and in the appropriate weather)..... the two boys were pretty much masters of all they surveyed.......

..... but it was not so – once they were safely reclaimed to the confines of the house.....

After my grandfather's death – the rule of law naturally passed to my grandmother..... and through the tyranny of her dark brooding presence – she was able to keep a grim controlling hand over all that passed as 'daily life'.....

Her surveillance over all things – was rendered infinitely more implacable by her almost complete loss of hearing.....

With communication, let alone conversation, almost impossible (especially for young children) – her presence took on a ghostly 'all-seeing' – 'all knowing' – 'all-judging' demeanour…..

….. like a sinister fore-shadowing of CCTV – she wandered silently through the house – ever vigilant and ever watchful for lapses in suitable behaviour and manners and dress – and especially – for transgressions in frugality…..

….. lest we be seen to be squandering her son's hard earned wages.

As a result – toys, clothes, books – in fact, anything at all that could be seen as being unnecessary for basic existence – had to be smuggled into the house with whispered entreaties such as, "hide it from grandma" or "don't let grandma see"…..

(Why the whispering I now ask myself)

Offending articles were quickly stuffed under beds – or thrown on the top of wardrobes….. thus life 'within' was forever furtive and under-handed – full of consternation and fear of being found out and exposed.

Once upon a time – my grandmother had been an accomplished violinist (as was her sister) – the leader of an orchestra – a musician from a family of musicians….. but once married – her music was forbidden….. that she might be free of distractions in the carrying out of her duties to her husband and her home…..

It is only now that it comes to me…..

….. why was her violin nowhere to be found in any of the rooms of the house…..

….. surely it could not possibly have escaped the inquisitive explorations of two little boys….. or the dispassionate clearing of her 'worldly possessions'….. was it disposed of years before….. to seal the dastardly act perhaps – to quell any lingering temptations that she might harbour – to hold it – and to play upon it once more.

All that was left from the joys of her past – was a simple upright piano – that I, nor anyone else, would ever remember hearing her play.

In the stealing of her music – her deafness took over from where my grandfather left off – and until this moment – I have

Dad, me and the Studebaker in its glory years

never considered – the broken dreams of a bright young women, used and betrayed – forced to renounce a life of colour and passion for a cold, dark and lonely prison cell…..

….. and who would have been there – to comfort her and to cup her tears….. *until this moment – I have never considered* – what, in another life, we might have shared…..

In keeping with pre-war fashion – our skirting boards and picture rails and large panelled doors were all covered in a thick layer of dark brown paint.

However – by the late '50's – the rush to be 'Modern' had seen picture rails torn down – panelled doors covered with white painted hard-board sheets and every horizontal surface in the kitchen over-laid with Fablon, Formica and Lino – the choice of which, appeared to be dependent upon their relative height above the ground.

The whole process seemed to require an onlooker – i.e. my

mother – to approve each act of 'liberation' (that would now go under the title of vandalism) with un-inhibited squeals of glee – all the time proclaiming….. "Ooh – how modern!"

Even as a child – although being pleased for my mother's enthusiasm – I feared that the situation was all a little odd and ill-considered – and before too long – my fears were proved to be surprisingly well founded…..

….. for slowly and sadly – as the corners and the edges of the shiny kitchen coverings became unglued – the resultant gaps soon became filled with dust and dirt and small crumbs of food….. the perfect antidote to a healthy young appetite…..

Although not with my grandmother – there *were* times of sharing in our home….. times of precious respite – as if we were all responding as one – to the irresistible calling of a divine 'half-time whistle'…..

As I think upon it now – my inclinations to be 'creative with my hands' were born – not in my father's workshop – but sitting with my mother on the floor of our 'living room'…..

Here she would draw effortlessly from strange hidden wells of patience and invention….. and as we explored together the simple resources of cardboard folders (lifted from my father's office) sellotape and scissors….. it seemed as if there was nothing that we couldn't make…..

Later – as I learnt to 'fly solo' – my creativity would become predominantly concerned with the making of army lorries – with opening doors and bonnets and tailgates and wheels that turned on matchstick axles…..

….. however – the effort required for their construction bore little relation to their on-going usefulness – they were meditations upon the perfecting of a single design – 'leitmotifs' for days of sickness and boredom – nothing more….. like delicate and glorious Mayflies – they would shine for a day and disappear….. their quiet sacrificial demise – though proud and noble….. was very soon forgotten…..

Cardboard lorries took their place beside Meccano cranes and plastic ships and balsawood aeroplanes that would hang by cotton threads from our bedroom ceiling…..

….. but all of these lofty endeavours were as nothing compared to the sticky triumphs of late December…..

As we entered the long-awaited (and much needed) season of 'Peace on earth' and 'Goodwill to all men' – of red Holly berries lighting up the house and Carol singers in huddled rows upon the frost covered grass of our front garden….. as we listened and waited through 'Silent Nights' and 'First Nowells' – my brother and I took our place within the mysterious and enchanting world of Christmas preparations…..

All around the newspaper covered borders of our old oak dining table – we would sit in obedient anticipation of our mother's guiding wisdom through the unravelling of everything that was festive and sparkling…..

….. before our eyes – flat lifeless tangles of coloured paper would be transformed into magnificent hanging lanterns and paper-chains would grow like summer daisies between our fingers (in proportion to the feelings of sickness in our stomachs from the glue upon our tongues…..)

But the crowning of the moment was without doubt – the making of the Christmas Cards….. for as my mother led us through the cutting and the folding and the painting of snow covered fields and trees and cottages and churches – she became as a loving and beautiful wizard – the mistress of all things wondrous and magical…..

….. and with the final mystical sprinkling of the silver glitter – it was as if a wand had been waved – a blessing had been bestowed….. for in an instant – we were no longer apart from our creations – we were taken in – we were taken through – into a place of 'Peace on earth' – of 'Goodwill to all men'….. of 'Silent Nights' and 'First Nowells'…..

….. and with this single act – simply and quietly – without the need for shouting or contrivance – my mother had showed us all – beyond question or doubt – that when it came to the really important things of life – there were things that adults 'knew' and children, most obviously, did not.

The onward march of technology within our home – was spearheaded – initially by an elegant floor-standing Cossor radio and later by an august looking Pye television set.

The Cossor valve radio was a present from my father's parents to my mother and father on their wedding day….. through many ups and downs it has travailed – with its gentle and kindly contributions to family life – a true and faithful friend to each of us…..

For a child – every sound that passed through its shiny brass meshed speaker grill – seemed to be imbued with an added sense of dignity and gravitas….. we came as to shrine – to cherish such broadcasting sublimities as 'Listen with Mother' or 'Uncle Mac's Family Favourites' or 'The Archers' or – sublimity of sublimities – 'Round the Horne'…..

'Round the Horne' followed on from 'The Archers' – both of which accompanied our leisurely Sunday Lunch….. it was the one true family moment of the week….. a time of uncharacteristic peace and togetherness….. of laughter and good cheer…..

….. and even though – for my brother and myself – the reason for this laughter would be ever a mystery – the tears of mirth that would fall from my father's eyes – were as drops of rain – on a parched and broken land…..

….. as it watches over me now – with its chunky Bakelite knobs and its small oblong dial….. through the soft glow of its warm golden light – my eyes are still drawn to the rows of exotic sounding names….. Luxembourg and Vienna….. Oslo and Budapest….. Moscow and Droitwich!!!

….. still I can feel their calling – and still I can feel the restlessness in my feet – from the romance of their song.

All that represented our limited interest and interaction with

the 'world beyond' – was conveyed to us through our radio.....
times of joy – of singing and laughter..... times of sadness – of
calamity and horror.....

From the latter – there is one that remains as vivid as the day
in November 1963 when it first spilled out into our unsuspecting
home.....

At the age of 11 years old – I had no idea who President John
F Kennedy was – and I certainly didn't understand the meaning
of the word 'assassination' – but from the harrowed tones of the
announcer – and from the unusually restrained gasp from my
mother's lips – I knew that it couldn't be a good thing.....

As I reach out now to touch its dark polished veneer – I am
sure – as I always have been – that those terrible words echo still
– within the wires and cables and valves and connections of our
faithful old radio..... a burden amongst many that it carries – lest
we stumble and forget.....

Such was the presence and the dignity of our Cossor radio –
that even after the television set was safely ensconced in its very
own 'Television room' – it was never completely passed by in
favour of the somewhat lofty pretensions of the newcomer.

The Pye television set did have one significant edge over our
radio though.....

..... it resided within a large square wooden cabinet behind two
thick wooden doors..... which meant that it was able to remain
– as a prima-donna – concealed and aloof until the moment that
the doors, like the curtains of a theatre, were opened to reveal
the ensuing entertainments.....

It also benefitted from an intriguing array of small adjustment
buttons – controlling 'Height' and 'Width' – 'Vertical hold'
and 'Horizontal hold' etc..... that, together with the mesmeric
wonders of the 'Test Card', turned out to be an endless source of
experimentation and fun.....

On the other hand – we soon came to learn that they could
also be an endless source of frustration and anger – as, one by
one, we all took turns on our knees – in a series of desperate,
and often futile, attempts to bring reason and order to a wildly

distorted or rolling picture…..

However – by way of redeeming itself – our television set would always close the evening with a small white farewell dot in the middle of its screen…..

….. after the usual tensions of our nightly televisual experience – there was always something strangely comforting about watching this friendly little dot as it got smaller and smaller – until that marvellous moment – when none of us could be absolutely sure – if it was really there or not…..

But neither the Test Card nor the Dot could delay the inevitable passing of the first innocent flush of TV euphoria – for it soon became apparent to the suspicions of the younger viewer – that the restrained and haughty sobriety of the single BBC channel – was selling them woefully short…..

'Listen with Mother' – that had been transformed through a humbling display of literary imagination into 'Watch with Mother' – only confirmed our worst fears….. what we instinctively craved were programmes that 'Mother' wouldn't want to watch – with or without us….. the very strange goings-on between Andy Pandy, Looby Loo and Teddy – just didn't rock our little sailing dinghies anymore…..

Of course – we were mercilessly nudged along this path of enlightenment – by the constant teasing of all the children whose worlds had been opened to the glories of ITV…..

The school playground had become rent apart into two irreconcilable groups….. the 'haves' and the 'have nots' of visual entertainment…..

….. while the one would huddle to share animated replays of the previous evening's fare – the other would gaze silently across in heavy-eyed envy – straining with every fibre to hear – as across the divide floated unbearably thrilling names such as 'Rin Tin Tin' and 'Boots and Saddles' and 'Rawhide' and the mischievously tongue-twisting 'Four Feather Falls'…..

As agonizing as it was – the situation may just have been bearable – if it hadn't had been for the final cut of the knife – the ultimate of taunts – the affliction to which there was no comfort or consolation….. like Oliver with his bowl – we came naked, pitiful and hungry – before our brutal and heartless separation from the TV Advertisement…..

As we wandered like outcasts through our desolate TV wilderness – life became a meaningless cycle of mocking and loss….. without the courage of heroic Collie dogs to inspire us – or the chirpy refrains of cartoon character salesman to lift our spirits – the future looked bleak indeed…..

….. something had to be done….. my parents needed to be made fully aware of the deprivation that they were inflicting on their children….. they needed to know – and they needed to act…..

….. and so – I fell back on the only means of communication that I knew….. emotional blackmail….. applied with relentless and artful cunning….. I had been an attentive pupil and I had been taught well….. now it was time to bring out the 'big guns'…..

Over meals and at bedtimes – during trips in the car and while waiting at bus-stops….. no opportunity was missed to speak of missed educational opportunities – of suffering school-work – of fading friendships…..

….. it was only a matter of time…..

And so it was – that our grand old Pye was replaced with a stylish new TV from Rediffusion….. with its enormous 17inch screen and its minimal modern case – this was not a machine that needed to hide behind shutters or to blend in with all the other pieces of furniture….. the Rediffusion was bold and assertive and demanded to have the attention of everyone in the room…..

….. we loved it from the start…..

….. we were now fully paid up members in the brave new glossy world of TV advertising….. what joy – what rapture – what enlightenment…..

….. we could sit and wonder at the whiter than whiteness of clothes washed in Daz and Persil….. the 'locked in flavour' of Hartley's jam….. the hitherto unexplored possibility of going to work on an egg…..

Basic Training

..... advertising jingles could now be sung and whistled in joyful affirmation of 'belonging'..... gardens and shops and playgrounds echoed to the seemingly endless outpouring of perky little tunes and catchphrases.....

..... but as far as children were concerned – there was one that rose above..... peerless and unrivalled in its perkiness and visual delight.....

'The Esso sign means happy motoring' was a gem of minimalism and understatement.....

..... just a series of disembodied heads bouncing around to the music – each depicting its own cheeky little racial stereotype..... (though all of them singing with strange quasi Mexican accents.....)

..... so chirpy – so cute – so gleefully patronising..... who could resist their allure or their pleas to 'call at the Esso Sign'..... who could be so cruel as to drive on by and disappoint these charming little characters.....

Although we would always sing along with unbridled gusto – in reality – 'Happy Motoring' was not something my brother and I knew a lot about.....

If we had come to discuss the matter – we would probably have come to the conclusion that it was something akin to those fleeting moments – between my mother's screams – her clawing at the dashboard and her attempting to jump from a moving vehicle..... and the hours spent in lay-bys – with our father obscured beneath an open bonnet – and our mother trying to distract us from the strange muffled 'words of encouragement' coming from the front end of the car…..

….. and yet – we still sung the song – just as later we would all be singing 'ground control to Major Tom'….. never let it be said that lack of empathy ever got in the way of a good tune…..

In the way of Father Christmas and the tooth fairy – it soon became painfully apparent – that no amount of visits to the Esso garage was going to change the situation…..

….. and so….. we were faced with our first undeniable clue as to the rarefied and dangerously disconnected existence of the 'Advertising Man'…..

….. if only we all could have had more compassion and understanding towards his plight….. maybe, we might have saved him from the sad pitiable creature that he has now become…..

By this time – my brother and my father and myself had all come to understand – that there was a protocol in our home that we could not challenge or question – *'After the screaming the guilt'*….. our guilt ! – for as with every criticism of my mother's behaviour – open or implied – there was always a mitigating and accusatory story that would follow …..

….. her contributions towards our family's lack of 'Happy Motoring' were definitely no exception…..

21

My Mother, In Her Own Words

I wondered if the person who really loves you
is the person who knows all your stories,
the person who WANTS to know all your stories.

Gabrielle Zevin

"When I was a child, my father would drive us to the top of a
hill and then pretend the brakes had failed and let the car roll
backwards down the hill. When we were all screaming and
crying, he would laugh and tell us it was just a joke."

My mother's stories were never meant for entertainment or edification..... they were always delivered in a raised angry voice and they would always start with the words 'When I was a child.....'

Although disarmingly simple – they were impressively flexible in their applications..... they could be used as a form of defence or justification – or they could be used as a form of attack – of accusation and rebuke towards 'wicked, selfish, ungrateful' children..... (and husbands too if need be).....

"When I was a child, we never had any toys or time to play, but I
was happy to help with the cleaning and the cooking and with looking
after my brother and sisters. I wouldn't have dared to complain or
refuse".

"When I was a child, I had to cover my sisters' ears at night with
pillows, so that they couldn't hear our parents screaming at each other
downstairs".

"When I was a child, we had to do what we were told straightaway. Once when I was reading a book that I had saved for months to buy, my mother asked me to lay the table, and because I just wanted to finish the paragraph I was reading, she snatched it out of my hands and threw it in the fire".

"When I was a child, I used to cry for piano lessons, but all my parents could afford was a cardboard keyboard that didn't make a sound".

"When I was a child, we used to have to go to the bomb shelter at night. One night my best friend and her parents, who lived over the road, received a direct hit on their shelter, and when we came out in the morning, their house had disappeared".

"When I was a child, I had no encouragement at all from my parents. Once when I took part in a Swimming Gala at school, no one came to see me. I was only thirteen and I had to walk all the way home across London at night because my father wouldn't get up from reading his paper. Because I won first place in Breaststroke, they said I could choose a prize, so I chose a tablecloth for my mother, When I gave it to her, she told me off for not choosing something for myself".

"When I was a child, we never had any affection shown to us. When I was in hospital with Diphtheria for 3 months my father never came to see me, and when they said I could go home I cried for them to let me stay in the hospital. When my little sister was only three, she caught Diphtheria too, and when she came home after 4 months I rushed to cuddle her because I had missed her so much. My parents were just ignoring her but when I picked her up my mother shouted at me to put her down because I would spoil her".

My mother's stories were the last word on every situation – they were the judgment bar – the stone upon which we fell and were broken….. in the face of the constant and vivid reminders of the harsh misery of her childhood – we had no place to hide

– save for the desolate shelters of guilt and shame….. they were the shining example of courage in the face of adversity – before which – we would ever be seen as wanting…..

….. my father's stories – on the other hand – were not like that…..

The stories that my father told, only appeared at bedtimes, and were only concerned with one single narrative thread…..

….. this 'thread' described the lives of a family of small furry creatures that lived in Nutwood….. whose telephone number – bearing in mind that my father was not known for his pushing at the boundaries of the English language – was Nutwood 1212…..

When asked about his childhood – my father would always say that he couldn't remember….. and as I always took my father to be a typical example of manhood – it lead me to the obvious conclusion that boys, as opposed to girls, had their memories wiped clean in the process of becoming men…..

This never really alarmed me – in fact – I came to find the idea quite comforting….. but the years have passed – and I still find myself waiting for this particular yoke to be lifted from my shoulders…..

As it was in the beginning – so must it remain….. which means – that it is now only right that my mother should have the last word on the subject of stories…..

"When I was a child we had no garden so we had to play in the street. One day, when I was 9 years old, the man in the basement dragged me into his room and took my clothes off and tied me up. My mother had been cleaning her carpets on the top floor balcony and saw it all happen, so she ran down the stairs to save me. After that, no one said anything, because they were worried what people might think".

This jolly tale is different from the rest – not only because of its appalling content – but because – 70 years later – it came to light that my mother had not told us the whole story.

I had taken my mother for a short break to the Grayshott Health Spa and had come to her room in the early evening so that I could walk with her down to the 'restaurant' – that we might have supper together.....

As she came towards the door – she suddenly stopped and turned and stared silently out of the window.....

..... and then – as if talking in her sleep..... she told me in a slow quiet voice – completely devoid of emotion.....

"..... after that man took me into his room..... I always felt that I was nothing".

..... by a strange twist of fate..... at around the same age
..... I came to the very same conclusion about myself.

22

I Discover The Beauty Of The 'Road'

Thus Nature, rejoicing, has shown us the way,
with innocent revels to welcome the day.

Nahum Tate

The boy is 8 years old.....
..... he is hanging suspended..... powerless – helpless – in mortal dread and reluctant wonder.....

..... he watches from a distance – while far above – from oceans beyond – a small evanescent circle of lucid green light shimmers quietly in the sunlight.....

..... a wreath – a crown perhaps – beckoning and beguiling – taunting and teasing – threatening and menacing..... and all with one softly murmuring voice.....

..... he claws in desperation – his lungs burning – his heartbeat breaking like thunder all across the flooded landscape of his senses..... but the thick dark waters hold him jealously – in their cold unrelenting fingers.....

….. with each flailing of his arms he grows weaker – he can fight no longer – his aching flesh – longing to surrender – to fall back into the darkness – forever…..

….. but the need to survive overpowers him – his body – his very soul – assert their irresistible longing for air and light…..

….. in the last reaching of his strength – he bursts out suddenly – into bright morning sunshine – filling each drowning breath with the cool clear air of an early summer's day…..

….. he is free….. he is free…..

….. from thwarted depths comes the angry stammer of a wrought iron gate as it clanks shut behind him – vowing vengefully that next time – he would not be so lucky…..

And so….. another school day begins…..

….. once more he has escaped from the madness within – the stifling restraints of his mother's tyranny over all things…..

….. for now – for just a little while – he can forget…..

….. the way that he must put on his socks – the way he must tie his shoe laces – the way he must brush his teeth and comb his hair – the way he must cut his food and the order with which the correctly diminished portions must then be placed upon his fork – the clothes which must be worn in respect of the anticipated weather for the day ahead – the screaming that accompanies the smallest deviation from these prescribed directives and – of course – the instructions for his conduct whilst away from home – instructions that will follow after him like a clawing black bridal train…..

….. for now – he can forget….. for now – he can breathe once more…..

He thinks of his father who – once dangerously exposed from the safety of his sleep – will hastily grab a cup of tea and a ginger biscuit and be gone – fleeing through the two large white gates – leaving the turmoil as just a small fading memory in his rear view mirror…..

….. how wonderful it must be to 'work' – to have a plan – a plan of escape – a plan that has been laid open to scrutiny and been pronounced 'acceptable'.....

..... but alas - such things are beyond the dreams of little boys.....

..... they must remain and run the full compass of each day's horror - of home and school and home again.....

..... they must hold their breath and bite their tongues.....

..... to be sure..... little boys must grin and bear it.....

His daily walk to school may be only thirty minutes long - but as he takes his first eager step each day - he enters instinctively into a holy place - a place where time has become effortlessly and amicably suspended - a sanctuary within whose warm embrace he has ceased to strive or to fret..... a sanctuary from which he may gaze out for a while - in awe and avid fascination.

As the world beyond his simple perceptions passes slowly and regally before him - life becomes but a series of ever evolving images - a numinous slide show of shapes and sounds and smells and endless tactile invitations..... he watches as through a kaleidoscope - the changing seasons and colours and glories of nature..... gifts laid freely and bountifully at his feet - as to a king his treasures.

The boy has discovered the timeless beauty of the 'Journey'..... a sanctuary - a shelter - an adventure for one..... a 'time out of time'..... a glimpse of eternity that will remain with him for the rest of his life.

Ah, the journey - the journey.....

..... where else do the worlds of time and space find such easy co-existence with the worlds within - such happy interface - such gracious accord.

The journey entreats us to step outside of reasoned things - to cease from that movement that is no movement - for just a little while - for just a moment.....

..... and as we let go into its open arms - we find there no coming or going - no leaving or arriving - no destinations - no departures..... neither haste nor languor.....

..... there is but the journey itself – unfolding into its own fulfilment of purpose and being.....

.....the journey..... our journey..... it has become everything.....

..... and as we cease to move – there in the stillness – as we step into the journey of the moment.....

..... we become dwellers within the vast cosmic 'Pause' of existence.....

..... for it is within the pauses – the spaces between – that we truly 'live and move and have our being'..... the spaces between the notes – between our hearts – between the smallest particles of matter..... the 'cracks in everything' through which the light of spirit comes shining.....

To this end – the journey is a chink in the armour of all that dwells deeply on the physical plane .....

For in the mind of this world of paradigms and deadlines – of labels and judgments – of successes and failures..... it is ok to be 'on a journey' – it is permissible – acceptable – even laudable.

On a journey – we are no longer wastrels – or in denial – or avoiding responsibilities – or lazy..... we are no longer helpless nor hopeless dreamers..... no – we are on a Journey – a journey to better things.

A window has opened before us – and as we gaze out on a vista entirely free from old encumbrances and limitations – we find ourselves standing in a place of renewed hope – of optimism and resolve – a place where every soul may start afresh – where everything seems suddenly possible.....

..... the journey..... our journey..... has become but a divine conduit to our healed selves – redeemed – justified – accepted..... loved.

Later..... for the man..... there will be no rejected husbands – or dislocated fathers..... there will be no jobless – or homeless – or loveless – or broken handed musicians.....

..... just as here – now – in a small Surrey village – on a bright summer's morning in 1960 – for a boy on his unhurried way to school..... there are no spelling tests – or multiplication tables –

or glutinous bottles of morning milk – and there are no scowling teachers – nor fears of rejection or ridicule or doing 'wrong'.....

..... it is now as it will always be – the journey calling – his soul aching..... his spirit – ever listening – ever attentive – for the song of the road – the railway track – the oceans before him – the heavens above.....

.....and as his heart reaches out – to fields and forests – rivers and streams – hills and valleys – to seas and skies.....

... he will find at last – a place of belonging...

... a place where his song may find its home – cradled within the greater song...

... the Song of Ages...

... a love song – pure and sublime ...

... the eternal song of love at the very heart of all things.

From the big red brick house at the bottom of Spinney Hill – the road winds gently up to the village of Ottershaw..... and after the allotment that adjoins his parent's garden – the right hand side of the road is lined by hedgerows that in turn border fields and farmlands and small copses of trees way across in the distance.

This particular path of Green Belt is interrupted only by a small run-down cottage that peers – almost completely obscured – from behind large overgrown hedges and bushes and free roaming undergrowth..... a cottage inevitably designated by young boys – ever on the lookout for mystery and excitement – as 'The Witches Cottage'.

For the first half of his journey – his right hand side is illumined by swathes of golden light rolling in from the meeting place between field and sky.....

..... this cannot be said of the land to his left.

After a string of uninspiring pre-war bungalows – prising themselves haughtily into his otherwise convivial itinerary come two long dark sinister looking buildings – with only a short

Salad Days

respite of privet hedge and slatted wooden fencing between them.

The first building is called 'The Isolation Hospital' – and the second – in splendidly 'Non-PC' local parlance – is referred to as 'The Mental Hospital'.

As the boy passes cautiously by – he imagines that he can feel the weight from hundreds of pairs of sad staring eyes – bearing down on him from the rows of small black windows above – so that – as he quickens his step – his short journey takes on a deeper hue – with the boy – as he walks the precarious line between darkness and light – unknowingly describing – in tarmac and stone – a simple metaphor for the life of the pilgrim.

As he leaves the first building behind – he reaches the hedge with its soft new shoots and the fence with its vertical wooden slats….. for the boy – and later for his friends – this will become the 'place of running'.

Sometimes he will run with the fingers of his left hand dancing across the wooden slats – and as he does so – he will delight in the sound that his effort produces – for – to the ears of a young boy – it will be the unmistakable sound of a small aeroplane engine – idling before take-off.

Sometimes his running will allow propellers of leaves – carefully skewered on thin wooden stalks and in defiance of all known physical laws – to whirr away freely and happily in the early morning breeze.

Sometimes he will run – just to express the joy and exuberance of life – and possibly to forget that – in his dreams – this is often the spot where he looks down in horror to discover that he is walking to school still dressed in his pyjamas.

No matter the format – his running will take him past the second long dark sinister looking building i.e. 'The Mental Hospital' – to the small converted chapel and the first signs of Ottershaw crossroads.

As he slows once more to a wistful amble – he comes to a large imposing building on his right that circumscribes a mysterious partly hidden inner courtyard in the manner of an ancient medieval castle. The walls are tall and built of crusty old red bricks – and although devoid of windows – are lined from top to bottom with rows of small thin vertical slits.

The local legend attached to this building – is that it is a Battery Farm for the incarceration of unfortunate poultry….. but until the day of its demise – the boy never sees or hears any proof of this…..

….. and his interest anyway is far more concerned with the fact that one of the castle walls borders the bus stop that is shared by the magnificent double-decker omnibuses of the London Transport and The Aldershot and District Traction companies.

Tickets must be shewn!

Everything about these vehicles is so wonderfully distinct from the other – from the livery through the seat upholstery to the beautiful chunky cast alloy ticket machines.

The Aldershot bus is wide and low with the passenger entrance at the front served by a fully closing door. The London

Transport bus, on the other hand, is tall and narrow with a rear entrance and just a simple permanently open jump on/jump off platform.

To have these two transports of delight in the same place at the same time is almost too much excitement for the esoteric inclinations of this particular young child to bear.

And then – as if this were not enough – there is the heart-stopping thrill of the 'bus stop protocol'.

The light green 48 and 48A buses of the Aldershot and District company simply pass through on their way from Chertsey to Woking and beyond – but the dark green 461A buses of London Transport use the island between the main roads and the chicken wall as a 'turn around' on their way back to Walton on Thames via Addlestone Bus Station.

Occasionally though – and for no apparent reason to young bus spotters – the 461A will spurn the chance of a quick double back to the bus station and continue all the way to St. Peter's Hospital.

Public transport obsessed youngsters – or at least one – find this anomaly tantalising in the extreme – as well as the fact that – although sharing the same plot of land – both companies stubbornly insist on placing their own distinctive bus stops side by side on this hallowed ground.....

..... a potent stimulus indeed for a flowering young imagination.

Often – and strangely always at this very point in his journey – he will pass the old man with the thick grey beard and long ragged coat and the slow stooping gate – the one and only 'local character' – our very own prophet of doom – with his placards strapped front and back warning in no uncertain terms that 'The End is Nigh'.

Only once has the boy found the courage to say hello to this strange old man – and as their eyes met for just a fleeting moment – the boy was shocked and somehow changed at the kindliness and the warmth that he saw there.

No one seems to know anything about the old man – except

for the fact that his days – and probably his nights as well – are spent in the continual sharing of this simple but urgent message.

Fourteen years later – whilst driving through the village late one summer's evening – the boy will pass the old man at exactly the same spot..... his beard thinner and whiter – his shuffle slower and the obvious cause of considerable pain and hardship – and his stoop now such, that his chin falls deep into his hollowed chest.....

..... but still strapped to his body – though maybe a little more faded this time – is the same dire warning.....

The End is Nigh

..... a man of patience..... without a doubt.

As the boy crosses the junction between Murray Road and Brox Road – his path – and the path of his school chums Paul and Ned (aka Stephen) converge with impressive military style precision.

No one questions the meticulous timing necessary for such an effortless act of synchronicity – whether it be by planning or the chance result of constant daily repetition – no one questions or seems in the least bit concerned to acknowledge – there is just the quiet expectation that this is the way things are.

It is at this point in his journey that a most profound and significant social exchange takes place.

Anyone passing by at that moment would merely be aware of three boys greeting one another with the short, friendly but 'rather common sounding' exclamation.....

'Watch Ya'.

However – the boys know – and cherish the fact – that deeper things are afoot.

It is not just a simple greeting that has passed between them – it is the flowering of the first tentative and tender shoots of the assertion of the 'individual' – not to be suppressed or denied or in any way taken lightly.

It is a password into the secret and magical society of childhood – a society that very soon will become full of similar such codes and ciphers and signs..... all instinctively created to protect the child's unique place in the generational scheme of things.

It soon becomes apparent to the newly initiated – that it is essential for the salutation to be exclaimed proudly – with volume being an integral element in the proceedings.

For the boy – it is the very first time in his life that he has expressed himself in a way that hasn't been determined by adults. It is thrilling and exciting – and when he understands the meaning of the words – it will be covert and rebellious – with unmistakable traces of wanton subversion.

Once this cheery interchange has been accomplished – with all its implications of comradery and subterfuge – the boys shuffle past the Otter Public House pausing only to gawp and wonder at the latest in a gleaming succession of XK Jaguar sports cars – all owned by the landlady Mary England – and all proudly bearing the number plate ME 93.

The boys never tire – it seems – of the hilarious similarity between the name 'Mary England' and the jovially jingoistic 'Merry England' (as if they are the first to notice this jocular fact) – so that – a soft exchange of knowing chuckles is regularly audible long after the main event has passed.

By crossing the road between the Pub and the small second hand car sales garage that nestles in the crook between the road to Guildford and the road to Chobham – they embark on the final – although perhaps a little more dilatory – leg of their journey to school.

The short path from the road crossing to Trident Garage is unquestionably bland and dull – and even the combined imaginations of these three boys can find no way of interacting with the adjacent scenery.

Still….. fun tinged with a hint of mischief is ever the order of the day – so that opportunities offered by the immediate environment for merriment and exploration are quick to re-assert themselves….. the final stretch up to the church and down again is no exception.

But first – they must traverse the busy and hazardous entrance and exit to and from Ottershaw's sole provider of petrol, oil and car maintenance.

Trident Garage comprises – a petrol station – a workshop – and a small car sales showroom. The various buildings are set back from the road to such a degree – that it is intuitively obvious to budding young motor enthusiasts that any interest shown by them in the cars standing on the forecourt – would immediately be perceived by the staff as unwarranted and potentially harmful intrusions into the security of the premises.

Consequently – Trident Garage is summarily ignored and attentions switched to the point at which the narrow unmade Church Road forks away gently from the main road ahead.

Along the side of the path that leads up the hill is a hedge – and behind the hedge is a wooden fence which – as it turns out – has been erected in such a manner as to produce a small child size gap between the hedge and the fence.

And so – the final adventure of the journey is born – the object of which – is to simply get as close to the school as possible without resorting to walking on the pavement – or at least – if it is unavoidable – to walk on the pavement for as little time as possible.

The boys in an instant become fearless jungle explorers – fighting through leaf and twig and thorn and brier….. partly for the fun of it – partly for the challenge…..

….. but mostly for another more worthy reason entirely.

By now – The Three Muskateers have been joined on their journey by other small groups of boys and girls….. most crucially – girls.

Other boys have already been warned to 'find their own

game' – but the girls – to a man – show no signs of wanting to join in.

The game is obviously, therefore, a 'boy thing' – and with this hasty assumption do the three lads embrace the age old folly that has been the blight and the downfall of the male sex from the beginning of time.

The logic, though deeply and tragically flawed, goes blindly but confidently like this…..

1. The girls/women do not want to join in because the activity is simply too dangerous or too demanding for them.
2. They would love to join in if they could.
3. The girls/women must therefore be impressed by the courage, the strength and the daring of the boys/men.
4. By thus impressing the girls/women, the boys/men must be making excellent headway up the ladder of male/female bonding procedures.

Big mistake!

At no point do the boys/men even remotely consider that the girls/women are not joining in because they think it is all too silly, a complete waste of time, and, quite honestly, typical of the ridiculous lengths that boys/men will go to impress them.

Even with the looks of amusement and disdain – if not contempt and despair – on the faces of these recipients of their macho entreaties – does the male of the species even begin to see the light – and so – and so – the sad charade continues.

Apart from all these frivolities and misapprehensions – there is in fact, a far more serious and practical reason behind all these early morning gymnastics.

At the school there is a middle aged teaching assistant called Miss Reed, who, in a moment of obvious derangement – has availed herself of a small three wheeled Messerschmitt 'bubble car' that – in reality – and definitely in the eyes of the boys who know about such things – is no more than an old aircraft canopy on casters.

Miss Reed who – despite being – by default – sweet natured – is nevertheless inclined to instil the fear of God in small misbehaving children by shouting – in a nicotine soaked growl – 'What do you mean by it' – in the ear of the unfortunate offender.

No one can decide whether the question is rhetorical or not – but as no one knows the meaning of the word 'rhetorical' – it doesn't really matter.

All of this would be of no account – and would all fit harmoniously and unremarkably into the daily life of the school – if it were not for Miss Reed's hideously misplaced sense of kindness in offering any child caught in the open a lift in her terrifying machine.

Oh the shame and the ignominy of being that child – to be driven right through the school gates – and to be forced to disembark in front of crowds of jeering faces and pointing fingers.

Our heroes will have none of it – with their senses ever heightened to the sound of an incoming Doodle Bug – they will always make sure that – at the appropriate moment – they are safely hidden behind the thickest and densest part of the hedge.

And so – our story resumes…..

At the top of the hill – and opposite the grand but decidedly unattractive façade of Christ Church Ottershaw – is the first of the many entrances to the Common – which – as the boys become older and braver – will become the return route of choice at the end of the school day – and the source of limitless opportunities for exploration and adventure.

After the church – the hedge fun manages to continue – although with the school now in sight – the game soon becomes half-hearted and stale – until – on reaching the long narrow lane to Mr. Foot's land – it is abandoned completely.

As the journey approaches its conclusion – there remains only a brief moment of freedom as the children walk fondly past the large regularly spaced oak trees that border the school playing field.....

... and then...

... with just a few more hesitant steps...

... they all arrive – 'hungry for knowledge and guidance'...

... at the modest steel gates...

... of Ottershaw Junior School.

23

Colebrooke Place – 'Seven Delightful Maisonettes'

Ottershaw Junior and Infant schools were built in Guildford Road, at the expense of Sir Edward Colebrooke. They opened as one school, run by the Church of England, in 1870, but school records show there was frequent absenteeism due to local fairs, circuses and children working as beaters in local shoots. The local agricultural economy also relied on the work of children, and so there were often absentees for the acorn and chestnut harvest in November, furze collecting for the bonfire in November and hay and corn harvests, as well as fruit and mangel-wurzel picking in summer.

There were also many epidemics, which affected attendance levels, often causing the school to be closed for significant periods. The worst was in 1865-1866 when there was a serious smallpox outbreak.

From the late 19th century the school steadily improved, offering a higher standard of education with a greater number of subjects being taught. These included gardening and bee keeping. Football and cricket were played at Botleys Park, and swimming lessons were held in the Thames at Chertsey.

In 1905 a separate Infants' school was opened in Brox Road, and so the overcrowding of the main school was eased. The Junior and Infants' schools were closed in 1967 when the First and Middle schools were opened at Bousley Rise. The old Junior school was converted into seven houses by 1985 and named Colebrooke Place. The Infants' school became a restaurant in the early 1980s.

Chersey Museum

24

Ottershaw Junior School 1959-1963

... for you have hidden these things
from the wise and learned,
and revealed them to little children.

Matthew 11:25

Everyone – it seems – saw my father coming….. maybe it was his self-deprecating manners – or his childlike sense of trust – or maybe it was his total lack of self-belief….. whatever it was – it became apparent to all of us who loved him – that even the honest and upright were hard pressed to resist the temptation to take advantage of his gentle soul.

In particular – my father was a sucker (even more of a sucker) – for anyone with a posh accent and a blazer and a car club – any car club – badge on the pocket.

One such young man – by the name of Chris Simpson – who tended towards the 'being a little bit oily' side of life – managed to hoodwink my father into accepting a rickety old MG VA in full payment for a long outstanding debt.

My father who should have – and probably did – know better – promptly appointed this sad old jalopy to the role of 'mother's car' – possibly in a vain attempt to make some sort of sense out of it all.

And so it was – that my first six months at Ottershaw Junior School were tainted by the sounds and smells and endless idiosyncrasies of this – now classic – 'Old English Sports Car'.

It would have been sufficiently upsetting to have had to endure the daily taunts of the other boys about arriving in such an 'old crock' – but these were by no means the sum of the afflictions inflicted by that sorry vehicle.

Mr. Simpson obviously considered himself to be 'a bit of a lad' – for in place of the standard flat non-offensive radiator cap – he had fitted one which acted as the unfortunate platform for a six inch chrome plated effigy of a naked female nymph..... the kind of figure that now adorns the small suburban courtyards and gardens of those with pretensions towards the 'Pastoral Conceits' of Ancient Greece.

To have to peer through the windscreen at this tasteless apparition every morning as it stood surrounded by steam pouring up from the ill-fitting radiator cap, was the last straw – and although my mother was reluctant to expose her little darling to the dangers of main roads and busy junctions – eventually – after much 'discussion' – my desperation won through and I was set free.

My first and most enduring impression of Ottershaw Junior School was the feast that it laid before my, as yet unsullied senses – the smell of crayons and stale ink and old wooden desks and the cocktail of odours seeping through from the kitchens – was accompanied by the shapes and colours of paintings and posters and the joyful pre-lesson badinage of twenty or so eager little citizens.

The responsibility of filling these small empty vessels with the wisdom and the enlightenment of the then adult world was in the hands of a modest team of teachers under the direction of the headmaster Mr. Melrose – known to the children as Smell Rose – naturally.

Strangely – this team were, for the most part, even-tempered good-humoured and friendly – especially Mr. Melrose who was strikingly tall and thin and was never known to lose his calm gentlemanly demeanour.

Mrs. Dawson, the Deputy, represented all that was modern and glamourous – at least to a 7 year old boy – and Miss Reed perfectly balanced out the equation with her smokers cough and her unfortunate taste in cars.

We had a PE teacher called Mr. Price who, in accordance with the principle that 'we can't always have fun' – was called upon to teach various other subjects in addition to Physical Education.

Mr. Price, not surprisingly, was of an athletic stature and although competent in other subjects – seemed quietly unengaged from any activity that didn't involve a ball – for most of the time, he seemed inclined to keep himself to himself.

There was the hermit like figure of the School Secretary, whose sole purpose seemed to be to keep the explorations of young boys under control by leaping out unexpectedly and expelling them from the passageway that ran beside the Headmaster's office. Finally, there were the 'dinner ladies' that tended to our nutritional needs with noise and chatter and general good cheer.

It is possible that other names and faces have fallen to the ravages of time – but it is equally possible that this small noble group were able to address all the requirements of the then modest school curriculum on their own.

There were four 'Years' in the school and four 'Houses' named Latimer, Ridley, Becket and Cranmer.

The colours for each House were red, yellow, green and blue respectively and of course, we were all blissfully unaware of the meaning of these names and the tragic course of events that enabled them to be eligible as House names.

I was very fortunate to have three 'Best Friends' – Stuart, whose father owned a large local building firm – Graham, who moved to Peterborough at the end of the second year and Stephen, aka Ned, who came from a large family of musicians.

My friends were easy going and unassuming and were not given to petty jealousies and rivalries – but most of all – they were good fun. The three of us were set apart by being 'Dinosaur buddies' – the Dinosaur being a small desktop creature – old wooden desk top that is – brought to life by tucking the thumb and little finger under the palm of one hand – placing the first and third fingers i.e. the legs – on the desk and lifting the third finger i.e. the head – with a finger of the other hand. (It makes me smile now to think of you trying this out for yourself).

Ned played the Clarinet and possessed the quiet modest confidence of someone who 'knows' something true and worthy deep within themselves – in Ned's case – a sort of musical gnosticism.

At the annual sports day – Stuart and Ned were the legendary and peerless Wheel Barrow champions of the school.

Although their technique was surely on the limits of sports day legality – their speed and mastery were so awe inspiring that no one in charge could ever have done anything but stand open mouthed in admiration and amazement.

Ned – who was obviously strong for his modest build – would hold Stuart's legs firmly around his waist so that, when the starting whistle blew, he would simply lean back – lift Stuart's arms off the ground – and run like crazy – with Stuart just flapping his arms around in mid-air for effect.

They were finished and drinking their lemonade while everyone else was still stumbling around and falling in ugly heaps on the starting line.

One level down from 'Best friend' was 'Good Friend' – in my case the identical twins Christopher and Gareth.

Although not playground chums, we would all regularly visit each other's homes after school for tea and general larking around while our mothers talked….. and talked – and talked.

Then there were classroom friends – the ones chosen by the teacher to sit next to each other which – of course – did not include playground buddies….. it is not hard to reason why – although this line of thinking did not seem to apply to the girls.

In our own classroom I sat next to Paul Beeson – king of farts and general knowledge and one of the sons of the two newsagents in the village. Paul was also the inventor and perpetrator of the infamous 'Ink Well Scam'.

At the front of each desk was a small ink well which was used to regularly top up our old fashioned quill pens.

With the useful countenance of a chubby little angel – Paul would place a small piece of blotting paper behind his quill so that – upon placing the quill in the ink – the blotting paper was dislodged to remain in the well and soak up the ink.

Once his well had dried up – he would politely ask permission to use ink from someone else's well – and so the procedure was repeated from desk to desk.

It was the aim of this plan – and Paul's dream – to dry up every ink well in the class and thus render all lessons impossible.

Of course it was never to be – and it wasn't long before the scam was exposed and stamped on firmly – but by that time Paul's endlessly creative sense of mischief had long since moved on to new and greener pastures.

Coincidently – our class included the son of the other village newsagent, namely Robert Lazell and we also had another set of identical twins – although not totally identical, as they were brother and sister.

There was Ian who was discovered to have a hole in his heart – and Steven – with a V – who was tall and wiry and seemingly unaware of the social impediment of being sent to school in the shortest of shorts – no doubt due to his rapid growth….. the cool guys, of course, wearing shorts that not only came down to their knees but also set the scene for the long trousers to come.

Last but not least was Howard – who lived in a strange but wonderful world of his own – a place of self-evident happiness and contentment….. for Howard – once set free from the confines of the classroom – would run around the playground with a huge smile on his face and with his arms flapping wildly by his side as if he were about to take off and fly.

Howard was so far out that he soared effortlessly above any of the attempts by the other children to tease or to bully – there was just simply no way to connect – and anyway – we all became quite fond of Howard and his eccentric ways….. and so – he ran and smiled and flapped and was happy….. as I hope he has been ever since.

Predictably – there is not so much to say about the girls – except perhaps for Christine.

For no evident reason, I always took it for granted that there was 'something between us' – a lamentable pre-disposition towards girls and later women that seemed to follow me and haunt me and afflict me from then on.

Although – in truth – there was something between us – there was a strange ritual that took place every time we were seated next to each other in the Art class.

Christine often wore an irresistibly soft light blue Kashmir jumper that was prone to producing small lumps of fluff all over its surface – as a result, it became my inclination and my compulsion to neaten the situation – by spending the lesson picking these woollen fluff balls off her jumper and then dropping them sneakily on to the floor below.

There was something strangely erotic about the whole affair, in that Christine would not encourage nor discourage my advances – but instead – would quietly submit to being 'picked at' in a most knowingly provocative way.

Nothing transpired from these events – and in time they became just another example of how children can experience things without knowing or caring what they mean..... just part of a growing awareness of life – an ever broadening tapestry – where sensations do not have to be pulled apart and understood in order for them to be followed by the appropriate actions..... just being and feeling and growing and moving on..... and when does it happen – that we become unable to do that anymore.

Apart from Christine – there was Alison – who was shy and unapproachable and Elizabeth, whose birthday party I was once invited to. 'Lizzie' was confidant and friendly and quite without guile – she had a best friend called Becky but seemed just as much at ease with the boys as she was with the girls.

Lastly – there was Karen – who managed to combine a pretty vivacious 'tomboy' appearance with a natural tendency towards reserve and sophistication.

However – there was a strange aura of foreboding about Karen – something that nagged and needled at my instincts – for although she was far from unfriendly – it became clear much later – that she had been an archetype – a chilling vision of all future romantic rejections – the one who would have her finger ever on the button of the un-bidden pre-emptive strike – the callous and indifferent dismissal..... the cold unspoken whisper.....

..... *'Don't even think about it'.*

At some point during our time at Ottershaw Junior School – Karen Mitchell and her family emigrated to Australia – which of course – though unprovoked – was the best rejection of all.

Despite the heady appeal of empty ink wells and fluff free jumpers – the highlight of the school day was, without question, the various mysterious activities that took place in the playground and – in summer when the weather was dry – in the adjacent playing field.

These activities were divided clearly and non-negotiably into 'boys games' and 'girls games' – mostly through the processes of peer pressure and choice – but – in the case of hopscotch, through a boys natural physiological programming that renders him completely incapable of understanding the rules.

The boys and the girls seemed happy and content to play their own games and perform their own rituals – although there was a crossover when it came to playground rhymes and taunts.....

(Na na – na na na for instance)

Girls played Rounders and boys played IT – which meant that for much of the time they were sitting despondently on the classroom steps with grazed knees and hands..... girls played Hopscotch and boys played Squash – which involved throwing a ball against almost anything at all..... girls played 'Houses' and boys played 'Garages' and Marbles and – with wanton disregard for the sanctity of life – pursued the most dangerous and terrifying game of Conkers.

Just once – one of the more 'mature' boys suggested that we chase the girls..... this proved not to be as easy as was first assumed – and as – in our haste to get started – we had failed to discuss a certain crucial part of the game..... none of us knew what do when we caught them.....

..... and so it was – that those of us who actually succeeded in our quest – were doomed to stand awkward and embarrassed before our prey – doing our best to try and start up a conversation whilst looking for the quickest and safest way out of the predicament.

It turned out that – in practice – there wasn't much enthusiasm for 'chasing the girls' and it was not repeated – not until much later anyway.

Some people talk of 'the Elephant in the room' but at Ottershaw Junior School we had a Stag in the shed – or at least the head of a Stag.

Nobody knew why, or were inclined to find out – it was just one of those strange 'school things' that children weren't meant to understand or pursue.....

..... like the Hooker pipe that my friend Stuart (many of my friends were called Stuart) found under the stage at Strode's Grammar School.....

.....some things..... they just 'are'.

On the whole, lessons came and went in a genial sort of way – all the time cleverly avoiding the inconvenient awakenings of interest and passion amongst all of those involved.

There were, of course, minor ripples in the otherwise still waters of school life..... for example – I could never really get the hang of 'joined up' writing – I could get it to join up for a while to please the teacher – but inevitably – the moment I turned my back – it would un-join again of its own accord.

For many years I would regularly re-visit this problem – but in the end I let it go – accepting that I was just not a 'joined up' sort of guy.

As the celebrated winner of an Art Competition, I had always sketched and painted to the extent that my very modest ability would allow – but with the move up from the Infants School to the Junior School came an abrupt introduction to the more serious and adult ways of doing things.

In terms of Art, this meant – apparently – that we had to now draw or paint a thick black border line around everything in the picture….. trees, tractors, flowers, clouds, bugs, butterflies…..

EVERYTHING !

Although it was not our place to question the generously disseminated wisdom of our teacher – black lines seemed to be instinctively at odds with my naïve sensibilities – and so – without any great feelings of loss or sadness – I found that I no longer felt the longing or the inclination to express myself through Art.

However, this sorry affair was, to some extent mitigated by our inauguration into the magnificent world of Paper Mache – where – within unbelievably acceptable levels of mess and noise and smell – coat hangers and wire mesh could be transformed into Horses or Tractors or Spaceships – or the boy next to you – almost anything in fact….. and although the end result wasn't always quite what was hoped for – it certainly looked less like a coat hanger than it did to start with.

Music lessons were also a source of liberation from childish notions of simple uncomplicated fun – especially in the choice of the songs that we were given to sing – songs that were no doubt chosen from an unfortunate collection entitled 'Jolly little songs from days of long ago' – which is exactly where they should have stayed.

Whether it was the unintelligible gibberish of 'De Camptown ladies sing dis song, Doo-dah doo-dah – or – the mind numbing repetition of 'Oh no John no John no' – Oh no not another bloody verse John no….. (oh the simple pleasures of racial condescension and forced marriage)….. it soon became apparent that proper grown up music lessons had very little to do with Music at all.

However – there was one bewildering incident – at least for a certain young man – that raised the bar of confusion and disheartenment into the realms of the sublime.

At some point between 'Uncle Mac's Family Favourites' – 'Listen with Mother' and 'Round the Horne' – my ears had obviously been opened – no doubt by accident – to the dubious delights of 'Contemporary Opera' – for – as it was soon to become painfully apparent – the name and the experience had become permanently lodged in the depths of my psyche – like some sort of malevolent genetic disorder – just waiting for its day of 'glory'.

As it turned out – this day of 'glory' was soon to arrive in the shape of a music lesson in which our teacher had chosen to bring the musical form of Opera to life right there in the classroom.

For most of the class, the plan resulted in a resounding display of apathy tinged with a natural inclination towards suspicion – but for one young boy – it was an epiphany – the moment he had been waiting for – at last he was the bearer of 'special knowledge' – and he wasn't about to deny those around him the gift of his enlightenment.

Thanks to the 'Avant Garde' leanings of the BBC's Third Programme, his enduring memory of 'Opera' was that it was made up of a random selection of notes and rhythms and dynamics – completely devoid of melody or indeed – sanity.

The teacher's plan entailed taking a short dramatic narrative and getting each pupil to sing rather than speak their allocated text – the flaw in the plan being that it was all to be made up on the spot.

As his moment arrived – the boy – full of misplaced confidence and alacrity – launched into the most disconnected series of notes that he could physically perform.

So sure was he of his understanding of the genre – that he

was soon lost and exalted in the mystical realms of the true performer…..

….. he soared up and down – he shouted and he whispered – he sung quickly and he sung very very slowly…..

….. it was a masterpiece – even he was impressed by the total lack of any kind of recognisable melody that he had achieved – just a random tangle of disconnected sounds – faithful in every way to the music that he had heard on the radio not long before…..

….. in short – he had nailed this opera thing for sure…..

He expected looks of admiration from his 'audience'….. he expected to be congratulated or maybe even applauded…..

….. he expected recognition for his keen sense of musical perception…..

….. what he certainly didn't expect – was to be told off for being 'very silly' and sent to stand in the corner for the rest of the lesson…..

The lesson that he actually learnt that day was to have very little to do with Opera – contemporary or otherwise…..

….. it was a lesson that was to serve him well during the years ahead…..

If you raise your head above the parapet – you're going to get shot down.

To be sure – school was a strange voyage of discovery – a voyage of absolutes – a voyage in which we were transported – sometimes from ignorance to enlightenment – and sometimes in totally the opposite direction…..

I discovered many things at Ottershaw Junior School…..

… I discovered that I no longer enjoyed painting and drawing as I once did and that I should probably not entertain any dreams of becoming an Opera singer…

… I discovered that I liked the colour combinations of certain foods – like rice pudding and jam – and chocolate pudding with cornflower sauce – and vanilla ice-cream and custard…

… I discovered that girls were hard to talk to and harder to understand and that I liked to be alone with Nature and all that seemed untouched and unspoilt…

… I discovered 'Jesu Joy of Man's Desiring' by J S Bach…

… John Ireland's setting of 'My Song is Love Unknown'…

… and – in the spaces – between the days of my afflictions…

… I discovered the words and the person of Jesus Christ.

25

Religion – Confusion And Truth

… I've also studied deeply in the philosophies and religions, but cheerfulness kept breaking through.

Leonard Cohen

On the whole, Church and religion meant very little to me. I had learnt from an early age that Church was cold, uncomfortable, incomprehensible and boring – and that Religion was just some meaningless stuff that adults talked about from time to time

I liked it when we said Grace – especially as I was truly thankful for all the lovely contrasting colours of my school puddings.

I also liked the 'Lord's Prayer' that we recited every morning in School Assembly – but I did have some reservations about some of its content.

Being unfamiliar with the use of 'Thee's and Thou's' – I interpreted the line 'Thy will be done on earth' to mean 'You're going to be done on earth'….. i.e.' You're going to get a good seeing to'….. which seemed to me to be extraordinarily disrespectful to the Almighty.

This just felt a bit odd – but the part that caused me to lay awake at night was the use of the word 'Trespasses'.

The problem was not that I didn't understand its meaning – the problem was that I understood too well.

Trespassing was what little boys did when they chose to climb over fences and gates in wilful disregard of the large scary signs that read 'Trespassers will be prosecuted'.

Now I knew enough about the world from cowboy films to realise that there were some pretty bad things going on out there – even if it was never made clear exactly what they were.

So it was the cause of great concern and consternation that Almighty God had chosen, in this his special prayer, to ignore all the other bad things and point his finger at the errant wanderings of small misguided boys alone.

Every day it was the same….. murderers and robbers and crooks were totally overlooked in order for his wrath to be directed solely at us.

Why was it just us that needed to ask for forgiveness – and who was going to be climbing over our fences anyway?

Fortunately, the prayer didn't last long….. but the guilt remained.

In a similar way, my experience of Church was doomed from the start because of my mother's strange approach to timekeeping.

Her deranged logic – to this day – dictates that any local destination is always '5 minutes away ' – therefore it follows that if you need to be somewhere by 10-o-clock – you must leave the house at 5 minutes before 10-o-clock.

As a result – after the panic of leaving the house – getting in the car – parking – checking that we all looked suitably smart….. by the time we entered the 'House of God' we were always at least 20 minutes late.

Of course this didn't in any way cause my mother to readjust her thoughts on the timing of these local journeys – nor did it deter her or suggest to her that a quiet discreet entrance might be respectively appropriate.

Oh no.... with noise and loud encouragements to 'hurry up now' we would all follow sheepishly behind my mother – regardless of the position in the service that we found ourselves – right up to the front of the congregation – there to push our way into the foremost available pew.

(To this day – whatever the venue – you will always find me sitting at the back – or – given the choice – not sitting there at all).

As it turned out – Church did have one redeeming feature – (apart from the Psalms and the occasional favourite hymn) – a diversion inspired by the necessity of having to cope somehow with the incessant boredom and the hard square wooden pews.

The idea was simple – I had worked out that the sermon was consistently 10 minutes long – not easy without a watch or a conveniently situated clock – and so – while the Vicar was speaking – the boy in the front row was counting from 1 to 600.

The game was to see who got to the end first – the Vicar or me.

Leaving the church proved to be almost as harrowing as our arrival – for it involved standing and watching my mother talking and talking with nothing for us to do but read the inscriptions on the nearest headstones over and over again.

The trauma of our arrival and departure and the brief respite of the 'Sermon game' came to represent my entire experience of Church – at least until I was conscripted without my knowledge or consent into the meagre numbers of the local Church Choir.

> *It ain't why, why, why*
> *it just is.*
>
> Van Morrison

Although an unwelcome and resented intrusion on my precious model-making time at home – as a reluctant choirboy I was eventually able to realise, accept and ultimately cherish – that I had walked through a door into another world – a place of rare and exquisite beauty – a place that enticed and nurtured the first tender shoots of my awakening spirit.

Apart from the transcendent moments of Evensong, when we all became lifted as one upon the wings of the Magnificat and the Nunc Dimittis – and apart from the feel of the crisp white surplices and ruffs….. the church part of being a choirboy touched me almost not at all.

It was the rapture of my senses that drew me in…..

….. the strange musty scent of the ancient wood and stone – familiar and comforting – like the stirring of long forgotten memories…..

….. choir practices on a winters night – the church cold and empty with only the small angled lights above our music to lift the blanket of darkness that enfolds us…..

….. our voices echoing – through the black vaulted spaces above our heads….. our song entwined – within a greater song…..

….. the presence of an 'other' – watching kindly from the shadowed reaches of this hallowed moment….. the stillness within – the silence between….. the two songs dancing – perpetual and perfect….. forever…..

> *… the words I have spoken,*
> *they are spirit and they are life.*
>
> Yeshua Ben Joseph

In terms of what is casually referred to as 'Truth'….. up to the age of nine years old – the 'adult' world in which I lived had managed to offer me nothing but well-meaning sound-bites at best – blatant lies and deceits at worst.

Through the eyes and the thoughts of a child – it had already become clear that there was no such thing as 'Truth' – only 'truths' – relative – self-serving – quicksilver and transient…..

….. until that is – my life was opened to the person and the teachings of Jesus Christ.

This was my first conscious encounter with Truth – not a

second hand subjective truth filtered and disseminated through the minds and agendas of children and adults – but a Truth that spoke directly and instantly to my heart…..

….. a Truth beyond truth – that stood outside of time and human agency – a gift from the ancient of days – that not only spoke to my heart – but somehow understood my heart – deeply, tenderly and lovingly.

There were no shining visions or blinding revelations…..

….. there were just the stories about his life – the words that he spoke and the parables that he shared…..

…. and the voice that spoke to me there – through these words and stories and parables – it was not the voice of a stranger – it was not remote or as if from afar – it was intimate and familiar – it was a voice that was already known to me.

I was not connecting – I was not re-connecting….. I was already connected and I was coming home….. to the home that I had never left or forgotten.

They too will listen to my voice,
and there shall be one flock and one shepherd.

The Prayer

The boy is 10 years old – he is kneeling in prayer….. his class has been joined by a newcomer – a boy called John, who is tall and gangly, loud and partially deaf.

John wears a large obtrusive hearing aid and is constantly calling out in a strange 'sing song' voice for the teacher to repeat themselves, as he could not understand what they had just said.

In every way – John calls attention to himself – and in every way he is mocked and ridiculed – without the least concern for mercy, compassion, patience or understanding

The boy is praying – but not for John…..

….. the boy is praying for himself….. he is praying that he may find the courage to be a friend to John – a friend that will stand up for him and walk beside him through the days of his lonely victimisation.

For the rest of his life – the boy will think of this moment – for, although John left the school soon afterwards – the boy will think of it and hold on to it as a source of hope – for until his moving to Surrey to care for his mother – it is sadly and without question – the only truly selfless act of his entire life.

26

The '11 Plus' Examination – And Its Wake

One foot in the academy and you are changed for the worst.
Heitor Villa-Lobos

With my days at Ottershaw Junior School drawing to a close – the time of the dreaded 11-plus exam loomed ever nearer.

As with all other school activities and endeavours – nothing was ever explained or elucidated – we were all just expected to comply with what was required of us. And so – as I approached the 11-plus – it was with very little grasp of why I was being compelled to do it – my understanding of Grammar Schools and Comprehensive Schools being limited solely to my parents' disparaging tones and expressions when discussing the latter.

What I did know, was that when you took a test – any kind of test – the general idea was to do well – and thus become the happy recipient of peace on earth and goodwill to men. Apart from that – it only registered on my Radar as being just another unpleasant 'school thing' – like Tetanus injections or Parents Evenings.

As I see it now – there are two reasons why I managed to pass the exam – and neither of them had anything to do with my academic abilities.

The first reason is very simple.

For a period of time prior to the exam – there had been a quiz show on television – probably the one and only TV quiz show at the time – and this show involved the solving of catchy little IQ puzzles and brain-teasers.

I would always watch this with my parents – mainly to enjoy their obvious delight when their little 'star' got the questions right.

This regular ritual resulted in me getting quite good at IQ type questions – which was remarkably fortuitous for – as it turned out – similar such questions constituted a major part of the 11-plus exam.

The other reason is a little less straightforward and necessitates a brief incursion into the realms of madness and delusion.

As the day arrived for the all-important Essay test – it was decided by my mother that I shouldn't be trusted with walking to school alone – but rather – be taken to the school by car.....

..... but instead of dropping me off – waving and then driving away – she got out of the car – and walked around to where I was standing – paralysed and petrified for fear of what was going to happen next.

My alarm grew as she bent over and draw her mouth close to my ear.

There was something disturbingly calm and purposeful about her manner – calm and purposeful not being my mother's usual way of imparting information – nevertheless – as if sharing a dark and forbidden secret – she proceeded to encourage me – in a low conspiratorial whisper – to use the words 'feverish excitement' as often as I could in the essay I was about to write.

I was stunned for a moment – but hastily re-assured myself – as I always did – that adults were privy to mysteries far beyond the reasoning of childrens' simple minds..... even though all the evidence suggested the contrary.....

..... and so – as I laid pen to paper – I dutifully – and in complete contradiction to my instincts – did exactly as my mother had suggested.

'Feverish excitement' was indeed inserted in my story – as many times as I could possibly make it fit – or even if I couldn't make it fit – I just put it in anyway – it didn't matter to me – I was intoxicated with the mania of it all – and if I was going to err – then I was certainly not going to err on the side of caution.

The luckless examiners must have been knocked completely off balance by this lunacy – and having been rendered at a loss as to know how to react – had come to the generous but erroneous conclusion that they must be witnessing the first eccentric and unintelligible signs of awakening genius.

Sadly – but not altogether surprisingly – my 'awakening genius' never progressed past the eccentric unintelligible stage – and – also not surprisingly – through the years to come – I never felt drawn to use that particular phrase ever again.

Four of us passed the 11-plus that year – and I was the only boy – a boy who was to find out over the next five years that he had actually made a huge mistake.

The fallout began almost immediately.

I was set apart..... I was suddenly an outsider – the object of derision – of suspicion and distrust.....

..... it felt like I'd done something wrong – like I had become a traitor to my friends and my classmates.....

..... I lived as though a carrier of a terrible disease.....

..... all of which was malevolently and assiduously reinforced by the coming of our new Headmaster..... Mr. Lewis.

Strangely – Mr Lewis bore an uncanny resemblance to 'The Hood' – the arch villain in the TV puppet drama 'Thunderbirds' – a not entirely inappropriate coincidence as it turned out.

With his dark bloated features – his thick black eyebrows – his deep resonant Welsh accent and his permanent scowl..... Mr. Lewis was one of those unfortunate breed of misfits who feel that they have the absolute right to take out their inadequacies on the small defenceless children entrusted to their charge.

Mr. Lewis hated me from the start – which I found perplexing and disturbing – for I had spent many years perfecting my quiet, timid innocuous school personae expressly to avoid just such a situation.

From the first day that he took our lessons – Mr. Lewis began a relentless campaign of emotional abuse towards me and me alone….. it was as if he had planned it all in advance – as if he had 'hit the ground running'.

Never did he miss an opportunity to humiliate and ridicule me – the venom pouring out of every pore as he triumphantly pronounced…..

"You may think you have passed the 11-plus – but you will be bottom of the Grammar School".

This calculatingly vicious daily gibe – coupled with the distancing of my friends – turned my final days at Ottershaw Junior School into a waking nightmare…..

If Mr. Lewis had only known the fear and trepidation that consumed me on my first day at Strode's Grammar School as a direct result of his childish malevolence – then I think he would have been proud.

By the time I had reached my final year in Junior school – I had become consistently bewildered by the various mysterious aspects of adults and of their behaviour especially.

Why was it that an adult could say a so-called swear word with total impunity – but if a child repeated the exact same word in exactly the same context – it was as if the heavens were suddenly falling in upon his head.

Why did adults complain of not being able to afford things when they had a cheque book in front of them which they could make out for as much money as they liked…..

….. I did – as soon as I was able – put this to the test with my own cheque book – and I found that it worked just as well as I had anticipated…. at least for a while.

Why were we told to refuse sweets from strangers – when good manners and gratitude seemed to be so important the rest of the time.

Why did some women have terrifyingly pointed breasts capable of poking your eyes out – while others had friendly round ones.

Why had no one informed the Aldershot and District Traction Company that they had mis-spelt their notice above the rear window of the driver's cab – 'Tickets must be shewn'.

Why did all my mother's relatives have names ending in 'Y'. (i.e. Milly – Flory – Elsey – Tommy – Freddy – Katy – Charley Geoffrey etc.) – and would the same thing happen to my name when I grew up.

..... and what happened to all the lessons that I'd missed because of illness..... the words un-spelt – the tables un-learned – the bugs un-drawn.

But all of these questions and others faded into oblivion when compared to the curious events surrounding the birth of my youngest brother.

Before the coming of Google – information of a secretive nature was always the proud domain of the one or two boys 'that knew about things'. These boys would occasionally hold court in secluded parts of the playground which were easily spotted by the quiet attentive huddle that surrounded them.

In this way – and certainly no other – I managed to acquire what I felt was a reasonable – if tentative – handle on the ways of human procreation.

That was until – in the summer of 1963 – my mother became pregnant at the age of forty.

All seemed well at first – but very soon surprise and excitement gave way to troubled bewilderment when my mother started announcing to anyone and everyone that this happy event had come about as the result of an 'accident'.

Now my experience of accidents was that they nearly always concerned things or people bumping into other things or people.

They usually involved falling out of trees or from bicycles or bumping into other children in the playground – and sometimes – they involved parents bumping into things with their car.

Accidents were violent and painful and nearly always left you with feelings of shame and regret – as well as with copious cuts and bruises and – ultimately – scars.

They were always unplanned – and they were always unwelcome.

Suddenly, all that I thought that I understood about 'sex' was slipping through my fingers like sand.

Had I been lied to or deceived – or maybe I'd heard it all wrong.

All through the summer of '63 – I wrestled with the problem of trying to reconcile these two seemingly unrelated things – the act of consummation and the process of having an accident.

I tried to imagine all kinds of likely scenarios….. my father running across the bedroom and tripping up….. but my father didn't run anywhere – and even if he did – he certainly wouldn't have been running around without any clothes on.

I imagined some sort of sleep walking accident – but every idea ended with the same conclusion….. surely they would have noticed – and having noticed – why would they then be acting surprised at the outcome.

Nothing explained the dilemma chasing around in my mind – although it did explain why teachers were so vehemently opposed to children running in the corridors.

It turned out to be a long and interminable wait – so long and so interminable in fact – before I was able to shed some light on the question through personal experience…..

… but still….. even though I know better now…

… it is very unlikely you will ever catch me running…

… and certainly not in a public place.

27

Mum Is Always Right!

The parents have eaten sour grapes,
and the children's teeth are set on edge.

Jeremiah 31

Nothing for my mother was ever straightforward or 'normal' – least of all – clothing and food.

Jumpers in particular were always one of her favourite victims.

Having shrunk a once baggy and comfortable jumper to the size where we were virtually unable to breath – she would cheerfully reassure us that it would be fine after she'd stretched it a bit.

The next day – we would be proudly presented with a hideous looking piece of clothing that – although still squeezing the breath from our bodies – now came down to our knees.

She was even able to turn the choosing of a simple Macintosh into a drama of Wagnerian proportions.

Whereas all the other boys had normal Macintoshes – my mother decided that mine should have a thick red detachable quilted lining – that once fitted – made me look like a small Michelin man on Steroids.

The scenes each morning involving this fiendish piece of apparel are indescribable – as is the heartless amusement that it brought to the other children.

Eventually I succeeded in hiding the lining so well that it was never found again – the advantage of living in a large rambling untidy house.

After a while my mother forgot about it – probably in favour of some other garment themed act of insanity.

Food – in my mother's capable hands – was also effortlessly transformed into an endless source of trauma and distress.

When it came to 'the kitchen' – there were two over-riding factors that determined my mother's approach to cooking.

The first was that she had no understanding or comprehension of the concept of Thermostats or Rheostats or probably anything else that ended in 'stats'.

Just as there are peoples that have no word for 'thank you' and no place in their culture for the notion of even wanting to express that sentiment….. so my mother has only ever been able to think and function in terms of on/off switches – everything else is totally missing from her cognisance of life.

Consequently – all appliances – whether Cookers or Toasters or Immersion tanks or Water taps or Central heating systems – were – in my mother's hands (which were the only hands that counted in our house) either fully on or fully off.

The second factor is her unshakable belief that food is a wicked evil poisonous thing that must be boiled or roasted or fried into absolute submission.

To this end – no matter how long the hapless piece of meat or vegetable or egg had been cooked – it would always need another 10 minutes….. for as well as being wicked evil and poisonous – food was also sneaky – and would often pretend to be dead when it wasn't.

My mother would also combine having everything full-on with the fatal compulsion to then go and do the hoovering or the ironing or even the weeding.

As a result – kitchen fires and floods were a regular part of the daily routine –as well as the hysteria that accompanied them.

My mother's culinary creations were surreal in the extreme….. toast was always burnt and scraped – cakes were also burnt but with the black outer edges sliced off this time – pieces of shrivelled Liver had the texture of a thick leather belt – eggs were hard and chewy – and vegetables !!!

….. maybe it's best to move on from vegetables and mention – in the way of consolation – the exceptionally delicious Bread and Butter pudding that my mother would always make at bed-times.

As with every other aspect of family life – my mother presided over an absolute tyranny in regards to what we ate – how we ate it – how much we ate – and general meal time manners.

Any slight deviation would be met with tirades of terrifying emotional violence and the constant reminders of 'starving children in Africa' – later to be upgraded to the threat of being 'put in the army'.

In our home there was one absolute and unassailable rule of law – it applied to all things at all times and it was the law that we were all compelled to honour and obey.....

MUM IS ALWAYS RIGHT

There was no compromise or give and take – no negotiation or mitigation..... there was – in fact – no place for communication at all – at least none that could be recognised as in any way resembling a normal mode of human interaction.

My mother was never ever in the wrong – and – for her – it was clearly a matter of life and death for her to maintain this delusion.

Any perceived attack upon her faultlessness was immediately met with a series of tediously predictable strategies.

If the shouting and screaming and throwing things didn't work – then they would be swiftly followed by the passive violence of self-pity and emotional blackmail – which in practice meant that my mother would either mooch around the house sulking and mumbling to herself – take to her bed with an illness – or walk off down the road in whatever state of dress she found herself.

She was able to keep this going for weeks – or at least until the offending criticism was unconditionally withdrawn – apologised for – and the recognition of her supremacy restored.

These sad broken patterns of behaviour were the currency of communication within our lives – and as children – in the absence of any alternatives – we soon learnt to employ the very same techniques for ourselves.

Whether it be to let some air in our bedroom – or wear a favourite shirt – or be excused the obligatory second dollop of food….. it was impossible to express preferences or utter polite appeals without them being seen by my mother as dangerous threats to her very being.

And so….. we screamed and shouted and sulked and were 'ill' – all the time sinking ever deeper into the putrid abyss of emotional blackmail and manipulative self-pity….. usually to no avail…..

….. but what else could we do.

How ironic that – towards the end of her life – my mother would develop such a hostile attitude towards all things Catholic – and be so willing to pour scorn and ridicule upon the notion of Papal Infallibility – whilst being so intransigent in the assertion of her own.

I would later come to understand that my mother's pathological need to be 'right' – meant that her love was like the love of an alcoholic or a drug addict…..

….. despite all professions to the contrary – no matter what – we would always take second place to her 'addiction' and we would always be seen as expendable before its throne.

It was the defining tragedy of our childhood – of our lives – that we all knew this instinctively to be true.

Indeed…..

Nothing has ever been straightforward or 'normal' for my mother.

28

My Health Begins Its Descent...

I feel sick – I feel sick
Mummy thinks I'm joking
but I'm really choking

I feel sick – I feel sick
Daddy thinks I'm lying
but I'm really dying

I feel sick – I feel sick.

My daughter Laura – age 6

Long before the boy moves on from Ottershaw Junior School - his life has become one long continual anxiety attack - with all its associated guilt and fear - self-loathing and self-harming.

Of course he doesn't think of it that way - for such has been the slow insidious erosion of his health - that the thumping of his heart - the violent bouts of sweating and dizziness and the daily struggle to breathe - are now - just a part of the natural soundtrack of his existence.

Although he doesn't know it then - deep within his body - something dark and malicious has been stirred - dark calling to dark ..... Disease - as the ancients understood so well - the inevitable and inexorable outcome of 'Dis - ease'.

Long before the boy has moved on from Ottershaw Junior School..... all the hopes and dreams that he cherishes for the life stretching out in front of him.....

..... they will be hoped and dreamed in vain.

29

...As My Spirit Rises

*... hallelujah the sparks flew up to heaven and I left the sober
people with their cold hearts*

Frazey Ford

It is often the way in life – that the darker and more violent
the storm – the brighter and stronger is the life-line that is
held out before us….. if only we would care to reach for it.

….. and so it transpired – that the days of my early childhood
had not finished with me yet….. they were in fact just saving the
best – for last.

I am standing in the corner of the school playing field – by
the large wooden gate to the road outside….. it is summer and
the field is alive with the noise and bustle and euphoria of small
children at play.

I am watching – as if from beyond the gate – as if I am already
looking back – sadly – but fondly on a scene from my past.

Within the mid-day heat and the cheerful commotion all
around me…..

….. I am standing – quiet and still…..

….. expectant and open…..

….. to what I somehow know is about to happen…..

In an instant I am raised up – into a place both within myself
and beyond myself – I am held there within the bright shining
wellspring of my being – a place of light – of profound and
infinite silence – a place where everything is transformed – and
everything is as it has always been…..

I see through the very same eyes – but I perceive with a vision now liberated from worldly influence and limitation.....

I am looking down upon a vast ever-moving – ever-changing landscape of mortal things – and I am suddenly aware of an affection and a compassion and an overwhelming love for it all.....

As the veil of my confinement falls away – I am released into the embrace of my true and changeless self.....

I am not young – I am not old – I just am – I am myself – I am the face behind the disfigured mask – the voice behind the muffled cry.....

I am the love song within the broken heart.....

I am free.....

Free from all the clawing machinery of the flesh – the levies and the burdens of all the tainted troops of drifting souls.....

I exist apart from it all – I am unchanging and real – I am my own unique being – I am eternal.....

All the broken pieces of my character now one perfect whole – where just a moment before they lay strewn across the universe like tiny pieces of shattered stars.....

Under the shadow of His wings – I am who I was always meant to be.....

Like a prodigal – I am returned......

... but in this world of men – I am now alone...

... and will always be.

The man is 65 years old – he has lost his sense of growing through time – he sees now only a vertical line – a line that exists in the moment – the eternal moment – a line that draws him ever back to his 11 year old self.....

..... and as hands reach out and fingers touch – all the darkness of the intervening years falls away – as if it never was.....

He is now as he has always been – as he always will be.....

He is the child – he is the boy – he is the man......

He is standing in a school playing field – it is summer and the sun is shining from a cloudless sky – everything remains and everything has changed.....

He is standing at the place of his awakening – the brief fleeting moment that he has kept locked away – like a precious jewel – like a guiding star – shining out across the years – shining to lead him home.

To see a World in a Grain of Sand
and Heaven in a Wild Flower
hold Infinity in the palm of your hand
and Eternity in an hour...

William Blake

Part Three

Through The Storm

30

More Tuscanny Dreams

Nothing happens unless first we dream.

Carl Sandburg

I have left the busy coast road behind – to meander carelessly along the by-ways that will lead me once again to the towers and cobbles of San Gimignano.....

My Jeep is murmuring away happily to itself as I follow the long straight road into the distance..... crops and tracks and small stone shacks line my passing – until slowly – almost imperceptibly – the road begins to wind and climb – up to the quiet unassuming streets and buildings of Volterra.....

I am following the echo of my daughter's laughter – the laughter that we shared as we explored the wild open beauty of Tuscany in our dashing little white Fiat 500.....

This time I have no *'Bella giovane donna'* to guarantee my finding a seat in busy cafes and restaurants and so I have to rely now on my own natural charm and charisma – which probably explains the gradual but undeniable loosening of my shorts around my waist.....

As I leave the town behind me – the hills and fields of late summer – now empty of their vivid carpets of poppies and sunflowers – appear strangely naked and intimate and I feel my hand longing to reach out and caress every curve and hollow.....

On top of a small rise – surveying its domain – stands a large incongruous 'ring' sculpture – held up against gravity and wind by the self-evident cunning of an ambitiously creative but practical mind.....

To each passerby, it will no doubt embrace its own meaning and significance......

To some – perhaps – it will be a wheel in recognition of the passing travellor..... to others – the top half of the feminine symbol – with profound implications deriving from the fact that the lower cross is buried unseen beneath the ground......

People who know about such things say that the artist – Mauro Staccioli – is asking us to *'to consider Tuscany's rolling hills as a work of art'* – and that *'the work seeks to develop a dialogue with the entire territory, emphasizing history, place, and the impact of humankind..... with the circle acting as a frame, that invites us to stop and consider the view, and to consider how the artist is asking us to see that view.'*

As for me – I see a large metal washer – just like the ones that used to fill up the drawers in my garage – together with other various nuts and bolts and clips left over from all the misguided car rejuvenation projects of the past.....

I have a feeling that I would probably have stopped and admired the view without the circular steel commentary of a higher mortal..... but who knows..... maybe it's best not to leave such things to chance.....

Soon – very soon – maybe tomorrow, or the next day – I will find a cool shaded grove – and I will pause awhile to write a song that is new and young and reckless – and I will offer it up to the keeper of rhymes – and then I will let it go and release it forever from the chains of my memory.....

I have nowhere to be – save for the unravelling of this moment..... maybe there is a room waiting up ahead – waiting to lay a soothing hand upon the weariness of the day – or maybe I will lie back into this soft black leather – open all the windows and let my senses dance and play with the sounds and the scents of the night.....

..... here amongst the dark billowing hills – I will fall into the rhythms of my own breath – and I will think of you in your lush and bountiful garden – with your floppy hat and your thick golden hair and your soft green eyes – there amongst your cohorts of bees and butterflies and small wild flowers.....

..... and I will listen for the song of your spirit – and I will ache for your beauty and for your touch upon my soul – and once again I will pretend in vain.....

..... that I am not missing you.

31

Waiting For The Rose

... you may wander in the moonlight in the garden of your soul,
you may listen for the whisper of your longing as it grows,
you may cry out for a harvest when the ground is hard with snow,
but as for me... as for me... I will wait for the Rose.

As things turned out – it was going to be a very long and lonely wait.....

..... but as the old man looked back over the years of his life – he knew with every part of his being that – if he could – he would not change a thing.....

..... whatever it took to bring him to this place of healing and light – of stillness and peace – it was all just fine with him.....

..... for the flower that he had been waiting for – the seed that had been slowly and patiently growing in the deep dark earth – lifting its head a little closer each day to the sun and the sky above – it was to be the flower of his own soul.....

..... there were no passing years – no journey – no moving on..... he had been rooted in one place all along – ever growing upward towards the light..... and the pain and the darkness – they were but the fertile soil – nourishing and nurturing the path of his unfolding.....

..... but 'fertile ground' – and 'growing towards the light' – and 'the flowering of his soul'.....

..... that was certainly not how it felt at the time!

32

The Eye Of The Storm

8th September 2012

My mother and I have come to the end of our first month in our small rented bungalow on the outskirts of Cranleigh.

Somehow, we have survived the sale of the 'family home' as well as the reasonably amicable division of finances and belongings, which was necessary to enable my long suffering step-father to spend what will become a happy and gracious but final six months with his son and daughter and grandchildren in Somerset.

Miraculously, my mother and I have also survived a month living in a mobile home while, at my mother's insistence, a large shower was fitted by our new landlord to replace the bath that was deemed inaccessible by my mother for an eighty nine year old lady with bad hips.

Somewhere in the middle of all of this, I managed to escape for a perfect four days in Florence with my youngest daughter Laura, but now, I am well and truly back in the eye of the storm – the violent unabating storm that is my mother.

The implications of my decision to leave my life in Devon are now becoming all too clear – I have moved from Narnia to live in a war zone with the only consolation being the very tenuous conviction that 'it is the right thing to do', and that somehow, there will be resolution in the months and years ahead.

What have I done !

I have been duped by the fairies of Totnes – I have been led into a trap from which there is no escape or mitigation. I am locked up inside a nightmare – a constant unrelenting nightmare….. and how could I have thought that it would be any other way.

Nothing has changed since the insanity of my childhood –

my brothers and I have simply been living in the highest order of denial….. but now there is no place for denial – or any other refuge of the mind.

There is no freewheeling with my mother – no peaceful interludes – no fluffy moments of humour and calm.

If she is not conducting a full-on assault, then she is plotting – and if she is not plotting, then she is thinking about plotting.

Her most insidious form of open warfare is that which is pursued with the intention of achieving total control over every aspect of my life, and to this end, there are two main theatres of conflict – my bedroom and the kitchen.

I am involved in the fighting of a relentless and hopeless rear-guard action to retain a hold on a small meagre piece of ground i.e. my right to exercise some choice in what I eat and drink and what goes on in the precious sanctuary of my room.

For my mother, 'control' is not something that can be discussed or compromised – it is not in any way a flexible commodity – it must always be absolute and it must always be imposed without leniency or weakness.

Her weapons of choice – as always – are shouting, screaming, sulking, illness and of course, emotional manipulation and blackmail.

The daily conflict goes – not something like this – but exactly like this…..

I return from my brief encounter with freedom – in the shape of an early morning swim – shopping in the supermarket and a coffee to ponder and prepare for the day ahead…..

You were a long time…..

(she does not wait for a reply)

I've had so much to do…..

(she feigns staggering and heavy breathing)

I'm exhausted – I've had to make your bed and clean your room and I've had to take all your clothes out of your cupboard because they were all folded up wrong and you'd put them in completely the wrong drawers.

What do you mean you've had to make my bed – I've asked you so many times to leave my room alone – why can't I have one space in this house to myself.

There you go again – you're always shouting at me – everything I do is wrong – I'm afraid to do anything – I'm afraid to open my mouth

*So what am I supposed to do – I've asked you – I've begged you…..
I've tried asking nicely but you just ignore me….. and how can you say I'm shouting – just listen to yourself.*

You're so ungrateful – I've been working hard all morning – I thought you'd be pleased.

YOU THOUGHT I'D BE PLEASED !!!
(now I'm shouting)

How could you possibly think I'd be pleased – when you know how much it upsets me.

You're a wicked man – I was just trying to help – I thought you'd be pleased – you don't speak to your daughters like this

Of course I don't – if I asked them not to do something that upset me then they wouldn't do it – they wouldn't carry on day after day after day.

(she screams – she cries – she throws her tea across the room – and then she limps dramatically to her bedroom – slams the door and lies on the bed sobbing loudly ….. a few moments later – she returns with a triumphant malevolence in her eyes to administer the 'coup de grace'….. her timing is impeccable)
Oh – and I've prepared a nice dinner for you.

WHAT….. WHAT !!!

What do you mean 'a nice dinner'

You need to eat properly – I've got the sausages and bacon ready and the potatoes and vegetables are all cooked in the saucepan – you've just got to heat them up

But I asked you not to prepare my food – I don't know what I'm going to feel like eating yet – I might not be hungry at all – I know that I won't want sausages and bacon and vegetables that have been boiled to death and left standing in a saucepan all day

How dare you – there's nothing wrong with the vegetables – how dare you – I've been cooking vegetables all my life – and if you don't eat the sausages then I'll have to throw them away – they are all defrosted now

Well you'll just have to throw them away then…..

What a wicked thing to say – you're so selfish – you never consider me – I've been working hard all morning – I thought you'd be pleased.

YOU….. I….. YOU…..YOU…..

(I am reduced to a stuttering red faced incoherent imbecile)
I'll never do anything to help you ever again…..
(oh yeah – not until tomorrow anyway)
You can do it all yourself – I'm finished with you – I feel ill – I shouldn't have to put up with this cruelty at my age – I'm going to bed to lie down – you can make your own dinner – I don't care anymore – you can eat exactly what you want – I'll never try and help again….. I'm finished with you
(and the parting shot…..)
I thought you'd be pleased !!!

(the door of her bedroom slams once more…..

….. and there she stays – loudly sobbing and moaning and complaining to herself…..

….. until tomorrow – when the whole sordid drama will be repeated all over again)

33

Russian Cars – A World View

Gaiety is the most outstanding feature of the Soviet Union
Joseph Stalin

My, not altogether unjustified, anxiety at entering Strode's Grammar School, coincided almost exactly with what would become the constant anxiety of living with a Russian made Volga automobile.

The path to its unfortunate acquisition was yet another example of my father's trusting and gullible nature, coupled with his inability to resist the chance of owning a brand new motor car – no doubt supplied by his 'friends' at Thomson and Taylor* at an unmissable 'special bargain price'.

Surely with this illustrious history to guide them, Thomson and Taylor should have known better than to associate themselves with anything coming out of the Soviet Union on four wheels and to this day I am unable to understand why they did so – or indeed how the country that invented the T34 Tank, the Videotape recorder, the Helicopter, the Russian Doll, Sputnik and Yoghurt could stoop to such a level as to become the designers and creators of the Volga Gaz M-21 G and its sad subsequent lineage.

---

*   Thomson & Taylor was a motor-racing, engineering and car-building firm, based within the Brooklands race track. They were active between the wars and built several of the famous land speed record breaking cars of the day.

Of course the 1963 Volga (by name and nature) was a thinly disguised copy of an American 1954 Ford Mainline but with all the contemptuous expressions of Western Capitalism replaced by good old home grown no nonsense 'people power' design features.

This blind adherence to political ideology resulted in the lovely big burbling V8 or silky Straight 6 of the US counterpart being replaced by a ludicrously underpowered 2.5 litre four cylinder tractor engine, which gave the car all the performance of – in the words of a great English poet – an asthmatic ant with some heavy shopping.

To compound the problem, the American standard issue Auto Gearbox – such a contemptable indictment of Western laziness and sloth – meant that the hopelessly misplaced motor was coupled – not to a 4-speed manual box which just might have made the situation tolerable – but to a 3-speed box – which in reality was a 4-speed box with the 3rd gear missing.

Bearing in mind that the car's bodywork was made from thick armour plated steel left over from WW2 – the vast chasm between the second and third gear ratios meant that – when trying to accelerate in order to overtake toddlers on scooters or old ladies pushing prams – or when attempting to ascend inclines greater than a small ant hill (to continue the ant theme) it was totally impossible to get from second to third gear – the drop in engine revs being just too much for the poor little motor to cope with…..

….. presumably they don't have hills in the glorious motherland.

Memories of outings in 'the car' will be forever scarred with the painful screams of an engine unable to get out of second gear – angry queues of traffic following behind at 20 mph – and waiting at the top of each and every hill for the steam pouring out of the over-heated radiator to gradually subside.

It is interesting to note that the KGB, if not actively responsible for the disastrous performance of the Volga, then certainly made good use of it..... their Volgas just happened to be fitted with powerful 5.4 litre V8 engines which meant that, conveniently for them, there was not a soul in the land that could out run them.

The sufferings and frustrations that this pitiful vehicle brought to our daily lives was seemingly without end – but one example should suffice in order to paint the picture.

Somewhere, in the small backroom that functioned both as a canteen and the Volga design office – the drawings for the carburettor and the office coffee percolator got mixed up.

The proof of this mistake was self-evident in the fact that if the car was caught in any kind of traffic for more than two minutes, the carburettor – which had been thoughtfully situated directly above the exhaust manifold – would 'percolate' petrol all over the hot metal of the exhaust pipes eventually creating a beautifully coloured prismatic puddle on the road below – this would almost immediately be followed by the engine stuttering to an undignified halt and requiring a cool down period of at least ten minutes before allowing us to resume our tortured travels.

As a result of these little 'idiosyncrasies', travelling in the Volga required us all to be constantly vigilant for all approaching lay-bys or indeed, for anywhere that would allow us to pull off the road in haste.

Each time I travel along the wonderful old A30 to Devon – I can still remember each and every lay-by where we all sat not so patiently waiting – and every house where my father went despondently begging for buckets of water and sympathy.

Understandably, I feel, I am astonished and incredulous to see that the Volga has now become a highly collectible and valuable example of 20th century automotive history.

Well let me state for the record – the Volga Gaz M21 is not a proud and rugged icon of the Soviet era – nor is it a fascinatingly austere counterpart to Western excess.

The Volga was and always will be a pile of irredeemable junk and no one should ever allow themselves to be tempted to pay a penny more for this car than its value in scrap metal.

*Volga-rity [vuhl-**gar**-i-tee] noun – the state or quality of being Volga*
- *characterized by ignorance of or lack of good breeding or taste:*
- *crude; coarse; unrefined:*

While I'm 'letting it all out' I may as well go the whole way and reveal my theories on the deeper and more sinister agendas that surrounded the production of the Volga.....

..... my unavoidable premise being that no country could have possibly come up with such a car in a serious and sincere attempt to enable its more privileged citizens to get from A grad to B grad in a suitably dignified and rational manner.

My first theory portrays the Soviets as devious aggressors – which to any lad growing up in the 'red under the bed' years comes very easily and naturally.

In this scenario the Volga – and its smaller ugly sister the Moskivitch – were both part of an ingenious plan to conquer the West by exporting hundreds of thousands of these Trojan horses and causing us all to spend our lives stuck in lay-bys, thus bringing our economy slowly but inevitably to a grinding halt.

Alas, the flaw in the plan was to ask us to actually pay good money for these ridiculous machines – if they'd been smart enough to give them away with packets of Cornflakes then without a doubt – we would all be calling each other comrade by now.

Bearing in mind that I do not put myself forward as in any way being an expert on Cold War matters – I do feel that my second theory throws a fresh and compelling perspective on the dynamics of East West relations – a theory simply derived from observing the long rows of grim faced officials standing lifelessly at all the pompous military parades that the Soviets so relished.

The Volga being the much desired and long awaited reward for the 'elite' of the regime, meant that these poor souls – after waiting and dreaming for 30 years – would eventually find themselves to be the proud owners of nothing but a lazy lacklustre lay-by loiterer….. no wonder they looked so grim.

If only we in the West could have thought outside the paranoid nuclear box for just a moment – we would have understood that their expansionist foreign policy was simply dictated by their desperate searching for a decent car….. all we really had to do was to ship over a few crates of Cortinas and they would have been our friends for life.

As it is, the whole sorry affair is now just another example of how the history of our world is so tragically littered with missed opportunities for peace and harmony.

As far as I can see, the Volga had only two mitigating features.

The first was the wonderful Drivers Manual that dripped with pearls of badly translated wisdom such as 'when wanting go forward – press down on throttle pedal – see Fig 20'….. or 'when wanting stop – press down on brake pedal – see Fig 21'…..

….. in my smug western way – I do find it impossible now to resist the temptation of imagining Ivan and Olga's first trip in their shiny new motor…..

… I'm sorry Ivan but I just can't find Fig 21
… Do hurry up Olga
… I'm trying – I'm trying
…. You're going to have to try a little harder my dear…..
… oh no ! …
… damn and bother !! …
… that will be thirty years down the drain then dearest one !!!

The second mitigating feature was of course, the magnificent massive chrome prancing Deer mascot perched proudly on the front of the bonnet, obviously designed to disembowel any unfortunate pedestrian that was subversive enough to get caught in its way…..

….. although, of course, for most of the time, this would necessitate the unfortunate pedestrian hurling him/herself at the Deer while the car sat steaming by the side of the road.

As things turned out, the Volga was to plague our lives for the following ten years – like some kind of unexorcisable medieval curse.

So the question remains – why would my father hold onto a car that quite simply didn't work or comply in any way with the basic requirements of a civilised form of transport – regardless of whether it was brand new or not.

Why did he surrender so dutifully to the unending psychotic demands of crazy cars – or crazy wives for that matter..... like a prisoner before his tormentor maybe – the Stockholm Syndrome not so irrelevant or comfortably remote as we might care to believe.

As a postscript to this story..... being in the early seventies the only remaining left hand drive example in the country – our Volga Gaz M-21 G actually came to outgrow us and went on to become a much sought after film star – hissing and stuttering its way through numerous 'Spy films' and the like.....

..... it is now, no doubt, enjoying a not so well earned retirement while writing its memoirs in between courses of expensive cosmetic surgery.....

..... скатертью дорога !

34

The Pink Shorts Make A Brief Appearance

... did you know that the Coral in the Great Barrier Reef
is the world's largest living orgasm?

My mother – age 94

The boy is 12 years old – it is the beginning of the Summer Holidays – his first long break at the Grammar School..... the day is hot and sunny and as he gazes out into the six weeks of school free bliss that stretch out before him – he cannot conceive of them ever coming to an end…..

….. the day is perfect – his hopes are perfect – all is perfect…..

….. but all too soon it would become clear once more – that his idea of 'perfect' and his mother's idea of 'perfect' did not always come together in tolerance and mutual accord ….. never in fact.

The very best thing about going to the 'Big School' is that he is now – not only able, but actually required to wear long black trousers – and such is their embodiment of manhood that he only – and very reluctantly – removes them when going to bed or climbing trees.

The plan for this particular perfect summer's day – is to wear his long black trousers, his school shoes and his white Van Heusen Drip-dry Bri-nylon shirt and meet his friends in Victoria Park Addlestone in order to generally mooch around with their hands in their pockets – effortlessly assuming the role that they were born to fulfil – of 'cool young men about town'.

They might, at some point, play a little cricket or throw a ball to each other – but it is without question the act of the debonair shuffle that is the order of the day.

This is the plan – and the cherry on cake of the plan is to travel to Addlestone by himself on the trusty old dark green 461A London Transport bus.

What could possibly go wrong…..

YOU'RE NOT GOING OUT LIKE THAT !!!

….. it's summer…..
….. you're not going out in long black trousers…..
….. what will people think…..

They're fine mum – honestly

They are not fine – you'll be much too hot in those…..
….. take them off right now – and you're not wearing a long

sleeve shirt in this weather either.....

..... I'm not taking you out dressed like that

(She is of course referring to her taking him to Addlestone in her new ultra-modern Morris Minor 1000 – the poor old MG now having been consigned to the garden with all the other crumbling wrecks)

You don't have to take me – I can go by bus

You're certainly not going on the bus – I'll take you in the car.....

..... but first go upstairs and put on these lovely shorts that I bought for you

(Now the whole picture is becoming clear..... from behind her back she instantly produces an article of clothing of such frightful appearance that the boy's heart almost stops in its tracks.....

..... in his helpless state of shock – he is only capable of blurting out what is blatantly and excruciatingly obvious)

They're PINK !!!

Don't be silly – of course they're not pink.....
..... they are coral.....
..... and you're going to put them on right now

What do you mean 'CORAL' ?

..... they're not coral they're PINK – and I'm not wearing them

You WILL wear them – you're not going out in this weather in long trousers

(The logic of her argument is lost on the boy..... he is experiencing an unspeakably traumatic 'out of body experience' in which he sees himself being dropped off at Victoria Park by his mother and like a man on his way to the Gallows – walking slowly and despondently across the park to where is friends are heartlessly crying with laughter at the very same pink shorts that his mother is now holding out before him.....

..... he is abruptly rescued from the nightmare by his mother dragging him by the arm with one hand whilst trying to tear off his trousers with the other.....

..... voices once merely fraught – now start hastily climbing up the ladder towards full-on screaming and hysteria)

I am not wearing pink shorts – they're girls shorts

They are not pink – I told you – they are a lovely manly shade of dirty red and you WILL wear them.....

(His mother would often use the word 'manly' in the completely mistaken belief that – like a trump card – it would instantly seal any clothing dispute with her sons in her favour)

..... you'll go to your room and put them on if I have to drag you there myself

But they're PINK – they are not CORAL or DIRTY RED or MANLY – they're PINK – they are BLOODY PINK and I'm not wearing them

(At this point – seeds of the 'Parrot Sketch' float out of the window and on into the universe beyond – flying off in search of happier and more congenial minds no doubt)

How dare you swear at me.....

..... you wicked selfish ungrateful child.....

..... get to your room right now.....

..... you can stay there all afternoon.....

..... and they are not PINK.....

..... they are lovely.....

..... just you wait until your father gets home

(Of course – when his father does get home – he will eat his supper and then fall asleep on the sofa..... but if the boy is really unlucky – his father might just mumble a few words about being 'put in the army'..... altogether not the dreaded deterrent that his mother would be hoping for)

..... and so.....

..... it is the beginning of the Summer Holidays – the day is hot and sunny and strangely peaceful.....

..... inside his bedroom – the boy stares out of his window and laments his lost afternoon.....

..... but he is nevertheless heartened at the thought that – if any lamenting is going to be done – it is a good thing to be doing it whilst wearing your favourite pair of long black trousers.

As it turns out – the whole affair proves to be a seminal moment within the boy's faltering steps to manhood – for as an old man, he is able to look back proudly upon the resolve of his 12 year old self as each time he ponders upon the unmistakable fact that – through all the long and meandering days of his life – not wearing pink shorts has, without a doubt, served him remarkably well.

35

Strode's Grammar School 1963-1968

It is the supreme art of the teacher to awaken joy in creative expression and knowledge.

Albert Einstein

Henry Strode, (1645-1704), was born during the English Civil War and lived in London through the Plague and the Great Fire. He was the son of a master cooper and joined the family firm in 1680 going on to make a substantial fortune in business in London. In 1704, he bequeathed to the Company £6,000 to establish a 'good strong substantial schoolhouse... for the learning and edifying of the poor children of the Parish of Egham'. There have been three schools on the present site. The school became a secondary school for boys in 1919 and was granted voluntary controlled status in 1950 as Strode's Grammar School. It became a co-educational sixth form college, known as Strode's

College in 1975 and was incorporated as a Further Education College in 1993. The first school was opened around 1706, demolished and rebuilt in the 1820s and again in 1915. The oldest surviving buildings are the almshouses of 1820s and 1830s construction. The main building constructed during World War 1 still forms the core of the College's complex of buildings. For almost 200 years Strode's School provided elementary education for the poor boys of Egham. Its second and third masters, John Paget and Robert Jones, served 97 years between them from 1710 to 1807. With changing educational needs, the School was closed in 1900 and eventually, a new school was built which opened in 1919 as a boys' Grammar School, with 62 boys, two full-time and three part-time teachers. The Grammar School expanded and developed, opening its first sixth form in 1924 acquiring an enviable reputation for academic success and artistic and sporting endeavour.

Strode's College Website

By the time that I entered its not so hallowed halls in the mid-sixties – the 'enviable reputation' of Strode's Grammar School had become somewhat of a distant memory as it struggled to hold on by a thread to the glory of its former life.

'Joy in creative expression and knowledge' – or in anything at all in fact – is not my enduring recollection of the sorry endeavours of the largely geriatric cohort of fluttering black robed teachers that stalked the school halls like flocks of predatory vultures.

The very best that we came to expect of the teaching staff was a very welcome degree of benign apathy – which was always such a relief from the usual round of sadism and perversion that was the normal order of the day….. with all due respect – which, in this case, means with absolutely no respect at all – in today's climate – the majority of the teaching staff would, without a doubt, now be committed to old people's homes – mental institutions or, indeed, prison.

I feel that it is long overdue for me to kick these particular skeletons out of the closet of my buried psychoses – skeletons being the operative word.

Of course I am guilty of allowing the pain and confusion

of those years to run away maybe a little overenthusiastically and unfairly with the tarring brush – so I'll simply relate a few typical (very typical) stories of what was evidently considered to be acceptable behaviour and let them speak for themselves.

I'll start with those who were too old and frail to have any impact on their pupils for good or for bad, except of course to contribute to the general atmosphere of tedium and irrelevant banality that was 'school life'.

Mr. Cope – nicknamed Horis, naturally – was known as the History teacher – which meant in practice, that after entering the classroom and condemning the atmosphere (in what was no doubt supposed to be a humorous tone) as smelling like a monkey house – would proceed to read out a chapter or two from the appointed history text book which we would then be required to write out word for word in our own exercise books.

After telling us to read and learn the day's dictation he would close the book at the end of the lesson and leave – ironic that he was so amused at comparing us to monkeys while being happy to drag the evolution of the teaching profession past the monkeys and back to the prehistoric swamp.

Despite this, I was grateful to Horis for enabling me to learn one very handy life skill. This skill involved learning to write whilst leaning my forehead on my hand thus disguising the fact that I had fallen into a pleasant semi-comatose state and was merely writing in my sleep.

My only memories of music lessons are that I liked music dictation because I was quite good at it and that I loathed Danse Macabre by Saint Saens – something that, in itself, has never really detracted from my musical development or from my appreciation of life in general.

There was the terrifying Maths teacher with his permanent scowl and a complexion so dark and menacing that he looked as if he may have never washed in his entire life. He had obviously subscribed whole heartedly to the Readers Digest 'Extend your vocabulary by learning a new word each week' article – for in every lesson he would use a new and random word throughout – which seemed to us to be rather sad and pathetic in a grown man.

There was the science teacher who, being middle aged, was still a relative novice in the subtle arts of school sadism and cruelty – but he did his best. He was always very keen to allocate large parts of each lesson to practical demonstrations – especially if this would enable him to incorporate a degree of inflicted pain into the proceedings.

For example, to demonstrate the workings of the accumulator battery, he would direct the whole class to hold hands while the two boys at each end of the chain were made to take hold of the positive and negative terminals – oh what fun filled gratification was had by the teacher as we all screamed and stumbled around the room in shock.

Demonstrating the self-igniting properties of Phosphorous didn't go so well….. or maybe it did.

Having placed a lump of Phosphorous on his desk, it did indeed – without any outside help or prompting – suddenly and violently burst into flames – however, the lively little lump didn't stop there – it carried on self-igniting things around itself until eventually the whole science lab was in flames….. the teacher's devious plan to incinerate a class of expendable 13 year olds only thwarted by our hasty and hysterical evacuation to the safety of the playground outside.

Before I come to the Chemistry teacher – I must introduce my classmate Lenny Watkins while I calm myself with a large mug of Chamomile tea.

Lenny was my friend – and sadly – a far better friend to me than I was to him. His parents were unusual, for they were free thinkers and intelligent and were not besotted or intimidated in any way by Authority or by the school teaching staff in particular.

Lenny was smart beyond his years and when it came to life at Strode's Grammar School, he was able to see through it all with an impressive clarity of thought and reason.

I would often watch him as he surveyed his surroundings as someone remote and detached, perceiving it all from a far off place of peace and sagacity – all of which, no doubt, led to his affinity with the songs of Bob Dylan and his dark bouts of depression, long before the rest of us knew what the word meant.

I have no idea why he entertained me as a friend considering the intellectual gulf between us – maybe because he mistook my tenuous grasp on reality as having a critical and revolutionary origin….. whatever the reason – it was a much needed saving grace in my life that he and my guitar buddies Stuart and Ian accepted me as I was – and still do.

Lenny was his own man – which inevitably made him the victim of choice for all the black-gowned bullies – but for one – this victimisation was to become a vile and dangerous obsession.

The Chemistry 'teacher' was a thick set man of late middle age – I will call him Mr. M not out of cowardice or misplaced consideration for his memory but because his name has become, not surprisingly, long since erased from my mind.

An inexperienced pupil could have been forgiven for taking his demeanour as being friendly and somewhat cheerful – that is until the full depravity of the man became apparent in the fact that his cheerfulness derived only from the pain that he was currently inflicting or was planning to inflict on some poor unfortunate boy.

One of his particularly memorable japes involved demonstrating the properties of the Force Pump by spraying water over the whole classroom – we were then all duly punished for having smeared ink in our exercise books.

Chemical experiment lessons would be a riot of Health and Safety disregard – with boys running around the room with open bottles of hot sulphuric acid and the like – lit Bunsen burners being placed on stools and chairs beneath small unsuspecting backsides and nearly everyone trying to find out what you would need to combine with what to cause a small but satisfying explosion…..

..... but with a tragic and pitiful inevitability – every lesson would sooner or later come down to Mr. M's proud and enthusiastic abuse of Lenny Watkins.

The usual outworking of this abuse would consist of Mr. M slithering around the room whilst talking about chemical reactions or something equally tedious until he was standing right behind Lenny's chair.

We all knew what would happen next.

Without any provocation on Lenny's part – Mr. M would wrap a piece of rubber Bunsen Burner tubing around Lenny's throat – pull it tight – then lift the lid on Lenny's desk, push his head inside and proceed to slam the desk lid up and down until, either he got bored with the violence, or Lenny became worryingly inert and silent..... whatever came first.

All this would be conducted with a silly and malicious grin on his face – as if it could be taken for granted that everyone in the room was enjoying the fun – and all without missing a single beat from the mindlessly regurgitated script of the lesson in hand.

At other times – he would bellow for no obvious reason 'Get in the back room Atkins' – he would then tell us to get on with such and such while he followed Lenny into the room and closed the door.

To our shame – none of us ever asked or even wanted to find out what happened in the back room – probably because this was not in any way shocking or unusual – or maybe we were just relieved that it wasn't us at the receiving end.

All was accepted by us boys with helpless but contemptuous resignation as 'being what teachers did' – who would we speak to anyway – it was the system – the whole abhorrent archaic system – all supported by the mystical adoration and respect afforded by parents – to whom teachers, like gods, could do no wrong.....

..... oh how things have changed since then – the pendulum now at the opposite end of its swing with never a moment's hesitation over the mean point of humanity and common sense.

On a lighter note – there were exceptions – those that I knew about and those of which I had no experience and to whom I now offer my apologies and my commiserations at being tainted by association.

There was the French teacher Mr. Roberts – who in his mid-thirties looked somewhat like a child compared to his colleagues. Mr. Roberts was just like a normal guy – he had no crazy inclinations – he spoke and taught without prejudice or madness. I liked his lessons – not because of any special leanings towards languages but because he taught calmly and intelligently and he could make things interesting.

I'm sure it was not his fault, but the fault of the curriculum that after coming top of the class for three years, I left school without the ability to speak a single word of French.

Mr. Mathias taught woodwork and technical drawing and for that reason alone – in my eyes – could do no wrong…… as a bonus, he was in fact a kindly and helpful man.

There was the pleasant but optically challenged German teacher who, to alleviate the tedium of the lesson, would tap his glass eye loudly with the arm of his glasses or remove it completely, to polish it, admire it, and roll it happily around on his desk.

There was the lovely Mr. Elliot who taught English and was obviously far too good and gentle for the profession as was evident in his violent facial twitch – gained, no doubt, from the merciless bullying he received at the hands of the sixth formers…… (Bullying, of course, was available as an O-level option in the 4th Year – but I decided to go for Woodwork instead).

Jock the Headmaster seemed well meaning and kind but was unable to make his presence felt and as a result was sadly ineffectual against the rampant prevailing darkness.

There was a general unspoken rule of law at Strode's and that was – if you were good at sport, and in particular, rowing – then no matter what – you would have an easy ride. For those of us on the outside of the sporting world – keeping your head down had to become a very necessary and practised way of life.

There was an unexpected postscript to my time at Strode's
– and one that was suitably expressive of the seriousness with
which the school treated the nurturing of its pupils' potential.

After the school had become a college I was musically
involved for a while with the then Music Teacher. One evening
after a small concert in the music room – and probably after a
few glasses of wine – he suggested that we have a look at the old
school records to see if mine was still in existence.

I went straight to Lenny's record in the mistaken belief that his
would be the most colourful – but strangely there was nothing
to distinguish it – no added notes or comments – and so it was
for Stuart and Ian…..

… mine however stood apart…

… there scrawled across the back of my record…

… a succinct but cautionary denunciation…

… written for the benefit of all posterity…

… as elegant and brief as it was dismissive and patronising…

'LONG HAIR BUT MUSICAL'

STRODE'S GRAMMAR SCHOOL

Established in 1704
for the learning and edifying
of the poor children of the Parish of Egham.

'Malo Mori Quam Foedari'

… whatever

36

The Summer Of Love Gives Way To Desolation Row

Nothing is real and nothing to get hung about

John Lennon

Madness at school – madness at home – apart from the blessed respite of the twenty minute train journey from Chertsey to Egham and back – my life was without any kind of reference point or anchor – and so – I spiralled easily and instinctively into a safe welcoming world of fantasy, make believe and self-loathing.

My physical slide began in earnest at the age of 14 with a bout of Glandular Fever that lasted for six months with just one short remission in the middle.

With its usual devotion to conscientiousness – the school did almost nothing to arrange for the making up of the lessons that I'd missed during my absence – presumably under the premise that it was all somehow my fault and therefore should not be allowed to inconvenience them in any way.

However, such was the vacuousness of the teaching that the missed lessons didn't actually seem to have any impact on the overall scheme of things at all – I'd already learnt too well that almost everything that passed as 'education' within the walls of Strode's Grammar School was in reality just meaningless, irrelevant and excruciatingly boring nonsense – what could I have possibly missed of any consequence.

My health – which had managed, by will power alone, to assume an air, although precarious, of convincing 'normality' – now fell into the open arms of what would become a fifty year period of illness and chronic fatigue – the summer of 1967 becoming a final and glorious few months of merciful respite.

For a brief moment during 'the summer of love' – the world of day-dreams in which I lived seemed to find a home and a keen accomplice in the colours and the pageant of 'Flower Power' – I needed no drugs to lift me out of the world of 'reason' and 'conformity' – I was never there in the first place.

It all started very quietly and insignificantly – like the news reports of scrap metal men landing on the Falklands just before the outbreak of full on hostilities.

Lenny of course was at the vanguard – with his precious copy of Sergeant Peppers and his subsequent poems about marshmallow lawnmowers and banana daydreams.

We were bewitched – but my first real inkling that something strange and exotic was truly afoot, was when one of the girls at our 'Sister Grammar School' – Sir William Perkins – with whom us boys had now taken it upon themselves to dutifully and enthusiastically explore inter-school 'cordiality' – turned up at one of these after school 'meetings' proudly sporting a painted flower on the back of her hand.

Within days we were all wearing flares and kipper ties and regency jackets and growing our hair – as much as was possible that is – and listening to songs about people going to San Francisco.

It was indeed the 'summer of love' – and we needed no prompting to throw ourselves whole heartedly into the pursuance of all the boy/girl adventures so happily endorsed and expounded on the crackling air-waves that would surround and guide us for the next three months.

The sun seemed to shine each and every day that summer and we soon fell into an enchanted and care free routine of laughter and song and the exciting discovery of 'loins'..... and the obediently following after to wherever it was that they were leading us.

After school we would cycle to the house of one girl or another and every weekend there would be a party with copious amounts of sophisticated grown-up consumables like Bulmer's cider and instant coffee and filter tipped cigarettes and endless unfulfilled rumours of Marijuana.

By the end of the summer I had discovered that sex – or at least what passed as sex for a then 15 year old – was almost as much fun as making model aircraft or changing the grease in the bearings of my racing bike.

For just three months in my entire life – I was deemed to be attractive and desirable by the opposite sex and I fell into the crazy unreality of it all with relish and abandon – girls were like sweets in a sweet shop – and like one dimensional cardboard cut-outs they were the perfect and willing complement to my make believe world.....

..... but of the callous cruelty that I inflicted as a result – on one in particular – I will probably never make sense or understand.....

..... the question ever restless for closure and peace.....

..... was I thoughtlessly and heartlessly culpable – or was I just a helpless and hopeless victim of the fates that bound me ?

As a last final swan song to my fading vitality – the school's ultimatum to 'cut your hair or do not return for the following year' – resulted in me walking out the back door of the Barber's Shop in Station Road, Addlestone – where I had been taken by my parents – climbing over various garden walls and fences and eventually taking a coach to Brixham to shack up with a beautiful 21 year old artist call Cherry who I'd met camping there with friends a few weeks before.

Cherry of course was quietly horrified by my unbidden arrival but was very gracious and kind and proceeded to supply me with shelter and provisions until the Police found me a few weeks later – as a direct result, I'm sure, of me not having read, at the time, any Len Deighton and so being woefully ignorant of the protocols of subterfuge and covert living in a foreign land.

I never did return to Strode's Grammar School but was enrolled belatedly but victoriously into Brooklands Technical College in Weybridge – there to study for my A levels.

The 'Guitar' now entered my life under the patient tutelage of my friends Ian and Stuart – flares and lime green shirts and all the trivial trappings of 'flower power' were now hastily cast aside in favour of whatever Dylan was wearing on his latest album cover – over-night, we became suitably deep and dark and moody and over-night, the girls left in droves – never to return.

..... but what did I care – the moment I heard Stuart playing an E7 chord on his old Hohner 'F Top' guitar I was hooked – and when he then slyly proceeded to bend the 7th note just a tantalising touch – I was transported, and my world for the foreseeable future was, in a moment, determined and complete.

I have been searching for that note ever since..... it was the very one that touched me as child in the hymn 'My Song is Love Unknown' and it would come back to me at various times in my life and in various guises like at the end of Hindemith's Harp Sonata.....

..... but no matter how hard I tried and how far I journeyed, I could never make it my own – just like the beauty of my beloved – or the sun setting over the ocean – at the top of every mountain there was always another mountain to climb..... or so it seemed.

In the midst of my failing health, my first year at Brooklands became a time of belonging and hope in the form of my friendship with Peron Schouten from St Lucia and the wonderful teaching of Mr Robertson.

Peron and I just sparked each other from the start – we would study through our break times and after college and – under the inspiring tutelage of Mr Robertson – we blossomed.

Mr R taught simply from the overflow of his passion – he was elderly but never had to raise his voice or reprimand – he commanded respect as naturally as the falling of a leaf on a bright Autumn day.

'O levels' failed at school just months before, were passed with A grades – Peron and I vied for the top two places in everything and discussions were even held concerning the Oxbridge entrance exam.

The flame burnt bright indeed – but it was to be short lived and its final breath abrupt and irrevocable.

The illness that had been patiently brooding for so long within me, now responded greedily and rapidly to the change in my life style and its necessary adjuncts of alcohol, coffee, cigarettes and 'dope'......

...... as the summer of 1969 shone for those around me – I was descending into a dark and pitiless hell from which I would only return as an old and, thankfully, wiser man.

The wild exuberant energy of Peron also succumbed that summer – in his case, to relentless migraine headaches...... his absences from college becoming longer and more numerous – until one day a message came down that his parents had come and taken him back home to St Lucia......

...... for a while we kept in touch – but then that too fell away.

Just like the previous year – September brought with it another bid for freedom – but this time one that was cheaper, less prone to romantic rejection and came with the promise of permanence and peace...... although just as susceptible to failure as it turned out.

I was never to try again – although the act was never far from my thoughts......

...... I hadn't really considered that people might care for me or miss me in any way – I'd never really spotted the signs – and after all......

... nothing was real...

... and there was nothing really to get hung about – at all.

Although nothing was ever mutually exclusive – the songs of Bob Dylan soon led to the Folk Blues guitar playing of Bert Jansch and John Renbourn and from Renbourn's album 'Sir John a Lot of' to Elizabethan Lute Music and from there to J S Bach and the world of Classical Music.

My crude but enthusiastic attempts at composing persuaded me – in the wake of the 'train wreck' of my A level exams – to start working part-time for my father – as the most available means to earn some money whilst I studied Music Theory and

Harmony at Trinity College in London.

Without any suggestion as to how the copious and implacable rules of harmony fitted into the broader creative act of composition – the OCD part of me sprung into hyper-drive when it discovered that music could be simply constructed according to what was 'right' or 'wrong'.

There were occasional confusions of course – such as learning that Parallel Fifths were 'wrong' or even 'bad' ….. up until that point, I'd always thought, in my naïve way, that they sounded rather nice.

I was a lone soul without bearings or compass – always accepting without hesitation that if there was any disagreement between my own inclinations and the teaching script presented to me – then it was up to me to go forward in the sure knowledge that it was I that was in the wrong.

And so – just as with the black lines around my paintings at Junior School – the seductive rules of harmony, as laid out so painstakingly by Mr. William Lovelock, inevitably led me to turn my back on the world of simple spontaneous and mistakenly enjoyable musical composition.

As the 1960's gave way to the 1970's, the silent shadow of my Grandmother's presence passed quietly and humbly from our midst….. our change in family circumstance almost immediately leading to our big old house being very abruptly abandoned in obedient response to my mother's sudden aversion to its size.

As with all of my mother's plans – they came with a blatantly contrived altruistic agenda that rendered them far beyond the reach of criticism or discussion.

In this case it was my father no longer being able to climb stairs due to his recent heart attack – it was of course futile to point out the obvious fact that my father actually climbed stairs all day at work without suffering any injury to his health, for screaming and shouting and bucket loads of self-pity always more than made up for any inconvenient lack of logic in my mother's arguments.

As with all things related to my mother and her demands –

the deed had to be sealed with immediate effect – and so it was that we exchanged our lovely old rambling house for a poky little 'jerry built' bungalow in the nearby village of Lyne – with almost no resulting financial benefit from the drastic downsizing.

Very soon, of course, it became my father's fault that we all now found ourselves in such a tight and miserable squeeze – and so, heart attack or not, he found himself building an extension bedroom on the side, knocking down the wall between the 'hall' and the 'dining room' and fitting a large sliding patio door – all under the generous guidance and supervision and correction of my mother's constant surveillance.

I'm sure he must have pondered all the while on how fortunate he was to no longer have any stairs to climb and how blessed he was to have such a caring and thoughtful wife.

My mother's haste to leave our glorious old West Dene – the house that had been my home and my protector for all of the nineteen years of my life – meant that we had completely vacated its numerous rooms and out buildings long before its new owners were able to replace us.

As a result, the old house stood empty and forlorn for over two weeks – an irresistible temptation for a young man with a very slender grasp on the concepts of honesty and trust and with a set of keys in his pocket that he'd somehow 'forgotten' to pass on.

Farewell to West Dene

On a dark night in September 1970 – two surreptitious intruders creep through the front garden of a large red brick house and let themselves quietly in through its impressive oak front door.

The old empty building, lit only by a single street light, echoes strangely with an uneasy and elusive foreboding…..

….. so many memories and so many hopes still clinging tenaciously to the musty air.

The young man and the young woman – wander silently from room to room – but after a very short while – being unable to absorb the grief of the parting that must ensue, with all its implications of betrayal and loss – decide to bid farewell in the most suitable way that they can think of on the spur of the moment.....

..... there on the naked wooden floor boards the sighs and the giggles of two naked bodies drift off into the night.....

... and maybe...

... just maybe...

... the old house became honoured more in that dark fragile moment by the gentle closeness and sharing of those two young souls...

... than it ever had been...

... within all the days of frenzy and convulsion...

... of the previous twenty years.

37

The Love Of Heaven

I like your Christ
I do not like your Christians
your Christians are so unlike your Christ

Mahatma Gandhi

As all the tarnished hopes of one decade give way – as they do – to all the bright young promises of the next – the spontaneous and 'innocent' excesses of Sixties Pop Culture gave way to the contrived excesses of Glam Rock and the obligatory puritan backlash of Punk.

By this time, it had become obvious to anyone with one or two brain cells remaining, that music, drugs and 'free love' weren't actually going to save the world after all.....

..... but what does it really matter – life must go on – and as the priests and prophets and gurus of the old order depart from their moral high ground for the safety of their tax havens and their country estates, the age old game of musical chairs continues with never a pause for question or breath.

..... for after all – is there not just one rule that really counts.....

Everyone is smarter than the one before

Every politician and every political party – every monarch and every dictator – every religious faith and every denomination – every regime and every cause – every rebellion and every revolution – every philosopher and every creed.....

..... I have grown weary of it all – I find that I no longer have any trust nor time for anyone who is incapable of saying.....

I'm sorry – I got it wrong

This is what I have come to believe.....

In this world of physical things – nothing is new and nothing ever changes..... for it is the heart that is the centre and the well-spring of all things ..... and our hearts can never change of their own accord or volition.....

..... in the first instance – there can be no 'corporate' struggle between right and wrong – for the only battle that matters is the battle within each individual heart.....

..... and just as the building will fall – no matter how grand its façade – if its foundations are rotten..... the cause will also come to nothing – no matter how honourable and just – if the hearts of those that support it are corrupted by bitterness and hate.....

..... for hatred cannot fight against hatred – nor intolerance against intolerance..... nor injustice against injustice.....

..... if they try – then the heart will be defiled from the start and the war lost long before the battle ever begins.....

..... in the end – only the cycles of suffering and madness will prevail – for there is nothing noble or worthy in hatred no matter what colours may hang from the banner.....

..... we may like to call ourselves 'radical' – in vain attempts to disguise the fact, that we are simply giving in once more to the call of our anger and our pride.....

..... but in truth – there is not, and has never been, a single radical thought in the mind of man.

There is only one truly radical force in the whole universe, and that force flies unerringly in the face of all human reason and instinct.....

..... it is the Love that bids us.....

..... *to love our enemies, to bless those that curse us, to do good to those that hate us, and to pray for those who spitefully use us, and persecute us.*

..... it is the love of Jesus Christ.....

..... and it is the Love that, from time to time, may be seen shining in the hearts of those that would seek to follow him..... whatever name they may go by.....

It is the root of all wonder

it is the mystery we seek

it is the song of creation

it is the cry of the deep

it is the laughter of a child

it is the truth that we speak

it is a dance pure and wild

it is the love of heaven

Memo

*We are one
and will always be*

*the sun rises for the wicked
as for the good*

*and the rain falls for the just
as for the unjust*

*if we reject and condemn religion
because of what has been done in its name*

*then we must reject and condemn
the whole human race*

for the exact same reason

38

Close Encounters

I always get the fuzzy end of the lollipop
Marilyn Monroe

It is 1973 – the boy is now a young man of twenty one and is working for his father as an engineer – a precision engineer.....

..... which means that for most of the time he stands and dreams of being a musician.....

..... but not today..... on this day – this ill-fated day – he is taking his younger brother to school in the brand new works Transit van.

There is a wide road with a central island – there is a small slip road to the school and there is a 'lollipop lady' all set for battle.....

..... in a moment of hideous error – he judges the slip road to be beyond the remit of the shiny white coated bastion of law and order.....

..... the 'lollipop lady' begs to differ – she catches the miscreant vehicle in the corner of her eye and in an instant is hurtling across the road with terrifying intent – her lollipop held out before her like an apocalyptic medieval lance.....

..... he tries to escape the impending confrontation but the acceleration of the ill-conceived V4 Transit is no match for this Olympian being.....

..... the lollipop is raised – the eyes are fixed and resolved – justice, retribution and deterrence are set to be acquitted in equal measure and the helpless vehicle is soundly and mercilessly 'thwacked'.....

..... it is a shocking experience – or maybe it is hilarious – the two startled occupants are not sure.....

..... little is said – the lad is dutifully and hastily dropped at school and the young man is left to ponder and fret on how he will even begin to explain to his father the strange malevolent looking scraping marks that have suddenly appeared all down the side of the once pristine petrol blue paintwork.....

Later – the young man will often re-visit the harrowing scene in his mind – never really sure of its gravity or its humour – but nevertheless certain that.....

..... compared to the many and varied forms of castigation and reproach that would be visited upon him through the years.....

... in terms of humiliation and defeat...

... being 'thwacked' by a lollipop lady was, without question...

... in a league of its very own.

39

All Fall Down

Wisdom that is proud
is no wisdom
at all

So what was it that I thought I knew – from what steady rock did I stand to survey the vistas of my heart – on what mountain crag did I rest to contemplate my hard won 'spiritual achievements'…..

….. it is of no account anymore – whatever it was – it is all as nothing now…..

….. for the very first time that my anger rose up against her – the anger that I thought was no more – on that broken day I knew – beyond any question or doubt – that I was helpless…..

….. all my fine words – all my proud and noble footholds…..

….. they had all fallen down into pieces – once again.

My one and only act of preparation towards the caring of my mother was the complete and thorough denial of everything that had passed between us….. as a result – I came to the situation as a runaway steam train hitting a slow bend at full speed.

After all the deranged outpouring of grief in the aftermath of my marriage break-up – I had come to think that my anger was now spent and that I had finally become a 'peaceful person'.

However, after just one week of living under the same roof as my mother – to my overwhelming dismay – it became obvious that I had barely scratched the surface of my pain.

No matter how hard I tried – it seemed that I had no defence against the 'triggers' within my mother's incessantly provocative behaviour – for, as I soon came to understand, I was not dealing with the trials of the present, but with the events and traumas of my childhood fifty years before.

Ironically, I was always at my most vulnerable when I was feeling cheerful or light hearted – if I had returned from swimming feeling re-charged or had simply been uplifted by the beauty of the surrounding countryside.....

..... without fail – my mother, like a shark before the smell of blood – could, and would, shoot me down in flames with just a single remark or just a single look.....

..... it took me a very long time to learn, that it was best to always fly very close to the ground and to keep any expression of my happier moments carefully hidden from view.....

..... it also took me a long time to learn, that it is discouraging and ultimately futile to expect any signs of sanity to be evident in the relentless out-workings of madness

..... for 'madness' is surely what it was and still is.....

..... it fills the air that I breathe – it clings to my skin like sweat before a storm – it hangs from the walls all around me like ancient dusty cobwebs.....

..... there is an aching and a churning inside me – to set it all down on this paper – to expose it all – every gesture – every remark – every demented act.....

..... I am crying out for 'justice' and 'peace' for a calm soothing hand to lay its gentle touch upon the relentlessly burning scars of my childhood – of my life.....

..... it is here now – it has never abated even for a moment – I am the child lying on the garage roof – shaking and struggling for breath – I sit here like a coiled spring – each word that I write like a needle twisting in some voodoo doll.....

..... I listen and I watch – and if this is set to be a 'good day' – then I will be able to delay the inevitable explosion within me for just a little while longer.....

...... I will hold my breath and I will still the restless hunger of my hurt – and I will close my ears to the question forever burning in my soul.....

WHY ?

….. why can nothing ever be straightforward or 'normal' for my mother…..

….. why must everything always be 'wrong'…..

….. the temperature too hot or too cold – the music too loud or too quiet – the lights too bright or too dim – the bread too thick or too thin…..

….. why am I ordered to use the dishwasher one day to save money but not allowed to use it the next for fear of it costing too much…..

….. and likewise – why must I drop everything one day to cover the flower beds in bark chippings only for them all to be removed the day after…..

….. and if all of this 'everyday madness' wasn't enough – why must there be the 'bad days' when the whole of her dissatisfaction with life becomes suddenly elevated to a supernatural state of malevolence and cunning…..

Exempli Gratia

I wake to a horribly familiar foreboding – like a poison hanging in the air – I can feel it before it starts – I can see it brooding in her eyes – in the contractions of her face as she sets her whole countenance to the task of provocation – a task that accepts no outcome but complete victory and annihilation – no matter how long or how violent the struggle…..

….. the saucepans are too large or too small and they don't fit the cooker hobs – the bread bin has no air holes in it for the bread to breathe – the shower mat is the wrong colour – the sofa is too small…..

….. she can't stand it for a moment longer – every offending item must be thrown out immediately– usually to be replaced a few days later with exactly the same thing…..

….. and if no reaction is forthcoming then the efforts become ever more personal and vindictive – they become as forms of punishment…..

….. she will threaten to call someone to take away the piano as I don't play it enough – she will throw out the pan that I use to stir fry because I am not using the one that she has stipulated to be the correct one for the cooker…..

..... *and if I react – if I dare to protest or raise my voice – then the 'finishing blow' is finally and gloriously inflicted.....*

..... *she will start ringing people (anyone will do, but Social Services were very popular for a while) to complain of my wicked and terrifying behaviour.....*

She has won!

..... *she is self-evidently vindicated and lauded as the innocent victim of arrant wilfulness and cruel and heartless selfishness.....*

..... *fortunately – the 'bad days' never come more than once a week – for the most part.....*

..... *maybe I should consider myself spoilt to have so many days in between to regroup my tattered threads of 'sang-froid'.....*

..... *but now.....*

..... *to continue with my supplications to the Universe.....*

..... why must everyone be forced to read or watch or listen to whatever book or magazine or music or film that is the current recipient of her approval and subsequent manic evangelism – and why must friends and family and strangers be sent away with piles of DVD's and books and photo-copies and CD's – to be suitably deprecated if they do not show immediate signs of gratitude and enthusiasm.....

..... why must unexpected visitors be vilified and abruptly spurned in favour of a hurried departure to her 'sick-bed' as a result of their thoughtless and selfish intrusion.....

..... why do all perceptions of criticism or contradiction instantly descend into a violent life and death struggle for her very survival – a struggle which must be won unconditionally without any consideration of cost to the offending party.....

..... why are the smallest encroachments on her 'domain' regarded by her as direct assaults and criticisms of her whole being – and why – when addressing the necessary but tedious chores of garden and household maintenance – must I also cope with an accompanying anxiety attack in anticipation of her bursting on the scene to inform me that I am doing everything wrong.....

..... why is she unable to accept my word, or anybody else's word, for anything at all – but must rather check all things out for herself before she is able to accept and move on.....

..... why does she see all that dwells in the past through inviolate rose coloured spectacles – and why does a person of such honest faith and such selfless devotion to prayer take such delight in Christian books and teachings that point poisonous self-righteous fingers at the 'error' of other Christians.....

..... why is it never possible for my mother to just 'like or not like something' – for it to be simply a matter of taste or preference – why must all things be either wonderful and miraculous or terrible and dreadful – and why must they change from one to the other in an instant.....

..... why did her children live in terror beneath the ever looming pendulum of being 'perfect angels' or 'devil's spawn' – never knowing when the fall from grace would come – never knowing when they would feel the horror of the sudden darkening of her face and the violence that would follow.....

..... why is my mother compelled so fiercely to live her life as if upon a railway track – her fixed steel grey patterns of behaviour, of thought, of attitude, forever rigid and unchanging..... her first perceptions, her first understandings, her first experiences, all unquestionable – irrefutable and absolute.....

Where is the breath of thought and discernment contained when all is habit and obsession – when all is set in stone – the cold hard unrelenting stone upon which we all fall and are broken.....

..... why did I dream every night of my life of smashing everything in our home in a desperate but futile attempt to break through the madness that held me in its merciless grip – crushing the life from my body – the light from my mind – the song from my heart .....

..... and why did I wake up each and every morning to the image of me hitting myself in the face over and over and over again.....

The questions remain….. but the questions – in truth – they are nothing…..

….. nothing but shadows of ghosts and lies…..

Only now am I beginning to understand…..

My mother is no different from any one of us – it is all just a matter of degree…..

But there are questions that are true – even if, in this life, we may never find the answers…..

What was born within us…
… and what has been laid upon us
of what have we been innocent…
… and of what have we been culpable
how many were the times of our choice…
… and how many, the times of our helplessness

But this is not the time for truth and enlightenment – this is a time for nothing but words – be they empty or not – be they small and petty or something other – this is the moment when pain may find its voice – nothing more…..

….. whether these questions are true or false – whether they have substance or not – right now, it is of no consequence – for these are the questions that allow me no peace – no healing – no sense of justice or resolution…..

….. I retch and I retch – but the vomit of my words seems as though it is without end or hope of such…..

I am tired now and can write no more – but still my pen burns between my calloused fingers – granting me no quarter – promising me no release…..

Why is nothing ever straightforward or normal for my mother?

….. oh my mother – my mother…..

….. even though I have barely begun to describe the disturbed contortions of her 'ways'….. I will content myself with just a few final questions…..

..... the most burning questions of all in fact.....

Why is my mother incapable of screwing the lids back on jars and the tops back on bottles when she has finished using them.....

..... why must she just lay them on top without completing the final twist..... and why oh why must I fall for this trap every single time.....

..... why is there always just enough adherence between the casually placed tops and the containers beneath to cause the latter to remain held for just long enough to clear the worktop but not long enough to reach a place of safety and repose in the relevant cupboard or fridge......

..... the result being of course – a dramatic slo-mo fall to the floor – the spilling of copious contents amidst numerous assorted pieces of sticky broken glass..... and the unavoidable and much resented cleaning up process.....

When I occasionally voice these and previous questions to friends or strangers or anyone that is inclined to listen – they will often say......

'Ah yes, but she is very old'

... to which I stoically reply...

'That's true...

... she was so much worse before'.

40

Two Formative Encounters

I just go where the guitar takes me

Angus Young

Due to mother's somewhat unmerited generosity towards her 'little darling's' wages – my time working for my father, although restless, did come to develop certain advantages in terms of spending power.

In what was to become my final year as a diligent but half-hearted engineer, I made two purchases that would come to influence my attitudes towards music and travel for the rest of my life.

In the early months of 1973, an 'up and coming' guitar maker called Jose Romanillos made an identical pair of classical guitars at his workshop in Fontwell Magna in Dorset.

The first guitar went on to enjoy an illustrious career in the hands of the sublime guitarist and musician Julian Bream – the second of the pair – for the sum of £300 – was doomed to a distinctly less illustrious path in the respectful but ineffectual hands of a troubled young man from Surrey.

I was awestruck by this guitar from the first – everything about it was a masterful expression of passion, flair and a profound and exquisite beauty…..

….. from its lightness and the understated elegance of its lines to its pale satinwood purfling and the design of its Rosette – created to imitate the magnificent architecture of the Alhambra Palace – it was just perfect in every way.

Although its promise was always far beyond the reach of my bewildered heart and my weak and stammering fingers – such was the soul of this glorious instrument – that the depths and the colours of its voice inspire me to this day.

The brightness of its tone was pure and light and silvery – but unlike so many others – this was but a gateway to the rich warm worlds of sound within – like the crisp outer coating of a dark chocolate that covers a soft creamy filling beneath.

These contrasting worlds of tone and timbre taught me the need for a sensitive balance between a firmness and a gentleness of touch – between plucking the string and coaxing the string – between making the sound and willing the sound…..

….. and so, I came to understand – that ultimately, the finest teacher that any musician can have, is the time spent sharing and exploring with a fine and trustworthy instrument…..

….. it was my good fortune and privilege to have such a guitar as my teacher and my inspiration – and to this day, I miss its beauty and its presence in my life.

José Luis Romanillos Vega was born in Madrid in 1932 and at thirteen years of age he was apprenticed to a Madrid cabinetmaking firm.

In 1956 he moved to England to work in a hospital in Epsom and a few months later to a hospital in London.

Five years later he made his first Spanish guitar in London.

She only loves him because he's got a Cortina

The Lambrettas

My second substantial purchase of 1973 was possibly not as soul stirring as my first but it was certainly life changing in its way.

In May of that year, and for the sum of £1200, I bought a brand new white Ford Cortina GT 2000 fitted, of course, with the all-important black vinyl roof.

However, buying a new Cortina GT and actually owning a new Cortina GT soon proved to be two very different things.

Due to the demand for these 'exotic' machines, the Ford Dealership in Guildford refused to part with the car (even after I'd paid for it) until they were in possession of another 'GT' to take its place.

As a result, for a period of about two weeks, I could often be found late at night sitting outside the showroom gazing at my shiny new but unattainable motor as it turned slowly and regally on its large raised turntable.

When it was finally released into my eager clutches, I was like a greyhound suddenly let go from it starting box.

During the next year and a half, I travelled 52,000 blissful and trouble-free miles around England, Wales, France and Spain – discovering the unfettered delights of the 'open road' – a reliable and sprightly vehicle and a good sound system.

Pamplona 1973 – my Cortina GT in a rarely seen stationary position

It is hard now to recall faithfully the impact that the Cortina had on my life – or the freedom that it brought to my sick and solitary existence.

Through the five years since the shining days of Flower Power, my health had deteriorated to a level at which my days had become filled with the limitations of weakness and illness, with my daydreams becoming the only means of finding any kind of fulfilment and purpose.

As I stepped within its shiny black vinyl interior I was, in an instant, made whole and dynamic….. I was the Bionic man with his replacement set of powerful man-made limbs….. I was Robocop infused with the life of a cyborg….. I was complete and I was alive – with all the energy and vitality that a fine 2 litre overhead cam engine and a loud four speaker Hi-Fi could offer.

As soon as I reached a destination, I was aching to set off for the next….. I listened to Rodrigo's Guitar Concerto as the sun came up over the plateaus of Pamplona – to Astral Weeks amongst the hills and valleys of Wales – to Hunky Dory beneath the wide open skies of Norfolk – and to Tubular Bells down the long straight tree lined avenues of France.

Petrol was cheap and speed limits were generous or non-existent….. I would gaze out at the world as though I were seeing it all through a TV screen – a world of elusive and ephemeral beauty that I could neither touch nor hold – a world on just the other side of the glass – a world in which I had no place nor standing.

Like my 'Romanillos' – I often think of my Ford Cortina and the simple joys that it brought me…..

….. according to the Gov.uk website – my Cortina saw no more hills or valleys or plateaus after the 1st April 1997…..

….. rest in peace my old friend.

41

Hatchford Park Nurseries – Glimpses Of Light

Villa-Lobos was larger than life, quite extraordinary. He didn't seem to be a composer. He wore loud checked shirts, smoked a cigar, and always kept the radio on, listening to the news or light music or whatever. Villa-Lobos wasn't refined in the intellectual sense, but he had a great heart.

Julian Bream

By the middle of the following year – plans were put into motion to prepare the way for my entrance to Music College. I forsook my father's factory and house for a bedsit in Cobham in which – encouraged by my landlady Christine – I began to teach the guitar as a means of supporting myself while I pursued the necessary studies to further my 'musical career'.

My trusty Cortina was replaced with a tired old Renault 16 with seats like armchairs and a cooling system that needed 'bleeding' every day, lest the heater pumped freezing air onto my feet and the automatic choke remained implacably stuck on 'Rich'.

Nevertheless, I was encouraged by these outward signs of my inner dedication and sacrifice for my 'art'.

Regular trips were made to Christine's more than generous cousin's holiday cottage near Ludlow to allow me to devote myself to uninterrupted hours of study and practice.

The small detached stone building, as it turned out, was without electricity or gas or running water so that, in winter I would begin each day by chopping logs for the friendly old Rayburn and breaking the ice on the well so as to access my day's water supply.

At the start of every visit I would be consumed by panic at the thought of such inconvenience and deprivation – but strangely, after a couple of days, the daily routine became as natural as the pampered luxury laden habits of home.

In summer I would go swimming in the lake at Hanley Child and walk the surrounding lanes in constant anticipation of meeting a warm and beautiful country girl there – but in all my time at the cottage, I never once came across another human being, let alone a beautiful and amiable soul-mate.

And so – I taught and studied and chopped wood and bled the air from my leaky radiator – but in truth these were but the fringes of my life at Hatchford Park Nurseries – the reality of that life was something else entirely.

After the all-consuming fear and negativity of family life, Hatchford came like an antidote – a much needed antidote of light and optimism – of free and creative thinking – of humour and simple honest eccentricity.

Alan and Christine, though very different in age and character, shared a passion for life that acknowledged and accepted no prescribed boundaries and conventions in their quirky but compelling enjoyment of all things.

Neither of them cared overmuch about 'money' – but Alan loved the sport involved in making it – and he loved the reckless generosity that it enabled.

Fortunes would come and fortunes would go, with only the merest hints of inconvenience occasionally surfacing through the laughter and the irrepressible free flowing congeniality.

For the first time in my life I found myself under the wings of people with a finely tuned but kindly perception for what was 'real' and what was 'phoney'.

When it came to music – it was from Alan, a so called 'non-musician,' that I learnt more than from any other person or teacher.

Alan could not be fooled by technique or bravado – he dwelt in the very heart of music and life – nights filled with fine red wine and the piano music of Jimmy Yancey would drift off into the early hours, as Alan would stand in front of his large open fire-place, glass in hand, lost in rapture and eulogy at this phrase or that phrase – endlessly lifting the needle on his long suffering old record player back and forth until he was satisfied that I'd 'got it'.

Oh that I could have shared his insomnia – how much more might I have learnt.

It was here amongst the wild unploughed fields, and the tumbledown old green houses and out buildings that I first came to discover the 'spaces between the notes'…..

….. it was here that I found my beloved standing in the kitchen doorway….. it was here that I first heard the ravishingly incomparable guitar playing of Julian Bream…..

….. and it was here that I first encountered the music and the person of Heitor Villa Lobos.

But now I must either stop, or dedicate the rest of this book and others to the 'Stories of Hatchford' – nothing in between could possibly do justice or even begin to express the debt of gratitude that I owe these two people.

42

Behind The Mask

If we take a snapshot of our thoughts
we reveal the deepest places of our heart
and we look upon a blueprint of our future

I awake to the light of another new day – never really knowing which is worse – the nightmares of my sleep or the nightmares of my waking hours.

My limbs are heavy and reluctant to stir – my breathing is slow and laboured – within my head there is a thick grey fog through which I must grasp for thoughts and words and images and ideas..... I reach out as for the hands of fleeting souls – silently receding into the mist.

This is how I live – this is how I wander through my days.

All is weariness – all is struggle and all is torment.

I long for light and I long for release – but the shutters have long since fallen on my life – the heavy dark doors are closed and bolted upon my solitary confinement.

I watch the world through the bars at my window – friends and loved ones – acquaintances and passing strangers – they come as prison visitors to pass their comforts through the small open crack in my door – the cool touch of their patience resting for a moment on my burning brow.

I long to hold them and to walk with them in the sunlight – but the walls are too thick and the locks too strong.

I must hide in the shadows of my solitude – in the haven of my distorted imaginings – where no one can reach me and no one can touch me.

The world outside has become an alien and hostile place – where even my own body has become my enemy – each day is a battle for survival – where selfishness and deceit and self-pity are my armour and my sword.

I cry out for a name to pin to my affliction – any will do – a name to hold up against my shame – but none is forthcoming – save for the labels of my disgrace.

I am but a malingerer – a lazy dreamer – a loser – a long haired bastard – a waste of my beloved's time.....

..... and so we are known – and so we conform – and so we succumb to the mantras of our affliction.

I live behind a mask in a world of lies and make believe – I live in constant fear of being exposed for what I really am.

I grasp at straws to satisfy my longing to know why – why am I this way – I reach out for an answer – for a reason – but I find only ridicule and contempt.

I must retreat once more into the deep dark worlds within myself.

I am nothing now but the substance and the manner of my daydreams.

I am alone – and will always be

And now you ask me why I write.

I will tell you.

I write for release – and I write to find an answer.

Sometimes I am a fly-fisher – playing words on the surface of my imagination – coaxing what lies beneath up into my hands.

Sometimes I am a sculptor – carving away – slowly and painfully – as if tearing at granite with my fingernails.

I am no writer – I just fiddle around until it looks right – until the clumsy stuttering of the words on the paper matches in some way the clumsy stuttering of the words in my mind.

But every line is another burden that I lay down by the side of the road – walking away a little lighter each time.

It is these 'inner words' – the words of my heart – of my soul – that are spilled out before you now.

They are my friends – they do not judge me and they do not

condemn me – they know me and they accept me for what I am – sometimes we laugh and play together – and sometimes we weep and share our tears.

I am no writer – I just fiddle around until it sounds right.

I go where these pages lead me.....

..... and now they have led me into the pit.....

..... I pray that they may lead me out again.

43

Dartington College Of Arts 1978-1981

Welcome to
Totnes
Twinned with Narnia

From the moment that I entered the narrow winding driveway that leads from the main road up to Dartington Hall – with its fields and woodlands to the left and its slow meandering river to the right – I knew that I had fallen in love with the South Hams of Devon and that, if I was going to become a student of music, there was nowhere else that I wanted to be.

Despite my doubts and my apprehensions, it soon became apparent that my many visits to Ludlow had achieved their aim, for in September 1978, I was accepted on to the three year Music Degree course at Dartington College of Arts.

It is a tribute to the convictions of the fantasy world in which I lived that, of all the concerns that I harboured, my poor health was not one of them.

I would always see myself, when other circumstances beckoned, as being whole and healthy there (wherever 'there' happened to be) believing that somehow, my sickness would remain at home while my healing would eagerly join me on the journey to my new situation.

Whether it was a Greek island or an Irish village or a folk club in Brighton, I never failed in my hope of a miraculous transformation – even though, each and every time, I would arrive to find that I was still 'me', and that all my sickness had travelled faithfully alongside me each and every step of the way.

And so it was with my dreams of becoming a music student.

When I imagined my new life in Devon, I saw only the path of a healthy and dedicated young man before me, taking it as a matter of course that the energy and the atmosphere and the light of my new surroundings would be more than capable of lifting me up from the darkness in which I had lingered for so long.

The inevitable result of this deluded self-deception was that, for the first real time in my life, fantasy met reality head on in what was to become a catastrophic and relentless colliding of worlds.

My daily survival very quickly became reliant on various hastily and intuitively constructed coping strategies.

I became quite good at essays and sounding as if I knew something – I learnt the useful distraction of a well-aimed flippant remark – I took up the Lute – I avoided all dangerously demanding social situations – I buried my head in the music of Stravinsky, Brahms, Villa Lobos and Van Morrison – and I raised my previously naive attempts at bullshit and deceit to a new and rarefied level.

Learning the Lute turned out to be a masterstroke, and a very enjoyable and liberating one at that. Its technique was much more forgiving towards the weakness in my hands than the guitar and, up to the level of modest Elizabethan song accompaniments, my fingers learnt to cope quite well with what was being required of them.

In this very pleasant way, the Lute enabled me to have the performing presence that the more extensive demands of the Classical Guitar did not.

If I had played the Piano or the Violin or the Flute or some other better known instrument, then the lamentable deficiencies in my playing would have been apparent for all to see – but the unknown nature of the Lute, and to some extent the Guitar, enabled me to hide my inadequacies with a good deal of ease and success.....

..... especially as most people were far more pre-occupied with the vocal and visual delights of the lovely young women that I was fortunate enough to accompany.

For many hours each day I would walk and sit and listen in the gardens and the fields of that magnificent estate. It was here that I found my sanctuary and my peace – far away from the constant demands for social interaction so highly regarded by places of knowledge and learning.

I sought my comfort in nature – I let my heart take its solace in the softness of the lute – I walked hand in hand with the great composers and I gave myself carelessly to the occasional romantic interlude and other welcome moments of shared camaraderie.....

..... and so I got by.....

Apart from my father's untimely death – each term passed by as amicably as the rest – until, that is, the spectre of the final solo concert loomed high on the horizon.

The guitar – which had been humming happily away to itself in the wings – was now required to step into the spotlight.....

..... but I wasn't overly concerned – I was still enraptured by the conviction that there was yet a way to break through the chains of my affliction – I just needed to push hard enough and long enough for my cell door to fly open – for the thick dark waters to part and set me free.....

..... in the last reaching of his strength – he bursts out suddenly – into bright morning sunshine – filling each drowning breath with the cool clear air of an early summer's day.....

All through my final year, the hours of my practising increased in direct accord with my ever burgeoning sense of desperation.

In the months leading up to Easter I was spending up to ten

hours every day pushing, always pushing towards that final and blessed moment of breakthrough.

As my hands became weaker each day, as my joints became stiffer and more painful, my resolve became ever more determined and intransigent.

I was continuing through nothing but the blind stubbornness of my will….. finally and inevitably, something had to give.

When the swelling and seizing of the middle joint of my right hand annular finger brought my frantic efforts to a sudden and agonizing halt – the medical help that I sought advised the fitting of a splint for a period of two weeks.

What I didn't know then, and would not know until many years later, was that in playing with a damaged joint, I had developed severe Tendonitis – or Repetitive Strain Injury – which is now understood to need constant but gentle movement all through its healing process.

When the splint was duly removed from my damaged finger – the crippled appendage immediately responded by curling under the palm of my hand like some remote inanimate claw.

Through the confusion and the denial of the following days and weeks, my final performance was put on hold for the immediate future.

As if in a dream, I shuffled my way through the final written examinations before packing my car and returning to Surrey – not knowing or suspecting, that it would be another 38 years before I was able to play again without crippling tension and pain.

And so my, for the most part, happy Dartington days came to their sorry and ignominious conclusion – as did my dreams of becoming a musician…..

….. but still I wander whenever I can in the gardens of Dartington Hall – always with the certainty in my heart that, sometime soon, I will step back into the unfulfilled days of my youth – back into the welcoming arms of friends and lovers – into the warmth and the sunshine and the promise of those scented summer days…..

..... I see it all now as if within a beautiful timeless cryogenic mist – forever waiting upon my return – upon my final concert..... upon my final and glorious healing and release.

Welcome to
Totnes
Twinned with Narnia

44

Broken Hands And Broken Hearts

... to have and to hold, from this day forward...

I am sitting on the floor in the corner of the room – my guitar is lying lazily across my lap as I slowly and laboriously pluck the open top string over and over with the first two fingers of my right hand.

My wife has left for the tasteful tree lined avenues of Virginia Water – there to spend her day as a Delicatessen assistant in amiable banter with such reassuringly personable local characters as Frank Muir, Bryan Forbes and his wife, Nanette Newman.

My day is not quite so exotic.

I am patiently and obediently following my doctor's advice to 'just keep on playing' with the consequent promise of my perseverance being that 'all will be fine'.

But all is a long way from being anywhere near the desired state of 'fineness' – and it is also far from being any kind of 'challenge' or 'opportunity'.

'All' is, in fact, a dark dismal unrelenting debacle – my life like a long drawn-out slow motion train wreck, with all the fear and certainty of disaster, but never ever quite reaching the bitter sweet deliverance in the inevitable finality of it all.

I sit here hour after hour straining with all my strength to uncurl my contorted finger – and once uncurled, to play a single note for as long as possible before my dismal digit re-asserts its stubborn inclination to snap back under the palm of my hand.

> *Music is the wine that fills the cup of silence*
> Robert Fripp

Yeah right….. maybe once more with feeling then…..

Five hours later my wife returns to find me unmoved, unseeing, dark, silent and brooding – still slowly plucking the same one note over and over.

> *… for better, for worse, for richer, for poorer…*

I just cannot accept that something that happened so suddenly cannot un-happen with equal suddenness.

I cannot give up on my dreams and all the years of my striving, no matter how vehement are the pleas of all those around me to let go, to pull myself together and to get a proper job.

Eventually I am left with no choice but to offer my illustrious skills and talents to the vagaries of the job market.

Here in the pitiless emporium of souls, I soon discover just how sought after are the charms and services of a failed out of work 'musician' – but I do get snapped up by a company specializing in driving rich vociferous drunks back from nightclubs and parties.

Every six months or so, I seek the help of one 'medical expert' after another – and every six months, year after year, I am told that there is nothing wrong and that I just need to keep on playing.

They smile and they tell me that it is all in my head, while they watch the clock and take my money, showing nothing but impatience and disdain at my protestations that the pain in my finger has now crept through my hand and up into my arm.

Eventually, after seven years, my inheritance from the sale

of my father's factory runs out and I give up on the idea of ever finding 'outside help' and so decide to go it alone.

... in sickness and in health...

I compare in painstaking detail the movements of every finger to see how one hand differs from the other.

I then pull and bend my fingers while being guided by the degree of pain that I am inflicting – in this way I am able to focus and work on the areas that seem to be the cause of the binding.

Many years later I will learn that when a tendon and the sheath through which it moves become damaged and raw – if they are not kept moving and free from each other, then as they heal, they will knit together as one.

Although I do not understand exactly what it is that I am doing – I learn to find exercises and movements that tear my knitted flesh apart – and in doing so, I finally begin to address the heart of the problem.

As each knot reluctantly surrenders, I experience a corresponding freedom of movement and surge in optimism – soon tempered though, by the realisation that this new found freedom is not the total healing that I seek, but just another small step on the ladder.

Although having to re-learn how to use my hand each time – I have undoubtedly turned a corner – and soon, though far from perfect, I am able to play a little and teach once more.

After a while I come to accept that I am on a journey – a journey that will take me another thirty years to reach its destination.

... to love and to cherish...

The years come and go – 'Black Wednesday' takes its toll on our fragile finances but we manage to hang on in there somehow.

Despite all the heartache and the disappointment – I find that I am content to rest in the knowledge that I love and am loved by my beloved – and in this alone if nothing else – I am, at least at times, to able to see my life as being blessed indeed.

In June 1990 our daughter Hannah is born at the Louise Margaret hospital in Aldershot.

In April 1992 our second daughter Laura is born at Frimley Park.....

... and in July 1994... my wife finally leaves me...

... she leaves with our babies on a fine hot summer's day...

... she leaves to find love and happiness in another man's arms...

... she leaves without a backward glance or a word of goodbye...

... she leaves and walks away – never to return.

... until death us do part...

45

The End Of The Beginning

Sixty Days in August

It's not nice when people don't love each other anymore
                                        My daughter Hannah – age 4

I am standing in the driveway outside my mother-in-law's house – I am shielded from the lights of the lounge by a row of small but dense Fir trees – I do not have to be here – I choose to be here – to torment myself once again – to cause myself hurt beyond that of which I have no control.

I am peering through a small gap in the trees – and like the trees – I am rooted to the ground beneath my feet – I am transfixed – in listless incredulity – as I stare into the warm golden glow of the house – the house where once I had been welcomed and embraced as 'family'.

It is dark outside but the curtains are not yet pulled – as if for my benefit alone – that I may see and hear and finally accept the hopelessness of my cause.

There on the sofa are my wife and my children – they are happy and they are laughing as we all once laughed together – but I am not beside them now – my place has been taken by another man – a man who has become seamlessly accepted as the new husband, father and son-in-law.

It is all so effortlessly simple – I am just a man replaced, nothing more – the house is full of cheerfulness and contentment – I am the only one, it seems, for whom there is a problem.

Even from where I'm standing I can hear their laughter as it echoes around the house – but this time it brings me no joy – no joy whatsoever – this time it cuts like a razor across my heart.

I am unwanted and unwelcome here – and if I were to knock on the door now – then panic and consternation would suddenly fill this happy scene – my children would be quickly ushered out of 'harm's way' and my father-in law would no doubt rise to defend the nest – to defend my loved ones, not against the stranger – but against me and me alone.

It feels like my whole life has been leading to this moment – I am finally and justly unmasked for all to see – the 'wicked selfish ungrateful child' must take his bow of shame at last.

I have often wondered at the stories of those who have suffered mental and physical trauma – Paramedics and Police after the scene of a fatal incident – victims of rape and other abuse. I have never been able to understand how they could come to blame themselves for what has befallen them – why their reason and their logic is unable to step in to their emotional confusion to assert the reality of their blamelessness and innocence.

Now I understand….. when all is distorted and unreal – when there are no points of reference or constancy to hold on to – then there is little to defend ourselves against the wild tormented hallucinations of our feelings and our emotions.

My life now has become nothing but pain and anguish and loss – every minute of every day and every night – like a claw tearing away inside my stomach….. and there is nothing I can do – nowhere in this world that I can go to be free of this misery.

I am aware that it is a madness that consumes me – part of me is watching on like a ghoulish spectator at some despicable blood sport – but most of me is helpless – and most of me is ashamed.

The focus of all my strength has become to simply keep this terrible moment from moving on – from becoming a normal way of life – I cannot conceive of this situation being allowed to be a part of the future – it must be set outside of time – frozen – just a passing aberration, nothing more…..

….. if it were in my power, I would keep the whole universe from turning – but right now, I will settle for August remaining forever August – until my beloved is beside me again and I can hold her and my babies once more.

As a result of all of this – I find that I cannot cope with anything that speaks to me of everyday life – of the passing of time – of life that moves from the present into the past….. I cannot read newspapers or magazines – I cannot watch the television or listen to the radio – I cannot wear a watch or linger before a clock.

I cannot sleep for more than an hour each night – I cannot eat save for the occasional biscuit or piece of bread – I cannot cope with public places and I seek only the company of a single quiet soul who is able to understand my grief – whoever they may be.

I walk away the nights and I sit through the days, with only my new found pastime of chain smoking to accompany me. When I sleep, then I sleep on sofas or in the back of cars – and sometimes in forests beneath vast vaulted cathedrals of leaves.

I stand apart and watch my ridiculous behaviour in helpless horror. All is insanity – except perhaps for my sudden violent aversion to alcohol – instinctively knowing where that particular road would lead, should I choose to embark upon it.

All is strange and all is alien to me – I sit for hours only to discover that barely a minute has passed – time has no meaning anymore – it has become a vindictive and malevolent thing…… it has turned against me to become a merciless and implacable foe.

My thoughts dwell on those who are imprisoned or tortured – I wonder if their minutes are also like hours or worse – but then I start to feel uneasy at daring to compare my trials to theirs.

The crazed whirlpools of my emotions give me no rest – they rise and fall as if upon a wild infernal carousel – in one moment understanding and forgiving – in the next – angry and resentful – full of vile self-righteousness and self-pity.

But in all of this – I slowly come to the realisation that I have never felt so strong and so alive – I feel as if there is a fire of energy within me – my head is clear like never before and my limbs feel willing and vital.

Somewhere amidst the pain, I make a subconscious connection between my new found health and my lack of appetite – it is a clue – and one that will be locked away until the time is right for it to be fully revealed and understood.

I have lost my love – my lover and my dearest friend – the friend that I need now more than ever – I cannot hold her or speak with her – she is gone and there is nowhere that I can go to find her….. for me – she simply doesn't exist in this world anymore.

I am as one bereaved – but there is no grave at which I can kneel and mourn – no headstone at which I can place flowers and remember – I am merely alone – as if the time of our being together – as if our love – has never been.

After 60 days – or so – the curtains fall on this sad and pitiful performance – the lights go down – the small handful of onlookers quietly leave and the doors of the theatre are closed and bolted.

Only one character remains – curled and broken – shaking and incoherent – lying in the corner of the stage.

For now – it is an ending – his life is spread across the

floorboards like a scattered pile of children's building blocks –
he lies exhausted and spent – shattered into pieces – with no
hope, but in the love and the kindness and the wisdom of those
around him – and of his God.....

..... which, as it turns out, is no small hope at all.....

..... for there in the silent darkness..... as he finally lets go to
all the years of struggle and fight..... a long forgotten word stirs
amidst the debris of his soul.....

..... and there in the deepest places of his being – as it rises
up from the source of all things – a river begins to move and
wander through the cracked dried-out valleys of his heart.....

..... a river..... not of water – but of light.....

And if between the waves of his unconscious self – he could
look down now for just a moment.....

..... he would see and know.....

..... that he is – in truth – having the best day of his life.

Now this is not the end
it is not even the beginning of the end
but it is, perhaps,
the end of the beginning.

Winston Churchill

Interlude

I will pause here for a moment to offer a breath of sanity and
hope – a reminder, perhaps, of the possibility that when love is
broken, Love may prevail without the need to succumb to the
irredeemable ugliness of wounded pride and senseless division.

May this short interlude of poetry give you the chance to rest
awhile beside the still waters, that you may consider the nature
of Truth and Beauty, of Forgiveness and Humility, and of the
Love that embraces all these things.

And now – words far too humble and gentle to have ever

fallen from my pen – as I read them once more, I feel partly ashamed and partly chastened before their simple majesty – but mostly I feel inspired and reassured that they have come to be written at all this side of heaven.

I include them now in the hope that, if I linger upon them for long enough, they may grow in me and cast out all that is painful and lamentable from the past – would that 25 years ago they could have been mine.

Who am I, who am I
to want you now you're leaving

who am I, who am I, who am I
to judge you now you're leaving

who am I, who am I, who am I.

Hannah Reid

Part Four

The Other Side Of Midnight

Two Songs of Courtship

1

If along the highroad
I caught hold of your sleeve
do not hate me
old ways take time to overcome

If along the highroad
I caught hold of your hand
do not be angry with me
friendship takes time to overcome

A Chinese Poem
7th Century BC

2

Beneath the laden air of perpetuity
corpulent retorts accuse and bewilder
falling like broken glass
on the remains of pressing farewells

masks lay discarded upon empty mantels
while trembling ghosts of courage
jostle to desert the empty room

beneath stars long since gouged
from their heavenly sockets
walls remember and silently weep

all that lingers now
all that prevails

just echoes of faith
and brave mounted words

stallions that fell

at the very first turn

An English Poem
21st Century AD

46

I Choose Life

Sic transit gloria mundi

All is darkness – all is confusion – I chase thoughts and images through the endless black labyrinths of my consciousness.....

..... I am sure of one thing only – that I am finally and completely lost.....

..... it is true, I know, that some may live as 'a feather on the breath of God' – but I am not as these – I am but a leaf upon the raging of the storm – I am without anchor or tether – blown this way and that..... helpless before the mercy of the wind.....

.....the sword that has hung over me for all of my life has finally fallen – it has fallen and it has severed my soul from its cradle.....

..... I am nothing now – and have always been – I do not belong in this world except as an object of contempt and disdain..... this is my purpose – I was born to hide and to cower in solitary shame – nothing more – to lay face down in the mud – with the cold cruel foot of my ancestors forever upon my neck.....

..... I look within myself and see only emptiness – it fills the spaces – I cannot see or hear or feel anything except for the pain in my heart – my feelings are remote and unreal – they perform before me like a procession of loathsome gargoyles – up and down and round and round – one moment speaking of hope – of faithfulness and love….. and the next, of despair – of vengeance and hatred…..

….. I have lived in the shadows – I have walked the streets alone at night – I have watched through windows at the lives within – but now I seek only solitude and sleep…..

….. I must tread softly now lest I awaken the dead – the dead that is my heart….. let me be – leave me to my fate – I will serve my sentence – just let me be…..

….. life has no place in me – I can't do it anymore…..

….. I am terrified to name the hunger that gnaws at my stomach – to name it and to lift my eyes to its entreaties – for what happens if I look into its face only to deny it sustenance – how do I go on if I say that I am crying out for my beloved – if I give voice to the words – if I give form to the shapeless agony inside of me…..

….. and worse – if I give credence to the charges that chase around inside my head – the charges that speak of a bleak and joyless marriage – if I accept them now – then I must also accept that my love is never coming back to me…..

….. each day is but a gaping wound – I am so tired of hurting – let me be – how do I live without being destroyed by the pain of it all – I hide from myself – I crave the peace of denial – the peace that is no peace at all – I long to return to my make believe world – but I am caught in these cruel threads of truth – I am unable to move – I am hanging here as if by a nail through my heart…..

….. but through the wordless mist of my falling comes a last reaching out to the skies far above…..

….. the only sounds that now remain from the tormented

cacophony of a lifetime.....

..... the silent unbidden cry of my soul.....

Lord help me

... just three words that will become my first faltering steps on my journey home...

... here in my silent tomb – I make a choice...

... I choose life...

... I choose to be a father and a brother – a son and a friend...

... I have looked into the warm dark seductive painlessness of the abyss – and I choose to remain here in the light...

... I choose to feel and to hurt... I choose to love and to grieve...

... I will know only God – and I will trust only God...

... I will take a chance on a God who is real – a God who listens and cares – I will take a chance that He is beside me now...

... for with all my being I am convicted – that there is no other way back from this place to which I have fallen...

... I will be angry at a 'cold heartless deity' no longer – I will trust and I will let go into the mystery of His love – and I will seek the peace that is beyond my understanding – the peace that has no part of this false and restless world...

... it is so close to me now – I can feel it – I can almost touch it – like a cool breeze through the cracks around my prison door – like the sound of children singing – like the touch of their love and their laughter ...

... through my darkest night – I will trust in the coming of the dawn – I will rest in its light and trust that I am being held there – even if it is beyond the reaches of my seeing...

... I will stand upon the bones of this mortal night and I will let the promise of this moment steal my heart...

... I will listen for the song that rises between the silence and the prayer – and I will curl once more in a warm sunlit autumn field – His spirit guiding me – unravelling me – cleaning away the rubble and the dross – and I will be laid open – my twisted broken soul – open at last to the power of surrender...

... I am lost in the darkness – but I am as equally lost in this moment of wonder and light...

... like Eurydice at the hand of Orpheus – I am being led from the darkness below– never to look back...

... this time...

... and are the stones that once made castle walls
and dungeons deep within

are they now engaged in raising
brick by brick
a temple.

Sic manet gloria spiritus

Memo

As time passes, it becomes clearer each day, that the hurt of heartache is like lying in the surf between the sand and the sea...

... sometimes the water plays around your feet – and sometimes around your body...

... and sometimes it rushes up and washes over you – and it seems in that moment as if there is nothing left but darkness and pain...

At such times – when the foam and the froth block out the sun and deny your very breath – the panic rises up from within you – and it is hard to remain quiet there and to not give in to the fear of drowning...

... and as the tides of pain ebb and flow...

... slowly... one day at a time...

... you get to know and understand their coming and their going...

... you become familiar with their ways – and you learn to be still and to wait for the moment to pass – knowing that soon, peace will return...

It is in this way – if no other – that we lift up our heads and move on...

... and it is in this way – if no other – that time begins to heal our broken hearts.

47

Learning To Let Go

Blessed are the poor in spirit,
for theirs is the kingdom of heaven

Matthew 5:3

So it was that I came to discover the truth behind words such as these – words that had fallen so easily and so carelessly from my lips and from my pen through all the years of my so called searching.....

..... words that fell as bright shooting stars across the night time skies of my slumbering spirit – fleeting insights that left only vague half-formed memories of something real and true.....

...... words that I appropriated and repeated like stolen mantras – sometimes for comfort, sometimes to impress, sometimes out of habit, and sometimes, very occasionally, in the unspoken hope and faith of them one day bearing the fruit that they promised.

But where was it that such fine and noble words – such vessels of strength and hope – where was it that they became so trapped and enfeebled.....

..... caught in the ever vigilant web of my Reason perhaps, as if by the 'umbrella' of a missile shield – bound as innocents before the sacrificial altar of my 'Self'.....

..... or maybe as homeless orphans – betrayed and neglected by my pride – passing quietly and unassumingly through my life and leaving only the faint echo of their beauty to ever reach through to the hunger in my ever restless heart.

I had always believed in God – it was believing in a God that loved me – a God that cared for me – a God that was present in my life – in the course of my life….. a God that gave a damn…..

….. that was the problem.

I didn't understand then just how much our idea of God, of his love, is coloured by our experiences of earthly love – in particular, the love that we receive or do not receive during the days of our childhood.

My mother's love was always erratic and unpredictable – one moment suffocating and smothering – the next, violent and full of condemnation and rebuke. My brothers and I learnt from an early age that Love was a very conditional thing, dependant on doing exactly as you were told and never doing wrong or criticising her in any way or being anything less than her perfect little darlings…..

….. not an easy remit to fulfil…..

….. but even then, there was no guarantee that a sudden and perilous 'fall from grace' was not waiting to descend for no apparent reason as a thunderbolt from a clear blue sky.

This is how I perceived the love of God – that I could never hope to be good enough to consider it as being a meaningful factor in my life – that it was a remote and capricious and fickle thing that could be granted or withdrawn on a whim – certainly nothing that could be trusted or relied upon or revered in any way.

As so many before me – I came to discover the hard way the path to that Love which is at the heart of all things…..

….. for it was only when the 'chips were down' – when my strength was spent – when all hope had run dry….. it was only in that hallowed place that the blessing of broken-ness, of emptiness, of 'poverty of spirit' stood quietly before me as 'the last man standing'…..

….. it was here that I finally let go to all the preconceptions and judgments and accusations towards God that I had carried in my heart for so long…..

….. sadly – it was only with a heart that was broken, that I truly reached out for my Creator – for his voice – his face – his song – the touch of his hand upon my hand…..

….. and it was only in my letting go to who I thought I was – in my ceasing to fight to protect the image in the mirror that the world held before me – the image that I had been persuaded from birth was that of my Self…..

….. it was only in denying the rule of this image that there was, at last, a chance for change that was true and not mere illusion – a chance for my heart to be freed from the petty tyranny of my Ego – a chance to rest in the truth that is Spirit and to allow God to embrace His child once more.

Whoever shall seek to save his life shall lose it,
and whosoever shall lose his life shall preserve it.
                                                                    Luke 17:33

48

The Ways Of Spirit

Everything can be taken from a man but one thing:
the last of the human freedoms –
to choose one's attitude in any given set of circumstances,
to choose one's own way.
                                                                    Viktor E. Frankl

So what can I say about the days and the months and the years that reached out from the wreckage of that broken hour. What can I write that is not mine and mine alone to visit and survey.

From the outside nothing had really changed – my emotions were still raw and unmanageable and as my appetite for food returned, then so did my illness – with the weakness in my limbs and the fog in my head and the aching in my bones once again resuming their dictatorship over every aspect of my daily life.

Family and friends did their best to keep their compassion and their emotional support abreast of the erratic unpredictability of my pain – but before long, and with the very best of intentions, they too became visibly weary and impatient with my persistent inability and reluctance to return to the 'real world'.

Indeed, from the outside nothing seemed to have really changed at all. I was still the 'wicked selfish ungrateful child', stumbling like a drunkard through the days of my restive spirit – seeing but not seeing – hearing but not hearing – yearning, but never ever enough.

Even from within, I was conscious of very little change, apart from a very tenuous feeling of having been 'spotted' by God and the growing awareness of the presence of a stranger within my heart.

This stranger had arrived completely un-noticed without any kind of fanfare or fuss – they were a stranger whose face was hitherto unknown to me – a stranger who was kind and patient and surprisingly loyal – a stranger who I would eventually come to know as Hope.

It would be pointless now to speak in any detail of the torrent of 'coincidences' that began to guide my life. It would be nothing more than the vain attempts of one who tries to describe the vivid colours of their dream to another.

No matter how much passion and enthusiasm and insistence they may command, no matter how much the listener may actually want to feel the drama and the excitement and the significance of the dream – inevitably, the dreamer will see the eyes before him slowly glazing over and the smile becoming ever more fixed and vacant.

Such coincidences, to anyone other than the recipient of their leading, are just that, coincidences – regardless of how miraculous they may be or how significant they are in the journey of the beholder – like dreams, 'God's coincidences' are personal and subjective and must always be quietly accepted and cherished as such..... and to each be his own.

Regardless of how or why – all through those tortured days of my reluctant 'awakening', hidden from view and with no apparent signs to its presence, another story was quietly and gently unfolding.

My life was, in truth, like the progress of a massive Oil Tanker or Container Ship upon the face of the seas – the course may be set and the rudder moved accordingly, but it is only over the passage of many many miles that the vessel begins to show any signs of obeying the commands of the Bridge.

In the moment of my 'crying out', my course too had been set and my rudder moved accordingly. My compass was now a full 180 degrees from all that had gone before. I was no longer falling ever deeper into the darkness – I was being lifted – slowly and imperceptibly – but lifted nevertheless, up into the light that came shining out from the heavens high above me.

Under the watchful but tender guidance of my new found companion, hope began to lead me into places within my soul that, only a short time before, I would never have dared to visit or even contemplate.

Hope shone like a bright Full Moon within the dark clouded skies of my anguish and my confusion – sometimes hidden from view and sometimes shining like daylight all around me – but always and ever present.

It soon became apparent, that it was no longer possible for me to stand as a helpless onlooker beside the blind vapid fatalistic march of my life.

I was required and ennobled to actually do something.

This new road, it seemed, came with lessons and instructions and exhortations on how to proceed, and although my inclinations and my trust were no more than visceral and childlike, it was soon obvious that they were all that were needed for the miracle of healing to take seed within me.

Although continuing at the time as a 'good citizen' in my obedience to the dictates of the intellect to define and to rationalise and to 'know' – it is only here as an old man, that I feel able to offer any kind of insight into the deeper currents of those troubled but enchanted days.

I see now that the ways of spirit can never be 'revealed' or 'passed on' or 'understood' through conduits of human experience – we may come to the gate, but clothed in the wisdom of the flesh, we may never pass through.

It is only Spirit that can reveal Spirit – and it is only God that can lead to God – everything else is but wishful thinking at best – wilful self-deceit at worst.

As for any child that has ever lived, our first faltering steps on the path to adulthood are concerned with the protocols and the joys of communication.....

..... and so it is with the nurturing of our emerging spirits.

God is Spirit, and just as Human Reason is the fundamental currency of our communication in this Physical world – Faith is the fundamental currency of our communication, of our relationship, with God.

However, and this is where it becomes somewhat strange and confusing, there is absolutely nothing we can do to become 'strong in our faith'.

This simple truth is diametrically at odds with the imperative of all Human Endeavour.

We seek to develop our minds and our intellects so we commit ourselves to study and learning and the acquisition of knowledge and understanding.

We seek to develop our bodies and so we commit our days to exercise and training and physical pursuits.

We seek to play a musical instrument and to express Music, so we practise and we play and we devote our hearts to its beauty.

In all things we address our attentions and our energies to the matter in hand.

But the ways of God, of Spirit, they are not as the ways of the Flesh.

God alone is 'the author and perfecter of our faith' – Faith is not our concern – our place in this mystery is somewhere else entirely – it is in the application and the persevering of our

Will and of our freedom to choose..... this is the dynamic of our spiritual walk.

Faith grows and becomes stronger in the moments we choose trust over fear and doubt – patience over intolerance – and forgiveness over anger and resentment..... or does it!

This is what we are called to do to be sure – to 'step out' in faith – ever moving from what is familiar to what is unknown – but there is yet a further twist in the patience and the humour and the benevolence and the nurturing of it all.

As we undertake, be it with all our strength and longing, to effect our Will and our Choice – we fail.

Sometimes we fail miserably and utterly and sometimes not so much – but always we fail. For it is not through our own strength that we are lifted up – it is in the honouring of our heartfelt intent that all is brought to its perfection through God's Grace alone.

We do what we can do – that is all – in the end it is by Grace that we are filled and that all we have cried out for is, in a moment, bestowed richly upon us.

49

Forgiveness

Resentment is like drinking poison
and waiting for the other person to die

Carrie Fisher

The act of forgiving – of learning to forgive – was the first tangible evidence that something had changed in my life – that something had truly shifted.

During the months following my wife's leaving, I was like a wild and wounded animal, either lashing out in vile self-righteous anger and recrimination or curled in tears of clawing self-pity, pathetically licking at my wounds.....

..... she had lanced the abscess – she was the only one who could – and through those dreadful days, all the suppressed rage and frustration of my whole life spilled out upon her gentle soul.

But very slowly, during my more lucid and generous moments, I became aware of the un-negotiable need to find forgiveness in my heart towards the one that I made such a show of loving and of longing to hold once more.

I had never thought of myself as in any way being a 'good person' – the natural tendencies of others to show care and kindness always seemed to require from me a lamentable degree of focus and effort – but nevertheless, the spectre of Forgiveness seemed to be forever before me, taunting me and provoking me and giving me no rest.....

..... but as I reached out to take hold of its hand, I quickly discovered that there was a vast chasm between the word that we all voice with such abandon and the actual reality of the act of forgiving.

We are all so familiar with the word – but what is forgiveness.

As I set out along its path it became clear from the many 'dead ends' that I encountered along the way, that it was far easier and, in the end, more productive, to focus my energy upon what it is not, rather than what it is or may be.

My first lesson was to discover that Forgiveness is not Pardon.

In order to pardon someone, we must first sit in judgement of them and we must then pass a sentence upon them if that sentence is to be commuted. To raise ourselves up to this exalted estate is simply to deny God's sovereignty – no healing or peace can ever come from attempting to perpetuate such a lie.

Likewise, it can also feel generous and kind to seek to find empathy and compassion for another's 'Story', that they might be found to be 'worthy' of our forgiveness.

Such 'methods' can seem attractive, even seductive at first – they promise to smooth the way – they promise quick results and they make us feel good about ourselves by flattering our sense of charity and of our being able to assert a degree of pro-active control over the situation.

In the end, such schemes lead nowhere but to the desolation of yet another dark and empty dead end street – it is only as we grow tired of all our fine 'Red Herrings' do we ask the question that is true.

Where is it that I go from here.

This is a good question – it led me to discover that Forgiveness is not an entity complete within itself at all – it is not something to be sought or grasped at or held in your hand.

Forgiveness is just one of the myriad colours that make up the wondrous prism of light that is Love – the Love that is God – the totality and the summation of all things seen and unseen

If we are to love, then we need to know that Love – the Love that we seek – the Love that we long for – it is not a `state of heart' – it is not a condition or a static force – it is not even something that we feel – although from time to time we may feel its touch within us.

Love is a dynamic – it has a rhythm – a direction – Love has a current – and like a river – Love needs to flow that it may be Love.

We are not capable of instigating Love – Love cannot be created within us – we cannot be vessels of Love….. we cannot contain Love – for we are not vessels but channels.

Love always gives – it does not take…..

….. we can receive undeserved kindness and affection – but if we receive Love – it is Love that we have given coming back to us.

As we truly become 'meek and poor in spirit' then we allow Love to flow through us – like a river washing away the stagnant pools – washing us in its healing stream.

Only then will our hearts resonate with the rhythm of love – the breathing in and the breathing out of love……

….. as we choose to let go to all that Love is not….. resentment – intolerance – anger – bitterness – jealousy – fear – the lust for revenge etc….. then we let go to all that would stand as a dam to its flowing.....

..... as we seek to bless, we will be blessed – as we seek to bring healing, we will be healed – as we seek to love, we will be loved – and as we seek to forgive, we will be forgiven.

This is the dance of Spirit and Flesh – the rocking of creation in the cradle of God's hand.... and as we let go into the rhythm of this dance – we will see the world around us begin to respond to the call of its beat.

Mercy and truth are met together;
righteousness and peace have kissed each other.
Truth shall spring out of the earth;
and righteousness shall look down from heaven.

I have known the pain and the futility of separation and alienation – from family and friends – from the beauty of Nature – from Music – from my beloved – even from myself.

We all know the truth in the statement that nothing worthwhile can ever come without a price being paid and a sacrifice being made – every Father and Mother and Brother and Sister and Loved One and Friend..... every Doctor and Student and Pastor and Businessman and Politician and Athlete and Artist and Musician..... even the Criminal will make sacrifices in order to realise the vision before them.

We all understand and instinctively accept this to be true, regardless of the extent to which we may succeed or fail in the honouring of this truth.

Sacrifices are made for many reasons, but the greatest surely is to remain true to those whom we love and care for even when they have hurt us or fallen away from us or have taken decisions and followed lifestyles that have caused us heartache and distress.

To remain true and to resist all temptations to protect ourselves and to make it easier on ourselves by pushing them away and setting them apart – this is to truly love.

Is it so hard then, to believe that Love itself has paid the price and made the sacrifice to free us from our place of separation from itself – that we all may find our way back to the home from which we have been estranged for so long.

A bringing together of all things in a way that no human mind could ever imagine or make manifest – a way that even stands as an affront to our own sense of logic and reason.....

..... the supreme and sublime act of forgiveness – the greatest gift of all from the Father to his wayward children.....

..... the redeeming of all things at the crossing of two blood-soaked pieces of wood.....

> *It is at the intersection of Creation and its Creator...*
> *... the point of intersection of the branches of the Cross*
> *Simone Weill*

..... nothing makes sense to me – nothing – without that I am able to come freely to this place..... as a prodigal to the feast – as a child to his father's embrace – cherished, restored and forgiven.

> *Love is a dynamic, it has a rhythm and a direction,*
> *Love has a current, and like a river, Love needs to flow.*

The tragedy of my marriage was not that it ended – but that I learnt too late that a person does not feel loved or know that they are loved, by being told that they are – but only by being shown that they are – every day – in every possible way.

Anger and blame are easy – they make you feel good – they made me feel good – they saved me from having to find the courage to face my own culpability in the failure of my marriage.

Only now – as cowardice and denial have finally begun to give way to the first delicate shoots of strength and honesty – only now can I face and accept the truth that I had nothing to forgive my beloved for at all – in leaving me she was just running for her life.....

..... and who could possibly blame her for that.

Ironically, through all the years of sickness and defeat – as I grew ever weaker, my will and my resolve grew stronger.

Mostly I lived by willpower alone – there was no strength in my body to carry me through – no lucidity in my mind – no faith in my heart – just a stubborn crawling on my hands and knees from one day to the next.

We are obsessed by what we judge to be good or bad experiences – we strive for what is 'good' and we shrink from what is 'bad', in whatever aspect of our lives we are considering in that moment.

This is the way of the world, to keep a scoreboard of the good things and the bad things, be they situations or circumstances or relationships or incidents of chance..... we covet the former and we do our best to avoid the latter, and our consequent state of happiness, or indeed misery, is determined by adding up the scores at the end of the day.

But I have learnt that true happiness is hardly ever found in the black and the white of life – in the easy things of life – in the things that we think that we want or need.....

..... Life is not so simple, but it is infinitely more beautiful than that which we aspire to or settle for.....

..... if we allow it to be so.

... all things work together for the good of those who love God

Indeed, maybe we should never look at our weaknesses and our failures and our adversities in isolation, but rather, we should acknowledge them and be grateful for them in the light of those areas of our lives that have been able to flourish and grow, not despite them, but because of them.

> *The deeper that sorrow carves into your being*
> *the more joy you can contain.*
>
> *Kahlil Gibran*

I chose with all my heart to forgive, not just my wife, but all those who had cast me out so abruptly in favour of another, and even though I failed miserably every single day, still I persevered, blindly and in constant shame for my failure and my pitiful generosity of spirit.

In this sorry way, after what seemed to be an interminable period of almost three years – on a bright Saturday morning during the Easter of 1997, I came, not to 'feel' forgiveness, but to be 'washed' in Forgiveness, like a wave of peace and contentment, consuming me in an instant – never to recede or withdraw its hand from me from that moment to this.

Later that day, something else happened that was to open my eyes to the possibilities that we are all connected, not just in obvious ways, but on deeper levels, far beyond the limits and the countenance of this physical plane.

All during the three years following the splitting up of myself and my wife, my eldest daughter Hannah expressed her obvious sadness and disapproval of the situation through her refusing to contact one of us while she was staying with the other.

Whether it was her way of protesting at the establishment of our two separate homes or whether it was her inability to accept or cope with the break-up of her family, there was nothing we could do to get her to simply pick up the phone and say hello.

Not until that day in 1997 that is, when soon after the events of the morning had passed, I picked up the phone to find that it was Hannah ringing up for a chat.

From that day on, she would regularly ring to speak with each of us with never a hint of reserve or reluctance in her voice.

Was this just coincidence…..

….. or could the ways in which we are united with our children embrace greater spheres of existence…..

….. could we all be united in ways that, at the same time, are too wonderful and too terrifying in their implications for us to consider or even attempt to comprehend within the walls of our mortal consciousness.

50

Childhood

¨ unless you change and become like little children,
you will never enter the kingdom of heaven

Matthew 18:2

Our wilful ignorance concerning the seasons of our childhood and our condescension towards its pre-corrupted innocence, is the very die that is cast that condemns humanity to its perpetual dysfunction – with all the sufferings that that dysfunction embraces.

Our first simple mistake along this path, is to assume that our children are our very own possessions – whether that 'ownership' be at the hands of biological parents, adoptive parents, 'community' or, as we are now experiencing more and more, by a 'State', with its own fickle, but very personal, agendas.

Our second mistake is to treat our children as if they were 'empty vessels', to be filled with whatever it is that current fashion dictates.

Childhood thus becomes an exploited commodity, often for no better reason than to allow us to feel better about ourselves and our own self-justified behaviours and endeavours – whether they be honourable and sincere or manipulative and abusive.

The truth is that the world is terrified of its children – of the accusations that are inherently manifest in Childhood – of the ever present danger of our whole sorry 'charade' being unmasked before the penetrating gaze of a child's clear unclouded eyes.

What we so proudly refer to as 'civilisation' is not and has never been the glorious onward march towards Utopia that we might wish it to be – it is a slow but inexorable slide into misery and oblivion with the defining features of the human race here at the summit of its 'achievements', being greed, selfishness, fear, stupidity, the adulation of Ego and the celebration of its broken-ness.

We try so hard and for so long and for what – the perpetuating of a lie, nothing more.

Creation is at odds with its Creator allowing only glimpses of His love to shine through the cracks in our castle walls – the walls we have so diligently constructed to keep Him out and to assert and maintain our independence and our separation from Him.

We spend our energy and our creativity devising ever more desperate ways of cutting ourselves off from the source of all life and to the imbuing of the resultant chaos with purpose and meaning, with worthiness and nobility…..

….. and as we gaze out in stupefaction at the horror that we have created – we hold our head high in triumph, proudly announcing that we could never believe in a God that would allow and condone such suffering.

As the charade of our independence and autonomy becomes ever more oppressive, controlling and paranoid, then it is beholden upon our so called education system to 'honour and obey' its master with increasingly hysterical attempts to fend off any perceived intrusions of Reality and Truth

The Reality and Truth that is God – omnipotent, omniscient and omnipresent.

Children know God and they know Life – and so they cannot be allowed to pass intact with all the secrets that they hold within them – for they enter this world still straddling the divide between Spirit and Flesh – the divide that is no divide at all except in the minds of broken adult human beings.

As they lay rocking in our arms they are also rocking in the cradle of Spirit – while we are busy confusing maturity with the hardening of our hearts – and contentment for the denial of who we really are.

Of course we deceive and comfort ourselves in being able to pass on the accumulation of our inherited wisdom – but mostly we are just complicit in sucking the spirit from our children's hearts so that they can become just like us.

And as they find their wings and their brief moment of clarity towards the deception that is the so-called adult world….. this world, that they have hitherto trusted and believed in, rushes to label them 'rebellious teenagers' – 'potential threats' – 'anti-social elements' – just so it can feel righteous and justified as its children are pressured and manipulated and cajoled into taking their place in line with the rest.

We who are broken and exiled take pride and satisfaction in thinking that we have something to teach our children…..

….. but if it is true, as I certainly believe it is, that when on that day the weight was lifted from my heart, my daughter's heart was also set free – then it follows that there are questions that cannot be denied.

What is it exactly that we believe we are able to teach our children – what do we hold in our hearts that we think is worth passing on to them – and what do we consider is our responsibility towards living and being a good witness to the truth of the words that we may speak (a question for our Politicians in particular).

What deluded sense of 'right' do we labour under – for how can we teach them of Love, of what is beyond our understanding save by God's grace alone.

Surely, our duty to our children is not the filling of empty vessels but the revealing and releasing and nurturing of what is already abundantly present.

I spy with my little eye something beginning with T…

… Clouds !!!

Laura – age 3

It was my daughters who gave me my first experience of

unconditional love..... they were my babies – my saviours – my teachers and my friends..... they were all of these things and so much more – as they are and will always be.

It was through them that I came face to face with the natural unreserved and unfettered energy passion and spirit of childhood.

It was through them I learned that the only honest and proper response to this open-ness and innocence was the complete and total giving of oneself – of one's very best.....

It was through them I learned that there is nowhere to hide in caring for your children – no place for compromised or diluted love.....

..... and it was through them that I learned to be un-selfish for the first time in my life..... for as our children give without fear or inhibition – so we are called to give in return.

My daughters taught me that laughter and joy could be found at unexpected times and in unexpected places:

... in helping them to make a stir fry when I thought that I just wanted to get a take-away and relax.

... in running into a freezing sea screaming when I thought that I just wanted to stay huddled and warm on the sand.

... in telling them funny stories at bedtime when I thought that I just wanted to close my eyes and go to sleep.

... in watching films over and over again until we all knew every line in every scene.

... in the discovery that all journeys could be filled with games and singing and that even traffic jams could be bottomless reservoirs of mischief and fun.

... in savouring the excitement of waking up to the adventures of each new day and in discovering that my life had found its colours not in following my own desires but in following theirs.

... in discovering an empathy with all parents, especially those who would suffer for love of their children.

They taught me things that I still need to bring to mind each and every day – although, I was able to have some influence on the choice of music that we all sung along to through all the many journeys that we shared inside a car.

Spice Girls, Bewitched, Bob Marley and Van Morrison.
Hannah – age 5
(when asked who her favourite pop bands were)

Until we accept and surrender to the gift of children we are forever lost in a wilderness of our own making – God has given us children so that we might recover that which we have lost within ourselves – that all may be children under heaven.....

..... that the path may be unbroken – that we all may be whole and equal – that every heart may lift up the next – and that in doing so it too may be lifted up

Parents are those that love and care for their children – and they are those that inspire love in return.

Our children are not our own – they are entrusted into our care and on whatever path they come to us it is not for us to judge or question – it is God's choice alone.

Let not the blessing ever be questioned or diminished.

We are asked, not only to learn from our children, but to care for and cherish every child as if they were our own – to treat childhood as a rare and precious thing – the gateway to our journey home.

So what is our true connection to our children, to our own souls and to the souls of all of God's children?

Who would be still now, here in the heart of the storm, yes and who would be hushed now, that the question may be heard.

Progress is man's ability to complicate simplicity
Thor Heyerdahl

Memo for a dead Prince

Forgive me for despising you, for being ashamed of you,
for rejecting you and casting you aside.

Thank you for your hopes and your dreams,
for your perseverance and your courage.

Thank you for carrying me here,
for lifting me up upon your shoulders.

Thank you for enduring all the pain and the confusion
and the shame of the darkness…

… that I may now know the peace and the joy
and the glory of the light.

51

Healing

What's it like there outside with the living…

Natalie Merchant

During the first few weeks of April 2012, not long after my move from Totnes to Cranleigh, I found myself driving across the majestic undulating hills of Oxfordshire on my way to a Private Doctor who lived and practised in a small village to the south of Oxford itself.

I drove as someone walking in their sleep, with no expectations in my mind and no hopes in my heart of any kind of happy outcome resulting from my visit.

I was simply following a dutiful desire to please a friend who had received help there for a long standing medical condition and was now very eager that I should benefit in a similar way. I just didn't know how to avoid the trip without upsetting her and deflating her kindly enthusiasm.

As opposed to the apathy and ridicule that I received from the medical establishment when seeking advice for my hand –

my visits to the 'alternative' sector, in regards to my poor health, were always met with instant diagnoses, heart-warming smiles and confident encouragements for a hasty return to abundant life.....

..... smiles and bravado and confidence that soon dissipated into thinly disguised expressions of boredom and frustration as my health stubbornly refused to respond in the appropriately positive and grateful manner.

Over the years I had become, as a necessity, hardened to such occasions and so, after the many tests and procedures involving blood and saliva and prolonged questioning, I was not really listening or was even particularly interested, when the elderly Oxfordshire Doctor pronounced, with the usual confidence and professional joy, the name Rampant Candida.....

..... especially as it sounded more like the title of a 1970's Swedish Blue Movie than the name of a respectable bodily ailment.

Nevertheless, upon my return home I did exactly what I had been advised to do – I changed my diet and took my pills and very soon two things happened.

The first thing was that my health got much much worse.....

..... and the second, was that my health got much much better.

Although it would take another five years before I was able to say with any confidence that I was completely fixed, the immediate improvement was undeniable and as welcome as rainfall on a parched and barren land.

However, what was not so welcome was the violent and unexpected emotional response that this sudden healing provoked within me.

Although I had always known that something was profoundly wrong, I survived from day to day by always finding a reason for my weakness and my fatigue.

Either I'd practised for too long or too little – exercised too hard or not enough – had too much to drink the night before or not had enough sleep – eaten too much or too little etc. etc.....

..... in the absence of any suitable diagnosis, there always had to be a plausible explanation.

But suddenly, I was playing the guitar and my fingers were getting stronger and more agile each day – I swam and my swimming became more powerful and assured – I ate healthy foods and my vitality responded accordingly – I would wake each day rejuvenated from the day before.

In every way, my body and my mind reacted in positive ways to exercise and work – they became stronger instead of weaker, resilient instead of vulnerable, willing instead of reticent and confident instead of fearful.

To get stronger instead of weaker – to feel energy instead of fatigue – to live in confidence and hope instead of anxiety and despair…..

….. what an amazing concept – what a brilliant idea – why hadn't anyone thought of it before.

In an instant I could see the whole sordid story of my wasted life with a new, brutal and devastating clarity.

As I experienced my profoundly traumatic re-connection with the human race, I was faced with the merciless reality of what it actually felt like to be a normal healthy human being.

I had woken from a nightmare and my awakening was more than I could bear.

I just wanted to give up – on music – on writing – on life itself.

If I had been a horse they would have shot me – my life had been nothing but a bad joke – it was all too late – there was nothing left now but to throw it all away with the trash – something that should have happened right at the start…..

….. but gradually, the storm in my soul relented, the moment passed, and as I got stronger, I discovered that I spent less time concerning myself with my own needs and was able to spend more time thinking of the needs of others, in particular, of the needs of my mother.

For the first time I was looking out instead of in – holding my arms out to embrace, instead of clutching them to my body – ever defensive and obedient to the all-consuming demands of my illness.

..... oh the Grace to be free to open up and give of oneself at last.

And now I look around me with an objectivity so long denied me, and I begin to see all the paltry limitations and boundaries that are set upon this giving.....

..... all the obsessive measuring and withholding of our worldly love – the judging of sickness to be 'worthy' or 'unworthy' – and the frugal and cautious allocation of sympathy when a suitable excuse for rejection cannot be found.

... from this broken down place where I hide from the living...

The world of the healthy takes so much for granted – the way that wounds heal and bones that are broken become whole again – the way that our immune systems rise to fight against illness and disease and the way that muscles and tendons get stronger as our joints remain supple and free.

In sleep we continue to breathe as our hearts continue to beat – countless systems carry on with their daily chores as the food we have eaten is digested that it may nourish and maintain our resting bodies.

But what if something is wrong.....

..... what of those who cannot take such things for granted – who try and try just to sink ever deeper into weakness, sickness and despair – what of those who must watch helplessly as their life slips through their fingers – what if it takes all their energy and resolve just to get through the day.

What of their dreams and ambitions – of their longing for love and happiness.

And what if no one knows how hard they try – as they suffer not only beneath their afflictions but beneath the added burdens of the world's contempt and scorn and its endless exhortations to 'success' – epitomised in its patronising, self-serving, mind-numbing platitudes.

"The indispensable first step to getting the things you want out of life is this: decide what you want."

"It may be that those who do most, dream most."

"There is only one thing that makes a dream impossible to achieve: the fear of failure."

"Every great dream begins with a dreamer. Always remember, you have within you the strength, the patience, and the passion to reach for the stars to change the world."

"The future belongs to those who believe in the beauty of their dreams."

"The only thing that will stop you from fulfilling your dreams is you."

"You see things; and you say, Why? But I dream things that never were; and I say, Why not?"

Well bully for you – whoever you are – whoever you think you are.

They all sound so positive – so encouraging – so uplifting and inspiring….. but the truth is the very opposite.

These little 'pearls of wisdom' are always written by those that have 'succeeded', and they are always inherently accusatory, dismissive of un-achieving, and sickeningly condescending.

For insinuated in each and every one, is the condemnation of those that do not 'succeed' for being responsible for their own failure. In this way, the 'succeeders' grant themselves the right and the permission to deny their sympathy and support and to feel justified and good about themselves as they turn and walk away.

So here is another one, written this time by one who has never had the misfortune to succeed in anything.

*"I will strive, not for what I can see, but for what is ever
beyond my seeing."*

Graham J Macey

You get the idea – it's easy – we can all create these pithy little gems – you try it – then you can quote it to your friends or the person next to you on the train, and when you do, you can feel yourself glowing with a smug self-satisfied but wistful air of superiority.

… I don't stand a chance among the living…

Truly – the world of the healthy takes so much for granted – never wanting to be reminded of what could so easily and suddenly befall it by those who have fallen by the way.

Of course some of these fallen ones are able and willing to make the effort to join in – to subscribe to the world of the healthy – and as they do – these plucky souls are welcomed and lauded as heroes and survivors – and rightly so…..

…..but what of those that cannot join in – what further hardships do they carry as a result – cast out – hidden away – unworthy of help or sympathy – what of their stories…..

….. and not just these – what of the Refugee, the Outcast, the Single Young Mother, the Homeless Old Man – those that are 'different'….. do their dreams have no worth – or should we just whisper in their ears…..

"If you can dream it, you can achieve it"

….. that should sort it.

… come tomorrow you won't find me here…

The game is everything and we must all abide by its rules – for every winner there must be losers beyond number – for all the shiny podiums there must be countless lonely rooms full of regrets and self-recrimination – and in the end, all that is really required of the loser is to not tarnish the victor's 'sparkle' – to keep out of sight and keep their shame quietly to themselves.

... 'cause I don't care to stay among the living.

This is the whole contemptuous charade of civilisation – this 'civilised world' that has now become but one big global Battery Farm, enabling and perpetuating the suffering of the many for the wealth and the glory of the few – and the rest just treading water to keep the whole damn thing afloat.....

..... when the only thing that really matters is getting to the top of the tree – in whatever field of life we have chosen or have had chosen for us – then there will always be those that need to be stepped upon on the way up..... always.....

..... no amount of awards or medals or shining reviews or bulging bank accounts or feelings of 'self-fulfilment' will ever make it alright or justified – or in any way meaningful.....

..... it will always be a charade – the desperate and futile attempt of the human race to find – by any means – its own purpose and glory – independent and in denial of its Creator.....

..... and what of me.....

..... a few years of caring for my mother in comfort and security and I seem to have become an angry, self-opinionated, finger-pointing know-it-all.....

..... so no change there.....

..... Lord have mercy.

If we are not our brother's keeper,
at least let us not be his executioner

Marlon Brando

Memo

Any person whose hunger
seeks a single apple
and yet takes two,
is a parasite...
... a leech
upon the blood of the poor,
and a cancer
within the peace and harmony
of all things...

... lucky for me
that I don't like apples.

52

Equality

... I realised that some people really can't think that way,
not because of their childhood or anything,
but because of the way they're created.

Sofia Helin

For the first year or so of caring for my mother, daily life was not unlike a battleground within which I was finding myself to be increasingly helpless before the relentless outpouring of my impatience and my anger.

But all began to change one evening in December 2013 as we all sat enthralled at the discovery of a dissected torso on the Oresund Bridge exactly at the half-way point between Denmark and Sweden.

We, the viewers, were captivated by the haunting ethereal sounds of the opening music and soon after, by the curious

Swedish detective with her tousled blonde hair, her long dark coat, her fixed humourless frown and her classic brown Porsche.

We were intrigued and drawn in as the radiant beauty of the actress was subordinated to the strange dark troubled and complicated beauty of the character – but gradually, as we settled down, we realised that we were becoming ever so slightly impatient and irritated by her intransigent behaviour and her callous rudeness to colleagues and public alike.

Saga was difficult, picky, pedantic, helplessly and uncompromisingly logical and fiercely and hopelessly asocial.

But then rumours started to circulate of Autism, and we all flew to our laptops to consult Google on the ways of the Autistic Spectrum.

Suddenly we all 'knew' Saga – we understood her and we felt for her.....

..... with just a click of our keyboards Saga was no longer Saga but an acceptable and non-threatening label – and so we were all now able to continue happy and content with our viewing in the reassuring knowledge that she was now safely in the box marked 'recognized human behaviour'.

Slowly, though, we started to be drawn in to her world and to care for her – and as we watched her trying so hard to understand and interact with the world around her – she started to break our hearts.

I began to realise then that I was no longer seeing only Saga, but my mother as well – I was beginning to understand that her anger and her violent defensiveness was maybe due to her just not being able to understand the world around her – of being constantly troubled by its strange ways and ever fearful of the threat that it presented.....

..... the heart and the sensibility of a small child – locked away against the cold unfathomable cruelty of the world outside.

As the weeks passed and one series of episodes gave way to the next – through the extraordinary skill of the actress and of all those involved in bringing Saga to life on the screen – the heart and the humanity of the character began to shine through.

As it did, I began to consider that, no matter how broken or 'different' a person may be, they have the inherent right to our respect and their dignity merely by the fact of being a human being..... no one should have their identity determined by another's approval or disapproval – by their acceptance or rejection.

This small step allowed me, for the first time, to find the courage to step outside the myopia of familial duty and the cowardice of wilful pretence, to say the words and face the reality that had been hidden away for so long.

My mother is not just difficult or challenging – she is not simply controlling and critical, and she is not merely neurotic and over-emotional.

My mother is a deeply disturbed woman, with mental health issues that clearly indicate, if nothing else, a substantial incursion into the Autistic Spectrum. She is different without a doubt, but I have learnt that there is no healing or value in constructing excuses for another's behaviour – in standing in judgment over them even if that judgment is benign.

My mother doesn't need to earn my respect and my recognition of her human dignity – whatever else has been laid on top, the person beneath reflects the image of God – that Divine and perfect Image in which we all stand as equals.

My mother, just as Saga, sees things differently and in her own way..... but then don't we all.....

..... until, that is, we are pushed and squeezed into the mindless machinery of the 'material dream' – all made possible and held in place by the monstrous regiment of 'labels'..... the simple but effective dehumanising of humanity in one simple stroke.

Hello there Father Ted...
... I hear you're a Racist now Father.

The plague and the abhorrence of labels – the stealing of the very nature and essence of the individual..... the true crime against humanity.

Labels make it possible for the acceptance of some and the exclusion of others, and when the humanity of the individual is lost or stolen it is but a small easy step to control and manipulate – to oppress and marginalise – exploit and use – to annihilate and 'ethnically cleanse.'

Labels may be what we do, the 'groups' that we belong to, the afflictions that we suffer, the passions that we pursue – they may be our acceptable, or not so acceptable, interface with the world around us – but they are not who we are.

But like the weeds that stifle the flowers and fruits of the fields – our labels become all that is seen, with our true individuality becoming lost to the labels of success just as much as to labels of failure.

It is the fear of this truth that sires the great deceit which is at the very heart of our march to worldly 'achievement.'

How much harder it is to be healed from the wounds of our success than it is to be healed from the wounds of our failure.....

..... the marks of failure and shame being so much more easily lifted from the fabric of our hearts than the stains of success and pride – for who among us would willingly and cheerfully let go to such as these.

And so we obediently accept the facades of 'adulthood' – we play our parts and we assimilate all the uniforms and masks and scripts and vocabularies that those parts require – for this world is a clever and cunning place, and if it doesn't get your allegiance one way, it will get it another.

It doesn't really matter which part we play as long as we play the game – as long as everyone contributes in some way to the Lie, which saves us all from having to face the Truth that God is All and in All and that under Heaven, all are equal and equally loved.

For true Equality cannot come through legislation no matter how well meaning it may be – Equality cannot be imposed and it cannot be faked just to make us all feel good – in fact, that is the very opposite of Equality – it is the belief and the acceptance that we are not equal at all, and that we need to be forced to conform through our words and actions and banners to whatever is the latest vogue.

In this way – all the pitiful euphemisms and deceits of Political Correctness are created to cover up the reality and the fear of worldly inequality – as they do so insidiously within any good Totalitarian scheme of oppression.

Maybe Totalitarianism is an unfair analogy – when it comes to issues of equality, maybe I should speak of a 'broad social assent'….. but then we all know how well that worked 80 years ago in Germany…..

Within the trite certainties of PC, equality becomes something to be inflicted – a weapon of restraint and control, like political ideologies and sadly, quite often, Religion – it becomes an object to be imposed, while the imposers, those who declare who is equal and who is not, remain aloof and inviolate within the 'self-made' towers of their absolute moral authority.

How can equality exist when our freedom to love is determined and compelled from above by a select few – this is nothing but dictatorship, with compliance judged by superficial behaviours alone…..

…… this kind of 'equality' is but hollow and empty – it grants no relevance to the inner convictions of the heart – for like anything of worth – true Equality grows from the inside out and not the other way around.

No wonder 'equality' has to be imposed with such violence when we see ourselves becoming nothing but the image and the appearance and the banner that we present – our identities defined almost solely now through our society's ever growing obsession with the sexual act – or lack of it !

As the glorious dance of the masculine and the feminine deep within the soul of every Man Woman and Child is lost to stifling labels and sensual greed – we turn our back on the love of our Creator, to seek our freedom in the frenzied and vehement brandishing of our chains – even to celebrate the very worst in us in the name of 'entertainment', as it becomes ever more faithful and deferential to the visions of Hieronymus Bosch.

"I saw a pretty girl and everything she has I want,
my aim is to be like her"
A child's social media comment

There can be no human dignity – no true equality unless life has meaning – unless there is a moral and ethical foundation to the Universe – if all is meaningless accident then we are just playing with words.

God is witness to our true individuality and He holds our Being in the cup of his hands just waiting for us to claim it – and in this claiming we do not become nothing – we become everything as we become reunited with ourselves and with our Creator.

In God alone are we equal and precious – in God alone are our dreams and aspirations, our fears and sufferings, our joys and achievements, all of equal worth – from the least in this world to the greatest – yes, even those who would deny us this freedom.

….. after all – if God is not God – if our future lies not in the hands of an omnipotent Deity but in our own hands and in the hands of meaningless chance – if we are relying on the 'blind' to show us the way – then we are all screwed anyway – so what do we have to lose by taking a chance on the existence of a loving and merciful Creator.

We are unique as individual snowflakes
upon a landscape of snow
we are one and we are distinct
perfectly and eternally equal
individual yet undivided

53

Sins Of The Fathers

How sweet the song when self is laid aside
21st January 2015

I am lying unmoving on my bed – the room is cold and dimly lit by a single flickering candle – I have opened the windows to let the winter's night air brush across my face – maybe as a penance – or maybe in the hope of it lifting me out of this dark brooding pit into which I have fallen.

I am weary – worn out – I have no strength nor will to resist the morbid visions that are flooding through my head – I listen over and over to their wretched script – as if I did not already know it all by heart.

'All is hopeless – all is lost – all was cursed from the day you were born' – and as if I needed proof – all the old stories of my mother's tragic and desolate childhood come parading back across my mind.

I let them come – and within the ingratiating arms of my wanton self-pity, I even reach out to welcome them back.....

..... the bitterness and relentless negativity of my grandmother, with her insatiable gluttony for 'self-sacrifice' that she wore like a medal around her neck.

All her shrivelled resentments – all her sour retorts..... they now condemn my present as they once condemned my past.

..... my mother's engagement ring that was dismissed as being 'unfit.'

..... the belittling and crushing of my mother's excitement on the night before her wedding.....

..... and not to forget her first kindly words at the birth of my brother..... 'What a shame it's not a girl.'

But the ways of the mother were surely as a saint compared to the selfishness and the meanness and the sadistic emotional and physical violence of the father.

The man who refused to get out of bed to fetch the midwife – trusting the birth of his youngest daughter to the hands of a neighbour while he continued to sleep.

The husband who let his wife cough up her cancer ridden lungs in a freezing unheated house – when one week after her death, he promptly attired his home with modern central heating – just for to keep himself cosy and warm.

The father who, as an old man, said of his daughter, who happened to be caring for him at the time, 'that one should have been strangled at birth.'

The small fortune (together with a list of the serial numbers of every note) that he had saved and kept secretly hidden under his bed, while his wife was forced to come crawling to him for pennies.*

The car that was forever being polished but, because of his reluctance to spend any money on petrol, was never driven – not until after his wife's death that is.

However…… as it turned out, my grandfather was to keep the best story until last.

The man who, as he got older and more frail, and more embittered by not being embraced as everyone's favourite 'grandad', managed, despite this, to grace his own funeral with an uncharacteristically heart-warming farewell – but not one that he would have planned or approved of.

The new vicar on the block, who although not really knowing my grandfather, was nevertheless strangely led to err on completely the opposite side to caution and brevity (the position that a small amount of common sense might have otherwise suggested) and present a eulogy of such shining proportions

---

* When the old man was admitted to a Nursing Home, he asked my uncle to bring him the brown paper parcel from under his bed. My Uncle, unable to resist seeing what was inside, discovered the notes and the long list of serial numbers and in a moment of genius, instead of removing a note, simply added a £20 note to the pack – thereby being awarded much mischievous delight in the sure knowledge that my grandfather would be spending hours and hours trying in vain to make sense of the discrepancy.

that half way through, my mother was inspired to turn to her sister and say.....

'We must be at the wrong funeral'

I think that this was the first time in my life that I felt consciously proud of my mother – proud in that moment to be her son, and to this day, its memory fills me with reassurance and hope.

But although I can feel a smile rising up from within me, I am not yet ready to give up on my brooding or the malevolent comfort of my nocturnal lamentations.

The truth is, that my mother never stood a chance – and I have come to understand at last how, in the absence of love and affection and kindness, my mother came to settle for pity instead – wherever she was able to find it.

This has been the daily focus of her life ever since – to inspire and generate 'pity'.....

... always falling back on 'illness' as her default position, if she was upset, had been criticised, couldn't get what she wanted, or was simply bored... no one ever knowing what was real or what was not – 'the little girl who cried wolf' without a doubt...

... staying up all night reading the complete list of side effects for her latest medication – and then ringing the doctor first thing in the morning to complain of experiencing each and every one of them...

... always acting out her feelings like a small child – unable to simple say 'I'm hot' or 'I'm cold' or 'I'm in pain' or 'I feel ill' – but having to accompany each desperate appeal for sympathy with a corresponding piece of melodrama...

... e.g. fanning her face while breathing heavily – shivering violently while clutching her arms tight around her body – crying out like a wounded animal and speaking in a small strained pitiful voice.

My mother was the little girl who always had to be the centre of attention – the little girl who would spend her whole life searching for the love that was so cruelly and heartlessly denied her.....

….. an innocent childlike heart, hiding away from the selfish brutality of the parents' mutual hatred of each other – from the selfish brutality of the world around her.

….. and me just being sucked dry by her broken-ness – living through her as an empty shell – like a proxy human being to her suffocating need to be right – to manipulate and control.

I am caught here now – beneath this poisoned inheritance – between the dark dreams of dawn and the dawn of my dark dreaming.

I want my life back – I want justice – I want to know why…..

….. why things were as they were.

I want to hear my stolen laughter – all the wild carefree laughter of my childhood.

I want to feel the fire and the vitality of my lost youth.

I want to see the flowering of my shattered hopes and the fruit of my broken dreams.

I want to hold my beloved once more beneath our thick Flokati rug…..

….. and I want all the music that I never played – all the songs that I never sung – I want them here in my heart now forever.

Lord, I am so weary…

… so weary of this wanting…

… I want to drive and drive until all my wanting is wanted out…

… and then to sleep a sleep that is deep and still and full of careless dreaming…

… and maybe in those dreams – I will find myself making love once more to a beautiful warm and sensual woman…

… Michelle Pfeiffer or Judi Bowker – or even both – but not at the same time – not unless they insisted anyway.

LORD, I WANT MY LIFE BACK … I WANT JUSTICE …
I WANT TO UNDERSTAND WHY

54

Surrender

The way I see it, these days there's a war on, right? And, ages ago, there wasn't a war on, right? So, there must have been a moment when there not being a war on went away, right? And there being a war on came along. So, what I want to know is: How did we get from the one case of affairs to the other case of affairs?

Private Baldrick

How does it happen – that we move from a moment of helpless unknowing to a moment of Divine Knowing – 'from the one case of affairs to the other case of affairs.'

Whether it comes as a critical mass of accumulated wisdom or by the sudden bestowing of revelation – whatever the means, in that moment we know that something wonderful has been laid upon our hearts, that we have been touched by something beyond ourselves and that everything has changed and will never be the same again.

The change that came upon me was not the embracing of an idea or an understanding of a concept or an acceptance of something long denied.

It was a gift – a gift that had been placed within my heart – the gift of the invitation to Surrender.

At last, I understood the meaning of the words that I had written so long ago, on a rainy night in the town of Jaca in 1973.

The beauty of the one who can surrender
without ever ceasing to care.

For to surrender to God is not 'giving up' – it is allowing Him to carry our burdens and to make everything 'right'.....

..... it is the assertion of our choosing to love and to deny the claim of all that would seek to break us and bring us low.

Surrender is beautiful and in every way the very opposite to all that we would perceive as the shame of worldly capitulation – it is the trusting of God with ALL our pain.

Through Faith, the power of Surrender is released – for it is an energy – a force – a connection to the Source of all life – to Love itself.

If we hold on to that which afflicts us for fear that it may be discarded if we let it go, then we are rejecting the power of Love to heal and to bring all things under the shadow of its wings.

If we hold on in heartache to that which is lost to us, then it will remain forever lost.

But as we surrender all that is gone – all that we mourn for – then as it lives and is restored in God it will also live in us as we live in Him.

With all my heart I know this to be true.....

..... for all that I sought after – all that I grieved over – all the happiness and love and contentment and peace that I searched for – all the healing and fulfilment that I craved.....

..... in my searching I had pushed it all away – the harder I searched the further it receded.....

..... but through Surrender, I have found all that I was longing for – it is with me now – it fills my heart – and as I remain in Him, I know it will remain with me forever.

Since that day, I have learnt that surrendering is not one single act of humility, but a way of life – a 'life skill' – a sanctuary – that we can use and be sustained by in countless ways each and every day.

In all the moments of my rising anger and impatience – my crying out for justice and resolution – I learnt to breathe and to place everything in God's hands – not to let it go that it may become nothing – but for it to live and find its resolution in Him – that for us there may be closure and peace.

For seeking marches while surrender rests – and in the end

seeking finds nothing but the echo of its own voice – while surrender rests and in knowing nothing it finds Truth in everything.

To surrender is not to submit – submission is passive but true Surrender is an active expression of will and can only exist within a relationship with the Father.

How could it be any other way in the light of this perfect Universe in which we live and breathe and have our being.

It has always been a source of disquiet for me – that so much of life seems to be determined by such random strokes of tragedy and misfortune – how can so many lives be blighted or cut short in such meaningless ways – broken and lost to nothing at all but the lifeless hands of 'fate'.

In the face of the perfect intricate web of our physical existence – the infinite frameworks that keep the balance of the Universe in place – all the ways of inter-dependence and inter-relation from the smallest to the greatest part..... in the light of the breath-taking design of it all.

..... must there not be a greater Truth for all of us.

It is my belief – it is my faith, that through surrender, everything becomes held in God – all our lost hopes and dreams – every cry of our broken hearts – every tear and every song of joy that never got to be sung – our lost loves – every life unlived or cut short before its time – every life tainted by illness and physical constraint – the lives of every aborted and still-born child.....

..... everything is held whole and perfect in God.....

..... and how could it be any other way – when we stand in the light of the Perfect Surrender, that all may return and be redeemed..... the bestowing on mankind of the majesty of His Spirit, that we might share and partake and be one with the very nature and essence of God.

And so, we too Surrender.....

... that every injustice may find its perfect atonement.

... every hurt its healing balm.

... every dark and troubled night its bright and wondrous dawn...

... and every tear its song of laughter and joy.

As we surrender to our Father – then all that seems lost is not lost – everything lives and breathes in Him – nothing is lost except those who would choose to be lost – all is as it was created to be – nothing is cut short – all is whole and perfect and complete in Him.

> *... not a hair of your head shall be lost.*
> *By your patience possess your souls.*
> *Luke: 21: 18-19*

As a leaf to the autumn chill
like a sail to the ocean's will
I will surrender

like a ring to the maker's mark
as a canvas to the painter's heart
I will surrender

as a chord to the melody
like a child to the mystery
I will surrender

hold on
the light is within you
hold on
your spirit is rising

when all is forgiven
then nothing is lost
there are no bridges to cross

as my sleep to the folds of night
as my dream to the morning light
I will surrender

my Lord
when this dance is through

I will come to you

55

Reconciliation

When the new day's light comes dawning
and the old has slipped away
I know that we will walk again my love
on that heaven sent healing day

Slowly – very slowly – peace began to rest once more upon our home….. it fell like flakes of snow upon our weary hearts and it moved softly and silently through the spaces between us.

It was as though a door had opened before my mother and myself – beckoning us each day, but always allowing us the choice of whether we stepped through or not.

Some days we did, and some days we didn't – some days we acted alone and some days through the grace of each other's example and encouragement.

However we chose to respond to the call of our healing, by the summer of 2017 it had become clear that the madness that had held us in its web for so many years had finally and manifestly lifted.

The truth of our release had presented itself in small fleeting and mostly unconscious moments, but by the time I drove my mother to see her oldest friend Pam in Somerset, the calm and the fun and the good humour of our five hour journey left me in no doubt that something magnificent and miraculous had happened in our lives.

Not once did my mother scream or grab the dashboard or complain about the route or the speed or the behaviour of other drivers, and not once did she try and open the door to escape from the moving vehicle.

In fact, the only concession that she requested for herself, was to be able to stop for copious numbers of 'tea breaks', which in their way, helped to turn our simple journey into an adventure of near epic proportions.

To this day, I still have to be watchful that I do not react out of habit to a trigger that no longer exists, but nevertheless, as each day passes, I am left a little more heartened and thankful, that after a lifetime of changeless misery, in just a few short years, we have come from a living nightmare to a place in which we can enjoy and respect and value each other's company.....

..... a place that resonates with humour and fun – with thoughtfulness and un-procrastinated apologies – with warmth and easy affectionate gestures and remarks.....

..... a place of friendship and love for sure.

It is now with a glow in my soul that I am able to sketch some of the many moments of this unfolding, together with some of my mother's more memorable and irresistible comments on life.

You'll know something is wrong when I stop talking

We are sitting in the lounge on an aimless Sunday morning – the wind and the rain are hammering against the windows, but here we are warm and lazy and peaceful.....

..... almost.....

..... we are listening to Julian Bream and John Williams on the CD player – I am writing and my mother is reading..... but things are not that simple – for whenever my mother reads she feels compelled to share her passion by repeating every other sentence with whoever is nearby i.e. me.

Once again, it is driving me to distraction, and I am on the verge of making a very pointed exit to seek the peace and the commentary free quiet of my bedroom..... this time though, I think of how this will make her feel and of how it will make me feel – the moment will be lost and its tainted memory will ever stand between us. Instead I choose to let go to my irritation and to accept the sharing of her enthusiasm as a blessing.....

..... and so it becomes.

Be careful there might be bones in the fish

Aaagghh..... why is it that she cannot resist warning me every single time – like asking me if I've cleaned the fluff out of the tumble drier or washed the lettuce or emptied the hoover bag or changed the water filter.

It will no doubt always be a mystery to her why such seemingly innocent remarks cause such anger and fury in me – but she is coming to accept it nonetheless.

This time I take a long slow breath while I surrender my anger and the scream on my lips – and slowly, it all becomes as nothing, as the moment passes and is gone.....

..... and after all, compared to the sufferings of this world – what does it really matter if my mother insists on a slightly higher level of diligence than I would otherwise have preferred.

We are following a group of keen elderly pink Lycra clad cyclists – my mother is visibly concerned – and not just at their apparel.

How do they balance on such thin tyres ?

Driving in the late Autumn – sunshine in shafts through the trees – tea and flapjacks at the coffee shop in Seal – sharing these moments – at last the two of us together, not tolerating not sacrificing, just being together – the sun through the leaves – Faure's Pavane on the radio – the murmur of the Jeep as it reaches out across the tarmac ribbon beyond – not mother and son – not carer and cared for – just two people, equally blessed by the beauty before them.

We are sitting together on the sofa – I take hold of her hand as she gazes through the window – she stares out into the distance and says in a very matter of fact kind of way.....

It will be a long time in heaven I think

She is sitting in the conservatory wrapped in a blanket and warmed by the winter sun and the small upright heater – I am sighing because I think she has come here to sulk as a protest against me not wanting to eat the liver she has cooked for me – but I'm wrong – she has let it go and now she is just enjoying the moment – watching the sun going down while listening to the Lark Ascending – number one in the Classic FM 'Hall of Fame' no less.

We are driving to Newlands Corner for chips and homemade soup – it is raining and my mother is reciting verses from her favourite poems.

The curfew tolls the knell of parting day, The lowing herd winds slowly o'er the lea, The ploughman homeward plods his weary way, And leaves the world to darkness and to me…..

She suddenly pauses as she turns to look back at a passing shop.

Didn't the board outside that Undertakers say 2 for 1 Funerals ?

She continues.

Let me not to the marriage of true minds Admit impediments. Love is not love Which alters when it alteration finds, Or bends with the remover to remove…..

Frensham Ponds – the pale winter sun lying lightly across the lake – Handel's Messiah falling like honey from the car's stereo – I take her hand as we close our eyes and fall asleep.

After an exploratory visit to a Care Home (aged 89) before my decision is made to move back to Surrey to look after her.

I'm not living there – it's full of old people !

Sudden impulsive displays of affection – they feel so strange but so right….. like giving myself to small willing acts of humility – such as checking the fluff drawer in the tumble drier or emptying the hoover bag whether it needs it or not.

I am walking through the Conservatory with a can of Cellulose Thinners in my hand – she looks up from her dozing and sighs.

Ah Thinners – that's about the only thing that I'm not taking.

I stand in the bathroom shaking with anger at her last thoughtless remark – a lifetime of pain weighs upon me and I feel brittle and helpless – but I choose to wait and not to react – I breathe very slowly and again I surrender into the moment.

A peace comes over me and, against all my inclinations to the contrary, I walk back to the kitchen where she is stooped despondently over the worktop – and there the unimaginable takes place as I put my arm around her shoulder and murmur a few quiet words of comfort and reassurance as she turns and smiles up at me.....

..... and is this not how my injustices are laid to rest – is this not how I am healed.

I return to the car park to find that she is sitting with the car door open yet again – there is nothing I can do to stop her – I needed some air she says – '*so why didn't you just open the window – one day someone will drive in and take the door off* '(as later they nearly did) – she says 'I'm sorry I disappointed you'..... she is learning for the first time in her life to apologise – my anger is diffused – I close my eyes and wait for peace to return.

Whilst shopping in the Co-op, my mother approaches an

assistant to ask.....

Do you sell Tom and Jerry's Ice Cream ?

It is Easter Sunday and I have taken my mother to church where she soon discovers that, as is usually the case, she has forgotten her glasses.

After looking up at a large banner that reads 'Christ is Risen', my mother turns to me and asks in an inappropriately loud voice.....

Why does it say Christ is Pisces ?

The woman next to us starts suddenly, looks at my mother with a distinctly disapproving scowl and then wastes no time in relocating to the pew behind us.

My mother's 'ways' are getting harder to focus on and I am feel guilty and uncomfortable as I write about the past..... I am learning to respect and care for her as a person – as my mother..... in fact, I am actually becoming fearful of criticising her, for she seems each day to be ever more innocent and vulnerable, honest and upset by the futility and the sadness of confrontation.

She is choosing to let go – to lift herself up above a lifetime of broken habits and behaviours. She has discovered the power of her will and the power of choice. I can feel her thoughts moving beyond the constraints of her fears, of her upbringing, maybe for the first time, like a child learning to swim, frightened but excited.

I know that I am witnessing the miracle of Change – and I also know that none of this is happening by accident.

Of all my mother's 'ways', one little idiosyncrasy lingers

tenaciously on however – that of never being able to take my word on anything but always needing proof – whether it be a question of the day of the week, the amount of her medication, or the date of my brothers' birthdays – she must always 'see' before she is able to believe.

On this particular day, I am tired and weary from another interrupted night and lose my temper at her blatant unreasonableness.

She says nothing, but shuffles to her bed where, even after all the evident healing, I still assume it be for the purposes of sulking and brooding upon my wicked behaviour.

After a few minutes I am alarmed to hear the sound of chuckling coming from her room and as I walk through the door it is with the expectation of finding that her mirth is but the first tangible sign of oncoming senility and that I should now prepare myself for the worst – but instead, my mother does something that is so utterly and exquisitely 'normal' that I am left awestruck and completely speechless.

With a child's mischief in her eyes, she reaches out for my hand, smiles a smile that is bright and brimming with warmth and candour and says.....

I know I irritate you sometimes and I make you angry,
but I do love you.

I kiss her forehead, tuck her in, walk to my room and pray.....

... Lord help me to love with my patience and tolerance,
help me to love with my will and with my choosing,
that by your grace, it may follow in my heart.

And so I have come to understand, that it is impossible to break down the walls that exist between us – that it is only pure unselfish unconditional love that can melt the walls away.

I have seen the futility of trying to `change' another human being and of all the harm that is wrought as we focus on those things that we think need changing.

There is only one way to lift up another human being – we simply love.

We look beyond the hurt and we focus our gaze on the divine seed within each broken heart – we let them see their beauty and their infinite worth reflected in our eyes and we never break that gaze for an instant.

It is only love that can set us free.

If we focus on another's so called faults, then we are chaining them to their pain and we are bolting the door to the prison cell of their broken-ness.....

..... but as we love them – as we show them the Love that is God – then we bid them to step out into the light of that Love.

Encore

(A short conversation with my mother)

It said in that shop 'Wild Bird Seed for sale'…

… so!

Can't wild birds feed themselves?

… they can – but don't you feed the birds in our garden?

Yes, but they're not 'wild'…

… they're sweet.

Part Five

Into the Light

My training has been everything but academic,
and I don't regret it.
I learned music from the popular musicians,
the dancers and the percussionists of 'Carnaval',
from the sound of the streets of Rio
and from nature.
So for me there are no boundaries
between classical and popular music.

56

Twelve Studies for Guitar

My music is natural, like a waterfall.

Heitor Villa Lobos

On the 22st December 2017, the last conflict within my war torn hands was resolved, peacefully and harmoniously with few recriminations being levelled or reparations being sought – there was no victory march – no wild celebrations – no drunken street parties – one day it just all seemed to be ok – that is all.

However, it would take another eighteen months before all the layers of tension that had accumulated over the years were finally laid to rest….. another eighteen months before the Studies that had carried and nurtured me for so long were able to allow me the chance to return some of their many favours.

It is said that these Studies are an expression of the inspired union of Brazilian Choro and French Impressionism. It is also said that, despite these and other distinctive influences, the final collection of pieces are a sublime example of the composer's own unique and enduring 'voice'.

As for me – I come to their calling, not as an analyst, not even as a musician, but rather as a painter before palettes of sound and time – of colours and textures – of rhythms and light..... I come to music that echoes the pounding rhythms of our hearts, of our fleshly hungers and passions..... to music that is rooted in the bowels of the earth just as surely as it reaches up and touches the heavens.

As these studies meander through the most 'guitar friendly' keys, each one rises effortlessly from its familial bond to humbly present its own wondrous character and heart.

One leads us deep into the heart of the Amazon, where the song of the forest entwines as it always has, with the song of the spirit above.

Back in the streets of the city, a morbid shuffle casts off its solemn mask to become, in a moment, a playful and a joyful dance.

There are those that ripple along gracefully, as a small village brook shining in the moonlight, while others remain forever wild and restless and far beyond taming.

There is one, at least, that is as close as you may get to making love without actually making love, whilst another tumbles childlike from the strings like a clear bright mountain stream at dawn.

For some, the notes must first bind seamlessly together, that the music within their buds be released.

As we come to these, we must find our patience and our faith, for first there is strife – then haste and bustle..... but later as our perseverance reaps its reward, we may reach up through the clouds of notes and harmonies to a place where all becomes still and serene.

It is here in the sunlight that there is nothing for us to do now but let the sounds and the timbres of the waterfall wash over us..... and as the music transforms into pulsating prisms of colour, we find ourselves floating amidst the glitter of the birdsong, high above in the rain forests of the Madre Tierra – suspended between staves of time and space..... just longing to stay here..... forever.

These studies have been my friends, my therapists and my teachers – and like all good teachers, they have been firm but patient, diligent but generous of heart – serious but always recognising the need for times of fun and relaxation.

More than any of Villa Lobos' guitar music, his studies have brought healing to my broken hands – the poetry of every movement – the energy and the beauty..... and like no other music, they have always accepted me, just as I am.

These short humble pieces of music, if we let them, can become as carriages to the deepest places of our souls – for, broken hands or not, this is where they have carried me, and carry me still.

They rang Villa Lobos in Paris and said – 'you know there's a wonderful English guy who plays your music so beautifully' – he said – 'surely that's an anachronism' – and I got the feeling, when he'd said that, that I wasn't going to be received with great enthusiasm. But anyway, I played to him, and he was very critical – he didn't like a lot of the fingerings... remember, I'd just recorded these pieces... we got to one point in the First Prelude, in the middle section, when he said 'STOP' – I was absolutely appalled, and he was very angry, he said – 'you can't play it like that' and I said 'Segovia played it like that' – he said 'I know' – and he said 'last year when Segovia was in Paris and I saw he was playing this Prelude on the programme, I telephoned him and told him not to play it'...

... and I thought, my God, what a man this Villa Lobos is – you know, I mean, very few composers tell you that they don't want you to play their pieces – I mean, that's incredible – I was absolutely terrified.

From 'Julian Bream – My Life in Music'

Memo

*We study, we practise, we learn,
not that we might play music
but that we might not get in the way of Music.*

*The highest aspiration of the artist
should be to let go,
to become as a channel,*

a nameless channel
through which all the Love in the Universe may pass,
all the Love and the Light that is God.

We practise that we may become nothing
and the Music everything,
for only as our song resonates
with the greater Song,
do we truly experience Music.

We forgive and we surrender,
that in becoming poor in spirit
we may become rich in His Spirit,
for only as our hearts resonate
with the greater Heart,
do we truly experience Love.

57

The Centre that is God

Let all my songs
gather together their diverse strains
into a single current
and flow to the sea of silence
in one salutation to thee.

Tagore

Music has a tonal centre that lives and breathes in the 'harmonic overtones' of each single note. There is nothing we can do to resist or deny its attraction, and to set ourselves free momentarily from its magnetic pull, elaborate frameworks need to be constructed and maintained.

It is true, that we can dance and play in the currents and

eddies of this attraction, but like a kite in the wind ever straining for release, we are forever being pulled back to the centre – the tonal centre of Music.

In the same way, the Heart has a tonal centre that resonates within every fibre of our being, and despite all our endeavours, there is nothing we can do to resist or deny its attraction.

As with Music – as with our Hearts – so with all of Creation, we are forever being pulled back to the centre – the Centre of all things – the Centre that is God. All the noise and clamour of this world, all the myriad pursuits of humanity, everything has but one purpose – to resist and deny the magnetic pull of its Creator – to render ourselves deaf and blind to God – to claim the Throne of Life for our Selves – and, as a result, to be set apart from His Love forever.

58

Back To The Blueprint

To arrive at being all, desire to be nothing.

John of the Cross

How would you detect a ripple on a wild and stormy sea – or a restless wind within a full force gale?

I have lived always with a raging storm within my heart – but as the storm dies away – the wind and the ripple of the water have become known to me.

There remains a troubling within me – a deep unease – like a fault line through to the depths of my soul.

What faces me now can no longer be hidden beneath turmoil and confusion – and so – at the very moment of my peace – the ice cold hand of judgement falls upon me once again.

How do I learn to live in the light of honesty and truth – to turn away from the dark fantasy of my life that I may discover who I really am.

What happens now – and where can I run to be free of these words that have stood as a headstone over all the days of my life.

Here lies a wicked selfish ungrateful child

It follows me like a gallstone of the heart – like something that I've swallowed that chokes my breath but that I can't cough up.

My afflictions now are not substance – they are not a burden to be lifted – a wound to be healed….. they are an emptiness – a place of hollowness within me.

I cannot be released this time – this time I need to be filled and the emptiness laid to rest.

I seek an answer through times of quiet – of fasting and prayer – of being still and waiting…..

….. if only I could just restore myself to an earlier point – to re-set and re-boot and safely start again…..

….. as it is – I reach out in the silence for some kind of blueprint – for some kind of master plan…..

….. and maybe this is the one that I am searching for.

> *The Lord our God, the Lord is one.*
> *And you shall love the Lord your God with all your heart,*
> *with all your soul, with all your mind,*
> *and with all your strength.*
> *This is the first commandment.*
> *And the second, like it, is this:*
> *You shall love your neighbour as yourself.*
> *Mark 12: 29-31*

59

The Silent Commandment – Meditations On A Ground

And you shall love the Lord your God with all your heart...
... and with all your mind...

The leaves of autumn are turning as I step out on the narrow way – the ancient path wherein the beauty and the truth of all things lie.

I have come from the desert of my days – from the dark recesses of my solitary shelter – I have come from the night of the Star – from the dawn of Love come down.....

..... and the light that I walk by is the Light of Men – it shines out from the well-spring of my quest – and the shadow that it casts before me is that of my hunger – the nameless faceless form of my aching spirit.

I have waited and I have longed for this moment for all of my life – for the whisper of the wind to call my name – for the surging of the tides to carry me – for the time that is no time to hold me in the cradle of its arms.

And now I have taken my place here, beside the traveller and the pilgrim – the outcast and the saint – each of us in his own way, slipping between the cracks in his broken heart – each of us in his own way, holding out his hands before this the year of the Lord's ineffable favour.....

From deep in the valley – a song rises up from the Ancient of Days – and as it does – all the coming together of the festivals of heaven and the seasons of the earth join in rapturous refrain.

These days of my setting out – they are light and they are contented – the air is filled with the glitter of birdsong and my path is lit by the shifting of the russet leaves and by the sounds of children's laughter.

This is not a time for introspection – it is a time of the heart and of the playfulness of spirit.

It is a time of Love reaching out to Love's embracing – of Love seeking its delight in the countenance of its face – the sound of its voice – the melody of its song – the colours of its beauty.....

..... my journey tracing the story of this tender reunion.....

.... for only Spirit can reveal Spirit – and only God can lead to God.

The Love of the heart – the First Love – its helpless instinctive and grateful response before the transcendent Gift of Life.....

..... this is the 'First Simplicity.'

For the heart – all is simple and easy and careless – she loves without caution or restraint..... but it is not so for the mind.

The two of them are like children, skipping and playing and teasing one another all through these slow golden autumn days.

There will come a time when they will come to respect and revere each other's gifts – but for now, they move by impulse alone.

The radiant and ethereal older sister and her bossy little brother who must always and everywhere be the one in charge – the last and definitive word on all things.

Faith is their teacher and faith their kindred bond – and as faith grows within them and between them – Mind will find its strength and its beauty in letting go to all that is ordained as mystery and in resting and rejoicing as Prince over all that remains behind.....

..... and Heart..... Heart will find security and direction and freedom and joy, in the presence and the guidance of her brother.

When the instinct of the Heart and the reason of the Mind are reconciled through Faith, then Wisdom is the flower of that reconciliation.....

..... and it is through this Wisdom that the love of the Heart and the

love of the Mind become received by God and loved by Him in return.

... with all your strength.

The coloured leaves have scattered now and the path is bare and hard with frost.

The low winter's sun flecks my sight as it passes behind this stark stubbled landscape of leafless boughs and branches – like a narrow but insistent searchlight.

Mostly it lies hidden beyond the interminable grey – but today it rests like molten amber all across the pale deserted frameworks of fields and hedges.....

..... but even so, my heart remains untouched and unsmiling before the splendour – for it too lies hidden beyond the grey of its sad retreat.

I move through winter's veiled address as if through a dream – a very cold and lonely dream – the slow onward rhythm of my step and the distant song of the wind – all that keep me going from this moment to the next.

I think on the warm sunlit days of autumn – the days of my setting out..... all was bright and carefree then – and my Heart and my Mind – to be sure – they were like children dancing around my feet as I walked.....

..... but now as the nights draw in and the days become colder and darker – as the heavens become as brass – I look to find that they have deserted me – to hide away in the darkness – subdued and silent.....

..... for as Faith leaves to seek its comforts in fear and doubt – Heart has become cowered and reticent – and all the genial hubris of Mind has turned to confusion and uncertainty.

Until this dark night has passed – until the dawn's breaking light – it behoves another to keep me company on this bleak and broken trail – it behoves another to stand and persevere.

And so Strength – as yet a stranger here – enters grudgingly upon the scene – the strong but indolent older brother.

Until now, he has been happy to remain in the shadows, watching while his loved ones laughed and played – happy for them to steal the limelight – happy to be overshadowed by their charisma and all their shining bravado.....

..... anything, in fact, for an easy life.....

But now he must learn to stand and to accept his role and his responsibilities – to hold his little ones close and to protect their innocence and their virtue.

This is his rite of passage – his coming of age – the discovery of Will – for as a spark to the kindling wood – Strength is aroused and released through Will.....

..... this is how he finds his fire and his metal.....

..... and this is how he loves – and is loved by God.

...in quietness and trust is your strength
Isaiah 30:15

In the bleak mid-winter...

... where the frosty winds make moan – and the earth stands hard as iron – and the waters like a stone...

... where all seems cold and lifeless...

... fruitless and barren...

... in the womb of the earth...

... in the womb of the heavens...

... far beyond the realms of our knowing, or our ability to incite...

... there are seeds that are stirring and reaching for the light...

... and in that silent stirring – all things will be reborn...

... as Heaven and Earth embrace...

... in the timeless celebration of new life...

... in the infinite outpouring of Grace.

The Holy Ghost shall come upon thee,
and the power of the Highest shall overshadow thee...
Luke 1:35

and with all your soul...

Winter is past – and with it, all the heaviness of Heart and Mind that seemed to last forever..... my children have returned now – a little wiser perhaps – but still singing and dancing together is if nothing at all has really happened.

The soft virgin colours of Spring now line my path – while new born lambs go skipping and all the emerging ebullience of buds and shoots and blossoms captures my heart.

I linger beside the still waters and I pause to rest in the soft green pastures – and the air is filled with expectation and promise as I am joined on my way by the salutations and the smiles of fellow travellers – all of us it seems, with an increasing urgency and purpose to our step.

We have escaped unscathed from the snares of the darkness – with each heart rejoicing in the quiet knowing, that all the while, the Lord has been walking unseen beside us – and that, all through this our darkest night, we were never alone.

The way is leading upwards now, and as we lift up our eyes to the hills – to the place of peace to which we are all now going – our mouths are filled with laughter and our tongues with the singing of the new song that rises from our hearts

It feels like we are no longer stepping but falling – into that holy distance where all will be drawn together – where all will be reconciled – where all will become as one.

For a little while we have sown in tears – while the heavens thundered and the earth cracked open..... but now we will reap with joy as we stand in the light of this new day – hungry like homeless orphans for the Bread that is Life.

We have come to a garden and to a hill and to a lonely wooden cross – where high above – with arms outstretched – ever waiting and ever watching – Love looks down and weeps, with tears of forgiveness and glorious surrender.

The Cross – the divine intersection between the Infinite and the Finite – between Spirit and Matter – between the place of Exile and the place of Homecoming – the meeting point of all things – where 'Love reaches out to Love's embracing' – Love paying the price that all may be brought into flawless union and harmony with itself – the redeeming and the making of all things whole and perfect.

> *"The kingdom of God does not come with observation.*
> *Nor will they say, 'Here it is!' or 'There it is!'*
> *For remember, the Kingdom of God is within you."*

I come through the tearing of the veil to kneel in silence before the foot of the Cross – to rest in the shade of its branches – to come in Spirit and in Flesh with all of my Soul – with all that I am .....

..... to kneel in shared rebirth with all things – with a passion like no other – and to know at last that this is how I love, and am loved by God.

> *In repentance and rest is my salvation…*
> *Isaiah 30:15*

> *… as [you love] yourself*

The warm sunlit path of summer stretches out into the distance – all is richly hued and abundant with life – my parched and thirsty soul longs to reach out for the First Fruits of my redemption but something keeps me waiting here – waiting at this sacred gate – waiting for a hand to lead me through.

I am caught here at the foot of the Cross with so many of my fellow travellers – we console each other and we discuss reasons and justifications for our reluctance – but, in the end, each of us is alone and unconvinced.

I have come to the Cross and I have drunk of its cup – I cannot go back now and I cannot stand still – I must move on......

...... to remain here on my knees in the chains of the 'repentant sinner' serves only to deny the fullness of its Gift – but I am quite unable, it seems, to take the next step.

I rest and dream a waking dream – and in that dream the key to the gate is held out before me – and I praise God for His Glory and I thank Him for His Grace but still – I do not take the key.

This stasis – this inertia – this is the place of my hunger and my emptiness...... I have found my fault line at last – for I have become poor in the spirit of this world only to resist being filled with God's Spirit – the 'worst of both worlds' – a pitiful wretch indeed.

With a cutting clarity it has become clear to me now – that my stumbling block – the stumbling block of all humanity – is the 'Silent Commandment' – for in truth, the Lord has singled out, not two, but three commandments as being above all others.

The Silent Commandment is the second, and the one in which the Lord exhorts us to love ourselves.

I see now that there is no worthiness and no noble purpose in my remaining here – and for this I feel convicted and ashamed...... the days of my restive musing and the nights of my shifting dreams – they have become charged now with one single voice.

Great is the sin – great your impotence – great humanity's loss and great the destruction that surrounds you if you do not learn to love yourself as you were created to do – for only through that love can you come to the place of my Blessing.

This is the very point of your fall from grace – it is the lynch pin – the moment when you succumbed to the love of worldly ego – to the love of sensual gratification and to the love of all the clamorous viscera of the flesh.

When you turned your back on my Spirit and the love of my Child within you – that is when you became as a slave parading as a free man – that is when you lost your true individuality under Heaven.

But you are not ashamed nor repentant of your folly, nor for the pain and the suffering that you cause – you even exalt its abhorrence with a name..... 'The Pursuit of Happiness'.

You are bidden to pick and eat of the fruit it is true – but not the tainted fruit of the worldly banquet – you are called to eat of the First Fruits – to see yourself through my eyes and through no others.

For you are not your own to worship or despise – you have been redeemed at a price and for a purpose – you have been fearfully and wonderfully made in my own image – to love and be loved by Me in perfect union with all things.....

..... the first natural desire of your hearts should be – not to please yourself – but to please Me.

Do not scorn or afflict the child within you in the name of Holiness – call it for what it is – Pride and Anger and Fear and the denying of my Love and my Grace and my Omnipotence.

To yourself first and then to others: Understanding – Compassion – Forgiveness – Patience – Tolerance and Love.

All your sufferings and your violence come from the tyranny of Self – but as you love yourself as my Child – as you nurture and chasten that Child in love and love alone – as you truly come to know yourself in Me, then my Love will come to make its home in you.

A heart in which my Love dwells cannot stoop to the selfish jealous controlling love of this world – it needs no defence nor seeks any – it cannot choose to bring indignity upon itself or to entertain that which is harmful or degrading to the flesh – for that is to bring indignity on myself.....

..... evil cannot take root in such a heart, for the heart that is filled with my Love does not seek truth, but becomes Truth.

My Child – I did not bring you home just to watch you crawl in the dirt – you are Spirit of my Spirit – Heart of my Heart – Blood of my Blood – Flesh of my Flesh – you are noble and fine.....

..... it is my desire and my longing that you love yourself as such – I say again – you are not your own to worship or despise.

My dreams reveal His Heart as His Heart reveals my dreams – around and around they dance until the way ahead seems suddenly clearer – as the clouds of my folly roll away and the sky is filled with light.

The barriers across my path are lifted now – and as the chains of this world slip away – I see the headstone of my shame lying shattered and broken on the ground beneath my feet.

The man has become the child once more – and the child has become the man – I am not young – I am not old – I am myself.....
I am the face behind the disfigured mask – the voice behind the muffled cry – I am the love song within the broken heart – I am at one with all things and I am my own unique eternal being.....

..... I am who I was created to be.

All the broken pieces of my being
now one perfect whole
where just a moment before
they lay strewn across the universe
like tiny pieces of shattered stars.

You shall love your neighbour...

I set out upon the path once more, but my progress is lighter now – for there is a dance within my step – and there is a song upon my lips – and there is a love-look in my eyes for all of God's Creation.

I am walking where the wild flowers reach out – where my heart and my mind are as honey eyed children dancing on rhythms of light.

I let the stirring of summer's reveries takes me in its arms – as I run through its valleys and chase the silent echo of eternity, there between its wistful glades.

I take my rest to kneel where the leaves of healing grow – my heart reaching out to fields and forests – rivers and streams – hills and valleys – to seas and skies.

I have travelled fifty days and fifty nights to this place of my belonging – this place from where Love may go forth – no longer to tarry as moths around a flame but to rise up on wings like eagles – that His Spirit may be poured out on all people.

This is the time of my empowerment – this is the of time of wind and fire – this is the time of the coming of Spirit – of Prayer and Fasting – that I too may be of the First Fruits and that my Love, now made whole, may reach out to my neighbour and from my neighbour to my special ones – to my family and my friends…..

….. to my beloved and to my children.

For is this not how it was ordained to be – first to God then to ourselves and then to all of God's children.

For how do I love my neighbour – my beloved – my children – if I do not love their humanity first….

….. and how do I recognize and cherish that humanity if I have not already learnt to recognize and cherish it within myself…..

….. and is this not how I am to love my enemy…..

We love, that with our seeing, we may see with His eyes – that we all may be His children – precious and equally loved for all eternity.

Behold, what manner of love the Father hath bestowed upon us,
that we should be called the sons of God:
therefore the world knoweth us not,
because it knew Him not.

Beloved, now are we the sons of God,
and it doth not yet appear what we shall be:
but we know that, when He shall appear,
we shall be like Him;
for we shall see Him as He is.

And every man that hath this hope in Him
purifieth himself, even as He is pure.

1 John 3: 1-3

We shall not all sleep, but we shall all be changed,
in a moment, in the twinkling of an eye, at the last trumpet.

As I return to the first commandment – the love of my heart is deeper and richer this time – it is not subject to the fickle impulse of first love for I have learnt to love as God's precious child – to know who I am, and to know the relationship with my Father that I was born to fulfil.....

..... to love God, to love myself and to love all of Humanity – with a love that shines as gold, refined and purified through the fires of my afflictions.....

..... this is the 'Second Simplicity.'

Each day the sun is sinking a little lower in the sky – and as summer gives way to autumn, I follow my path back to the place of my beginning.....

..... to the joyful celebrations of reaping and gathering – to the sounding of the Trumpets, where all is redeemed and made perfect – where all is reconciled and made whole – where all is atoned for, that every prodigal may be invited to the Feast..... that in Him who lives and reigns forever – all may be one.

My journey has reached its end – my journey has just begun – my journey has always been – my journey.....

..... it never was.

I complete the circle like a halo around a flame – the circle of the festivals and the seasons – the circle of our Lord's Commandments – the circle of this eternal moment.....

..... and with each return of the circle – I dwell deeper in the Heart of Love – my own heart becoming as still waters there – reflecting the glory of God with ever more fidelity and grace.....

The circles continue – as simplicity leads to simplicity...

... until the veil is at last drawn away and I step lightly from the threads of this coat of flesh – from this mortal coil...

... to be set free...

... Light returning to Light...

... Love returning to Love...

... released into eternity as naturally and as effortlessly as the seeds of a dandelion clock drifting out across the meadows at dawn...

... and there where all is quiet and still...

... only the words of Jesus Christ remain.

> *On that day you will know*
> *that I am in my Father,*
> *and you are in me,*
> *and I am in you.*
>
> John 14:20

Memo

> *Christianity is not a religion,*
>
> *it is a relationship with God*
>
> *through our Lord Jesus Christ*
>
> David Pawson

60

Existing Is Easy – It's Living That Is So Hard

> *'I'm so tired –*
> *I feel like I'm walking half in this world*
> *and half in the next'*
>
> My Mother – age 94

Just when I was beginning to think that our lives had reached some kind of peaceful plateau, once again, all has changed.

Out of the mists has appeared before us now another mountain top – another season to navigate and traverse – a season ever more dominated by sickness, tiredness, pain, memory loss, hallucinations and all the unpredictable vagaries that are the bowel movements of old age.....

'Just think, while we're sitting here, there are men all over the world excavating for things – all sorts of things'

..... there can be no complacency or freewheeling or relaxing one's guard in the care of the dying it would seem. I feel like a miner, scouring the depths for further resources of patience and compassion and love – cutting deeper and deeper into my soul – always in search of another level – always in search of another seam of gold.

Everything that I've learnt must be learnt all over again – with each day's peace being but a brief evanescent victory garland for yet another battle fought and won..... this time.

Yesterday's degree of compassion is of little use today – nor yesterday's patience or surrender or concern for my mother's dignity..... every day I must start anew.

'I want to change my name'

It is just beginning to sink in, that the days of peace and humour and sharing – those days that seemed like the summit of a sunlit peak that we had climbed and reached together – those days have passed.

I thought that they would carry us through to the end, but now I must face the truth that they are probably never coming back – at least as no more than a pale reflection.

Madness has returned, but not the dark malevolent madness of the past, the atmosphere that surrounds us now is a somewhat lighter and more jocular relation – a strange but harmless cousin to the wicked stepmother of old.

'It's funny that I didn't see St Paul when I was in Ephesus'

It is true that she no longer seems inclined to pick up her walker and throw it at me – and for this I suppose I should be grateful.....

..... but every day my mother is losing her grip on reality a little more – or maybe 'reality' is losing its grip on her.....

..... the spectre always hanging over us of my mother being forced to spend her final days bewildered and anxious in the well-meaning but alien surroundings of a Care Home

'I heard that Henry VIII has just destroyed all the Monasteries and killed all the Catholics – how awful'

Three or four times each night she cries out – for me to take the dog out of her room, or to send the man away that is sitting on the end of her bed, or to get her coat and her paperwork so that she can go to the office and finish the accounts, or to answer the front door – the variations are endless, but all share the same command, that I instantly rise from my sleep to settle the situation and calm her anxiety.

'I didn't call –
I was just talking to the man at the end of the bed'
(I am tempted to reply)
Maybe you can ask him to empty your commode
before he leaves

Our days are no less trying – with every pain and discomfort and passing unease met with an insistent request to see the Doctor or the Nurse or the Chemist with the absolute conviction that all can be fixed on the spot with the appropriate pill..... to be sure – my mother doesn't really 'get' old age.

'Can we go to Spain for a few days?'

(Not that this is very different from before – maybe just by degree perhaps).

I feel like one who is 'punch drunk' – still trying to catch my breath from one barrage while I find myself overcome by another.

Sometimes I feel like the guy in countless old war films – the last guy in the platoon who volunteers to hold the position alone so that his comrades may escape – and everyone knowing that he won't make it back but still making brave and cheerful plans for their eventual reunion.

There may be many battles, but there is but one war – the war that must be waged against the incoming darkness.

Every day and every night, it attacks on all fronts without pause or cessation.

Like the solitary soldier, I am alone now, fighting with all that I am to keep the light shining in our hearts – to protect it and nurture it and to keep my shield held firm against the arrows of fear and doubt and resentment and self-pity.

'I'm sure the clocks are running slower these days'

This is certainly not the happy and glorious ending that I had in mind when I first started writing these pages – but it is the truth nevertheless.

To alleviate my sense of helplessness before the demands that each day lays upon me, I seem to have developed many and varied coping strategies to help me through – and like a sailing ship before a storm – I too have trimmed my sails and battened down my hatches.

I am supported and comforted by simplicity and routine and especially in the coming together of the two – maybe like holding one's breath and keeping very still so as not to disturb the source of a physical pain.

I shop and I swim and I write, I play the guitar late at night and I listen to music in the car and whenever I can, I dream of dispensing with everything that won't fit in a Jeep and then getting behind the wheel and driving away to wherever it is that the wind chooses to take me.

I attend to my mother's needs for entertainment and scenic stimulation and to her voracious appetite for films and dramas and old sit-coms – which, in effect, means anything involving Michael Kitchen, Maggie Smith and Penelope Keith.....

..... although I sometimes think that I could save myself a lot of trouble by just sticking a picture of Michael Kitchen on the TV screen – thus allowing my mother to depart this life in blissful adoration and contentment.

'I want to start Piano lessons'

I keep to the safe margins of my routines and I fight my battles as they come – but there seems nothing I can do to escape the fact that I am scared – scared of how long these days will endure and how troubled and demanding they will become.

I am scared of losing the strength to infuse my mother's final hours with moments of happiness and levity..... for existing is easy – it's living that is so hard.

In truth, no matter how hard I try, my life just seems to just lurch precariously between welcome but fleeting moments of lucidity and serenity.

I am like a climber working his way from one foothold to the next – ever fearful that each successive crevice will allude him and that he will be doomed to just hang there on his lonely mountain crag forever.

And yet – all that really matters is this moment – for right here and right now she is alive – with her totally undiminished and undefeated capacity and longing and thankfulness and passion for the 'Beauty of Life' – wherever she may find it.

'When I'm feeling better, I'd like to go dancing'

Maybe this is the inspiration that keeps me going – that fills my heart with hope and determination – maybe this is the real distinction between the living and the dead and one that has very little to do with all the flowering and the wilting of the flesh.

(As we are passed by a couple of speeding motorcyclists)

'I think motorbikes are marvellous'

Maybe I worry too much – maybe my purpose now is simply to find ways to brush aside all the indignities and embarrassments of age and to make light of all that would seek to weigh down upon us.

At times, life can feel over-run by all the incessant unresolved dialogues of the mind – but in the end, it just comes down to choice – and the only choice that really matters is the one that saves another person from staring into the trials and humiliations of their own death for just one more day – or one more hour – or one more minute.

'I can't remember whether you have arranged my Lasting Power of Eternity'

Over the last few weeks I have noticed one particular aspect of my mother's behaviour becoming more and more obsessive and anxious.

She is concerned now that, at all times of the day or night and no matter how cold the air outside may be – that there is always an open window in the room and sometimes an open front or back door.

These are no idle requests and they cannot be ignored or persuaded away.

I have come to accept that maybe her spirit is ever watchful these days for a way of escape, should it become necessary in a moment of unexpected emergency.

J'attendrai Le jour et la nuit
J'attendrai toujours ton retour
J'attendrai car l'oiseau
qui s'enfuit vient chercher l'oubli dans son nid
Le temps passe et court
En battant tristement
Dans mon cœur si lourd
Et pourtant, j'attendrai ton retour

(My mother's favourite French song – she can't always remember who I am but she can still sing the whole song from memory)

P.S. *'At my funeral I want everyone to wear brightly coloured clothes'*

61

One Day At A Time

… here it comes… here comes the night

Bert Berns

My bed – it is no longer a place of repose – of sanctuary – of rest and recharging – a safe harbour from the storms of the day….. it is now a broken thing – it is ever tormented and restless – for there is no succour here – no quiet – no rest…..

The night may begin reassuringly with its own peaceful rituals – the smoothing of sheets and creases and the puffing up of pillows – pills and hot water bottles – biscuits and water and cups of tea – thoughts and stipulations for the following day – apologies sometimes – and sometimes humour…..

….. but later – as I fall into the candle lit darkness – as my sleep reaches out to beckon me in – the voices start…..

….. far out across the swollen hills – a slow murmured cry – rising from deep within the jilted heart of the God's lovelorn creation….. the gentle cry becomes a troubled groan – rhythmical – cyclical – rising and falling – in crescendoed insistence…..

….. the small plaintive voice of a lost child calling for its mother – the cry of a wounded animal unpredictable and dangerous – the voice of calm and genuine need – the voice of boredom and attention seeking – the voice of anger and impatience – the voice of confusion and helplessness…..

….. so many voices – and me never quite sure – what is real and what is not….. what must be attended to and what must be ignored…..

….. when to be firm and rebuking – and when to be gentle and kind…..

….. and can she really hear people tapping on her window at night – mother, brother and sister…..

….. can she really see cats and rats and mice under her bed…..

('The Cat and the Rat sat on the Mat' ….. a sort of gothic Janet and John for older readers perhaps).

And so….. the long fractured night shuffles mockingly into place – as weariness falls like black clouds all across the vistas of my defeat…..

'Can you ring my mother,
I want to go home to my own bed now'

So many voices – both from without and from within – but it is with the latter that the real danger lies…..

….. 'it's all so unfair' – 'she is so unreasonable, so selfish' – 'and it's not just old age, she's always been this way' – 'you're right, you don't deserve all this crap, you've had it all your life' – 'it's not right' – 'you shouldn't have to live this way'.....

So runs the tape in my head – giving myself permission and justification for my anger and my impatience – incitement and encouragement even.....

..... it all sounds so true – so plausible – so reasonable –and yet it is here – right here that I am lost.....

Patience is hard – loving is hard – but if I give myself excuses – if I listen to the voice of my tempter – the voice of my cowardice – then there is no chance – no chance at all.

(Waking me up to ask)
'Are you asleep?'

It has taken a lifetime – but I have come at last to this place where I am no longer helpless before the will of my whinging tormentor.

For no matter how dark and tense and broken the night – all can be brushed away with a single kind word – an arm around her shoulder – a kiss upon her forehead – affection and kindness for the child starved so cruelly of such as these.

As I bend to lay my hand upon her frail but still proud countenance – I am struck by how strange and scary it feels – for I have spent a lifetime building and maintaining a wall between myself and my mother – a wall to protect and defend myself against all the violence and the madness – a wall that has become a wall against the world – against my God – against myself.

'Someone has left a baby on the wardrobe –
what a terrible person to do that'

These moments of comforting – they are so much more than gestures and words..... they are an arm raised against all that came between us – that would come between us still – against all the brutality and cruelty of her childhood – of my childhood – these moments are a confirmation that together – by God's grace – we have overcome – and that it is Love and Love alone that now holds sway over our lives.

And so at last – quietly and naturally – in the very heart of the night – the unimaginable happens – I walk to the side of her bed – the side closest to her window – I sit on the edge of her mattress – I take her hand and I pray with and for my mother.....

..... and as the first fine cracks in a mighty dam – the tyranny of the years begins to slowly fall away.

'I'm exhausted – I've been packing boxes all night – packing boxes and shovelling coal'

The focus now – of each day and night – is to maintain and nurture her simple human dignity – to resist the negative thoughts – to not fall into the habit of treating her as a burden..... for she is a person – she is God's precious child – no less in the difficult times than in the times of light.

She may be frail and disorientated with her memory failing a little more each day – but strangely, her thoughts now are more lucid than ever before – the tangled ball of twine finally becoming a single thread.....

..... my mother has found her peace – as at long last, have I..... and maybe my mother has been hanging on in hope and faith for this very moment.....

I am learning to let go – one day at a time – to see my days here as a privilege and not a chore – an honour and not a degradation.

'I must go back to school soon –
can you tell my mother'

The years are passing – and maybe they are taking with them the final chapters of my health and the dexterities of both my body and my mind – maybe my dreams of driving once again across the hills and valleys of Tuscany will remain forever just that….. dreams….. the way things are going – maybe my mother will outlive us all…..

….. maybe this is true…..

….. but my faith tells me otherwise.

Every night I prepare my mother's porridge for her as she likes to eat it long before I myself have woken up.

While I go through the simple routine, I find myself reminiscing on the days of my first coming to Surrey to care for my mother, and how I perceived my own needs then, only in the context of being subservient to hers.

I am smiling as I think on how easily and naively I slipped into the role of reckless self-sacrifice – how quickly I was to assume that it was all about her and how differently things have worked out to the way that I imagined they would.

How mistaken I was in those early days to think that I was simply putting my life on hold for a while and how astonished I would have been to know then, that all the faith and the peace and the self-respect that I had searched for, for so long in vain – that I would have found them all in such abundance through caring for a very difficult old lady…..

….. for although it is God who has shown me how to love myself – it is without doubt my mother, who has shown me how to like and value myself.

A Midnight Conversation

(It is 4 am and she has called me into her bedroom for the third time tonight)

What is it !

'The Trifid grows in the secret garden
and the secret garden is in your mind'

What !!

'The Trifid grows in the secret garden
  and the secret garden is in your mind'

I don't understand !!!

'The Trifid grows in the….. '

…..yes yes – I heard that – but what does it mean !!!!

'The Trifid grows….. '

It's ok – I understand – just try and get some sleep now…..

I awake this morning with unusually charitable feelings towards my mother – bearing in mind that I am rising from yet another long broken night's sleep.

I walk bleary eyed in to the lounge with generous offers of tea and porridge making on my lips – but, to my surprise and mild apprehension, I find it empty.

It is now 9 am and there are still no signs of stirring from her bedroom.

No matter – the tea and the porridge can wait…..

….. she has been so tired lately…..

….. there is no hurry after all…..

….. I think I'll just let her sleep.

62

Stepping Lightly From Her Threads

...where everything and everything
has fallen by the way
and only love...
... only love
remains

My brothers and I are walking slowly back to our cars – we are walking together and we are walking in silence, thankful for the wordless sharing of our mutual grief.

In the pale blue skies above Guildford Crematorium, all is still and hushed and waiting – and as the night comes on – I find myself kneeling once more before all the troubled passing of my silent moons.

But as I sleep my fitful sleep – as I dream my restless dream – somewhere, in the unseen darkness, a stone is softly rolled away and a beautiful childlike spirit steps lightly from her threads, and as naturally and as effortlessly as the seeds of a dandelion clock, goes drifting out across the meadows at dawn.....

..... and somewhere.....

..... between the stars of that shining distance.....

..... I know.....

..... that she is walking with her Lord.....

..... through all the days of love and light

..... that reach out now before them.

Rest eternal grant unto my mother, O Lord
and let light perpetual shine upon her,
may she rest in peace.

63

She Was My Mother

Grief only exists where love lived first
Francesca Cox

I return once again to the empty house. It has been just over a week since the funeral, but still I feel nothing apart from an overwhelming sensation of being lost.

The days are haunted and unreal and the nights cold and interminable. I am ever restless, and find myself constantly in a state of wandering. I wander from room to room as if looking for her – I wander into town as if to buy her shopping – I wander through my mind that I may find her there in my thoughts.

I know that I miss her, but I can't feel that 'missing' – my heart remains cold and hard and unapproachable.

All is strange and unfamiliar – the phone rings from time to time with offers of help, but I don't want to see anyone or talk to anyone except for my two brothers and my two daughters.

I have little appetite for anything at all, especially food, but today I find myself walking to the kitchen to make myself some toast and marmalade.

This is something that I never usually eat, but it is my mother's favourite – her staple day and night – and I suppose I am doing this so that I can somehow feel her here – feel her here beside me..... or maybe I just fancy some toast and marmalade.

I find that there is a single small brown loaf still remaining in the bottom of the freezer and I manage to separate a slice and put it in the toaster. It is all so familiar. I let myself go into this simple act – the act that I performed for her so many times each and every day of our time here together.

I leave my toast defrosting and go to the fridge to take out the jar of marmalade from the place where my mother last left it – together with a thoughtful little reminder of herself.....

….. for there is just enough adherence between the casually placed top and the container beneath to cause the latter to remain held for just long enough to clear the shelf but not long enough for it to reach a place of safety and repose on the worktop…..

….. I watch unable to move or intervene as the jar performs its dramatic slo-mo fall to the floor – there to spill its copious contents amidst numerous assorted pieces of sticky broken glass…..

I stare at the mess before me as I start to feel something like a breaking within me – I am suddenly consumed with weariness and can no longer find the strength to stand any longer.

I see myself falling as if I am watching it all from afar….. a man on his knees – sobbing like a small child – tears and marmalade and broken glass all becoming as a memorial – my one last offering to her.

> *She was a proud woman*
> *she was a brave woman*
> *she was my mother*
>
> *Sgt, Gerry Boyle*

64
1963 – A Slight Return

Nothing for my mother was ever straightforward or 'normal' – least of all, it emerged, her obedience to the dictates of the stipulated School Uniform.

Understandably, most parents were concerned to take into account their child's growth rate, when buying expensive things like school blazers and coats, by allowing a certain amount of growing space in their choice of size.

This prudent attitude towards school clothing, when subjected to my mother's own particular slant on life however, resulted in her buying me a Blazer so large, that I was still 'growing into it' three years later.

In the early Sixties, for young boys in their last year of the 'Little School', various ploys were taking shape with the sole purpose of exploratory pushing at the boundaries and restrictions of childhood – no doubt in anticipation of the move to the 'Big School' that was now looming ever larger on the horizon.

For the boys at Ottershaw Junior School, and no doubt, for boys throughout the land, this was a period of wild and dangerous ruminations.

In practical terms, and for the sake of maintaining a semblance of dignity and 'cool', the failure of the short-lived 'chasing the girls' exploit soon gave way to the safer but no less radical activity of gum chewing.

The chewing gum, so favoured by our American cowboy heroes, translated its way into our lives in the shape and the colour and the texture of 'Flags of the World' bubble gum.

Each pack of gum came with a large brightly coloured card with a Flag of each country on the front and a picture of local dress (or some such cultural stereotype), together with a few lines of interesting facts, on the back.

The idea, of course, was to collect all the various cards and mount them proudly in the scrapbook supplied by the gum makers for a 'small extra fee'.

What a surprise it was to small gullible children, just how many bloody flags there were in the world !

Buying the packets of gum wasn't a problem as, for parents and their purses, the whole endeavour fitted neatly under the heading of Geographical Studies – however, getting through the huge required amounts of sweet chewy pink gum most definitely was.

No opportunity could be missed for a spot of chewing and casual discarding – which led me one fateful day to finding myself in mid chew at the very front of the classroom as our teacher walked through the door.

Now the result of being caught with a piece of bubble gum in my mouth was far too terrifying to contemplate, so there was no alternative left to me but to place the offending item hastily in my blazer pocket and then to forgot about it for the rest of the day.

Who would have thought that a small piece of dried bubble gum could be so tenacious and so strong.

Nothing I tried was able to separate the gum from the pocket, or indeed the pocket from itself – going to my parents for help was of course out of the question as violent recriminations were plentiful enough without going out of my way to find them – and so, I had no choice but to accept that I was stuck with a single pocket blazer for the foreseeable future

This actually transpired to have little impact on my life right up until the moment when it became the nonchalant air of choice for young men about town to walk everywhere with their hands in their pockets…..

….. all except for one not so nonchalant young chap who was forced to walk everywhere with one hand in his pocket and one hand dangling free.

This whole episode did have an upsetting and disturbing postscript even beyond having to conceal the fact from all and sundry that my blazer only had one pocket.

My sprouting OCD meant that, as opposed to most of my peers, I had managed to complete the whole album of 'Flags of the World' and was able to sit back and enjoy all the exotic colours and cultural tips while they were still at the chewing and the casual discarding stage.

Every card was a proud and colourful celebration of each country's unique appearance and culture and an unambiguous seeding for later global exploration – all except one.

When it came to the country of Peru, for some obscure and malignant reason, the pictures of the indigenous population had the nobility of their vibrant 'peasant' attire utterly ruined by the painting in of coloured Bowler Hats on their heads.

By the end of the year, my move to the 'Big School' had

necessitated the blessed purchase of a new unsullied but equally oversize garment and experiments in liberty had moved away from intrepid gum orientated dissent to more subtle acts of insurrection, such as the wearing of Chelsea Boots and the singing of 'She Loves You Yeah Yeah Yeah' quietly but rebelliously under our breath.

But still the question lingers in my 11 year old head – why had the bubble gum makers chosen to so cruelly lampoon and ridicule this country alone – it was like drawing a pair of spectacles and a moustache on the face of Brigitte Bardot.....

..... yet another riddle to be locked away in the large box marked 'Unintelligible Adult Behaviour.'

Ah, my mother – my mother – bless her sweet soul.....
..... and now.....
..... the poem that was my mother's poem.....
..... the one she chose to be read at her funeral.....
..... it has now become my poem.....
..... passed on from mother to son.....
..... her final precious, trim and well-fitting, gift to me.

Sonnet 116

Let me not to the marriage of true minds
admit impediments. Love is not love
which alters when it alteration finds,
or bends with the remover to remove.
O no! it is an ever-fixed mark
that looks on tempests and is never shaken;
it is the star to every wand'ring bark,
whose worth's unknown, although his height be taken.
Love's not Time's fool, though rosy lips and cheeks

within his bending sickle's compass come;
Love alters not with his brief hours and weeks,
but bears it out even to the edge of doom.
If this be error and upon me prov'd,
I never writ, nor no man ever lov'd.

William Shakespeare

65

Newlands Corner – The Last Day

… the kingdom of God
is in your midst.

A ll through the summer of 2019 – we floated along as if becalmed in the middle of an endless ocean – slow and shapeless – quiet days and quiet nights – just waiting for the wind to come.

And now it is the day of my leaving….. I have come here one last time to Newlands Corner – here where my mother and I shared so many lunchtimes of homemade soup and chips – our favourite spot, to be sure…..

….. I am thinking about what she has left me – how she hung on to life until all that I needed to learn from our time together was learnt – until every drop of blessing had been squeezed from her last dying breath…..

….. a mother's love indeed.

….. and as I sit here gazing out on the majesty of the Surrey Hills, I feel like I am melting into the universe – the universe in which and with which I am now at peace…..

As a child of my mother, I learnt that to speak was futile and served only to bring violence down upon myself. I learnt to be silent and to keep everything hidden within me. As a child of my mother I learnt to hate myself and to believe that I was nothing.

As a child of my Father in Heaven, I have come to discover my own voice, and to find that it is pleasing to me. I rest in knowing that through Jesus Christ I am one with all things. As a child of my Father, I have come to love myself as I should, and to know that this is pleasing to Him.

As children of this world, my Mother and I were hopelessly and irredeemably broken – at odds with ourselves, with each other, with the world around us and with our God.

As children of the Kingdom we have come to walk, as we will always walk, hand in hand, together, mother and son, now and forever.

'Judge and you will be judged'

As I flick once more through the pages of my journey of the last seven years – I am struck by how full of judgements they are – upon teachers, parents, grandparents, politicians, pop stars, Russian car makers, writers of 'inspirational quotes', myself and even lollipop ladies.

I fear that these judgments say less about those that are being judged and more about my own bitterness and mean-ness of spirit….. and anyway, to raise my voice in such a way is to surely bring more discord and disharmony to the perfect patterns of God's design than that which I would disdain.

'Who am I, who am I, who am I
to judge you'

….. but maybe the words needed to be said – and as I continue to release the cries of my heart into God's safe keeping – I trust that my heart will one day become more generous and forgiving…..

….. to love as I am loved – to forgive as I am forgiven….. to see only the child of God within another..... not because they 'deserve' my love and forgiveness – but because of the One who bids me to do so..... to love without condition.

'For we walk by faith, not by sight'

Whether we know it or not – whether we like it or not – whether we accept it or not – we all live by faith – but faith in who or what is the question – for without doubt, the focus of our faith will determine the path of our lives.

Faith for me – the journey of faith – has been a bit like giving up smoking – in the beginning there was only confusion and restlessness – lots of effort – fear and doubt – stumbling and falling – picking myself up and starting over.....

..... then as things settled down, shame and self-vilification turned to smugness and intolerance – to intemperate enthusiasm and a preachy self-righteousness and judgmentalism.....

..... thankfully this too passed – and as my eyes opened to the miracle of my release in the face of my own weakness and helplessness – peace prevailed.

The past is now like an old film – black and white – set apart – something I can watch for a while and then turn off – for now the barbs have gone – and death has lost its sting.

You who have followed me page by stammering page – step by step through these fractured texts – along these barb-wired borders of my soul – from doubt to the first faltering steps of faith – precocious and naïve – fatuous and fickle.....

..... I have stumbled beneath the burdens of sanctimony and pious anger – I have judged and I have waived the pointed finger.....

..... but I have not edited these words – be they shameful or merely over-zealous..... for the echoes of truth can be heard even within the darkest nights of my journey.

And now – as the sun sets upon my last night before my travels begin – I ask this one thing.....

..... of all that has passed between us – whatever causes your anger to rise up – I pray – let these words go.....

..... but if any of my words bring you peace and help you to walk in love and light – then thank God for his hand upon me, and may these words remain with you as you hold these things in your heart.

66

Farewell

Words – like little children they shine,
and just like little children – they grow and move on,
so that the hands that were once held out for love and direction,
are the very same hands that now return to lead us home.

I have come now to my last stop – my last port of call – my last Galette – my last fond farewell.....

...'one more cup of peppermint tea before I go, to the valley below'

Everything that I have written here – it is only with the desire for honesty and healing – to try and express somehow the mysterious meanderings of my journey home – sometimes stumbling – sometimes running – sometimes crawling on my hands and knees.

My hope is that I have merely offered up my thoughts to the judgments of the silent walls that have surrounded me – nothing more.....

..... but if there were to be something more – then let my words be but pebbles dropped upon the water, to maybe disturb the surface there, of all the complacencies and the certainties of this troubled age.

Some of what I write is written with the elation and the

trepidation of a small child learning to walk – and some of it is written as an escaping convict, wading through the mists and the mires of his fear…..

….. the fear of trying to 'write' – of not being able to let go – of clinging to maps and plans – to the futility of trying to make something happen.

And now – and now – I have come to understand at last – that writing finds its breath only through the words that sneak up behind you – while you're busy focusing on those that you are laying out across the blank spaces beneath your pen.

Writing is like trying to fall asleep – or to play music – or to fall in love…..

….. as in all things – writing, like life, is not a process of learning – of seeking to be filled…..

….. it is a process of learning how to stop trying – of how to be still – of being emptied at last from all the noisy stuff of human travail…..

> ….. *of giving wings*
> *and the freedom of the skies*
> *to the light*
> *that is already within you.*

The Upper Room; Mon Oncle Jean; Totnes

Coda

Of Angels Singing

67

Tuscanny At Last

Vous papillons épinglés
une belle nuit d'été sur ma page
vous amoureux déchirés
couchés sur le papier bien sages
c'est à mon tour regardez
j'ai une voix pour chanter
j'ai des pieds pour courir
j'vais quand même pas rester
toute ma vie à écrire

Camille Dalmais

The mist in the half-light is trembling – before the covered murmur of the big straight six...

... dignified and poised in its venerable restraint – the lightest touch of my foot – the only request that it seeks, to calmly address the affairs of the day...

... with authority and grace – my trusted old companion – hand in hand through the dust of our winter years – down these vacant tracks of my restless surrender...

... this ragged journey back to the dawn of my days...

... fields of sentried sunflowers are reaching out to the horizon...

... the warm dusty air of summer hangs in the spaces between us...

... here by the side of the road – a fitful silence holds out its hand to beckon us in...

... far out across the distance...
    ... a dark-eyed young woman comes dressed
    in wedding white...
        ... and there is a dance within her step...
           ... and there is a song upon her lips...
            ... and there is a love-look in her eyes...
            ... as she walks softly by ... and is gone.

My journey has reached its end...
    ... my journey has just begun...
        ... my journey has always been...
        ... my journey – my journey...
            ... it never was

... the sunshine echoes with the laughter of the flowers...
    ...as I rest upon the bumper of my chariot...
        ... my song is lost in a greater song...
        ... like a small child – to the passing throng...

Heitor is smiling...
... his melodies and rhythms float out across the hills – wherein
lies their home...
    ... I close my eyes to savour each breath of my guitar...
    ... Heitor leans across as if to whisper...
    ...and there is mischief in his eyes
        as he draws deeply on his cigar
            throws back his head
              and laughs...
  ... 'not bad...
      ...not bad at all...
            ...for an old white guy'.

To know oneself
means having nowhere to hide

and just as there can be no subterfuge
in musical performance
there is finally none in life either...

... particularly in the face of death.

When all the tragedy and drama is finished,
the bombs have stopped dropping,
Wotan has dissolved Valhalla
and life is over...

... what are we left with?

Two sounds continue to resonate
in the still air and infinite silence...

... birdsong and children's laughter.

If we are still there to hear them
we might think they are angels singing...

... and we would be right...

Paul Robertson – *my friend*

In order to create
there must be a dynamic force,
and what force is more potent
than love.

Igor Stravinsky

You will never find the dawn
by searching for the sunrise –
neither will you find Me
this way

Thank you to the following fine establishments, in which the majority of this book has been written...

Buckfast Abbey
The Bull's Head in Ewhurst
'Take it' (now Yangaz Bistro) in Cranleigh
The Onslow Arms in Cranleigh
The Sun Inn in Dunsfold
The Plucky Pheasant at Newlands Corner
and of course – Newlands Corner Café

... and to these equally fine establishments...

The Church of Jesus Christ Redeemer of Mankind
Mon Oncle Jean in Totnes
The Rania in Cranleigh
The Roger Tichbourne in Loxwood
The Wing Hung in Shalford
Cranfold Physical Therapy Centre in Cranleigh
The Natural Life Shop in Cranleigh
The Cranleigh Leisure Centre
Specsavers in Cranleigh
and the Brighton Implant Clinic

... for their much needed and much appreciated edification, support and succour of Body, Mind and Spirit.

With a special thank you to...

Paul at D'art Design for the front cover
and
Rick Williams for 'The Flamenco Dancer'

... and to...

J C American Autos
Ele's Tyres and Servicing
and Autogas4u in Wimbledon

... without whose skill and patience, I might well now be driving through Tuscanny in a Prius!

Lightning Source UK Ltd.
Milton Keynes UK
UKHW021509121119
353381UK00006B/644/P